LIVES OF THE MASTERS

VIPASSANA

S. N. Goenka

EMISSARY OF INSIGHT

Daniel M. Stuart

Shambhala

Shambhala Publications, Inc.
4720 Walnut Street
Boulder, Colorado 80301
www.shambhala.com

FRONTISPIECE: Photo courtesy of Daniel M. Stuart

Cover art: Robert Fenwick May, Jr.
Cover design: Gopa and Ted2, Inc.

9 8 7 6 5 4 3 2 1

FIRST EDITION
Printed in Canada

⊗ This edition is printed on acid-free paper that meets the
American National Standards Institute z39.48 Standard.
♻ This book is printed on 100% postconsumer recycled paper.
For more information please visit www.shambhala.com.

Shambhala Publications is distributed worldwide by
Penguin Random House, Inc., and its subsidiaries.

LIBRARY OF CONGRESS CATALOGING-IN-PUBLICATION DATA
Names: Stuart, Daniel Malinowski, author.
Title: S. N. Goenka: emissary of insight / Daniel Stuart.
Description: First edition. | Boulder, Colorado: Shambhala, [2020] |
Series: Lives of the masters | Includes bibliographical references and index.
Identifiers: LCCN 2019049592 | ISBN 9781611808186 (trade paperback)
Subjects: LCSH: Goenka, S. N., 1924–2013. | Teachers—India—Biography. |
Marwaris—Biography. | Vipaśyanā (Buddhism)
Classification: LCC BQ960.O89 S78 2020 | DDC 294.3092—dc23
LC record available at https://lccn.loc.gov/2019049592

Contents

Series Introduction

BUDDHIST TRADITIONS are heir to some of the most creative thinkers in world history. The Lives of the Masters series offers lively and reliable introductions to the lives, works, and legacies of key Buddhist teachers, philosophers, contemplatives, and writers. Each volume in the series tells the story of an innovator who embodied the ideals of Buddhism, crafted a dynamic living tradition during his or her lifetime, and bequeathed a vibrant legacy of knowledge and practice to future generations.

Lives books rely on primary sources in the original languages to describe the extraordinary achievements of Buddhist thinkers and illuminate these achievements by vividly setting them within their historical contexts. Each volume offers a concise yet comprehensive summary of the master's life and an account of how he or she came to hold a central place in Buddhist traditions. Each contribution also contains a broad selection of the master's writings.

This series makes it possible for all readers to see Buddhist masters as deeply creative and inspired people, whose work was animated by the rich complexity of their time and place, and how these inspiring figures continue to engage our quest for knowledge and understanding today.

KURTIS SCHAEFFER, *series editor*

S. N. Goenka and Illaichidevi Goenka in 1976, meditating together at the formal ceremony for laying the foundation of the meditation pagoda at Goenka's first meditation center in India, Dhamma Giri. Courtesy of the Vipassana Research Institute.

Preface

IT IS A DIFFICULT task to write a historical and critical book about one's own meditation teacher. It is an even more difficult task to write about a personality like S. N. Goenka, one of the most influential meditation teachers of the twentieth century.

Like many, I first met Goenka by way of video and audio recordings, on one of his ten-day courses in the North Indian city of Jaipur in the state of Rajasthan. Though it took place more than two decades ago now, it was an encounter that I will never forget. It set me on a path to study the teachings of the Buddha, and I find it unlikely that I would be a professor of Buddhist studies today were it not for that first remote encounter with the man I now think of as my teacher.

I feel lucky that I encountered Goenka and his teachings in India and that I felt the urge early on to understand the Asian contexts from which his teachings emerged. This led me to study Pali, Hindi, Sanskrit, and a number of other traditional languages in which the teachings of the Buddha have been transmitted. It also led me to want to spend time in Asia and look as deeply as I could—with my limited capacities—at the sociocultural dynamics at work in the various contexts in which I found myself.

This book is based on more than a decade of formal historical and ethnographic research, as well as an additional decade of personal engagement with practices and communities around the globe that owe their inspiration to this great teacher of *vipaśyanā* meditation.

I began a formal, ethnographically informed, historical study of Goenka and his movement in 2008. Since that time, I have spent a combination of more than four years in India carrying out fieldwork and many more years working on archival material relevant to the history of the tradition. Since I have worked on a number of other projects during this time and have published several other books, this research material has had to wait for publication.

But it has also had to wait because I have, at times, found it painful to analyze the actions and identities of Goenka and his close disciples in the light of historical perspective. These are people whom I love and respect. It is a challenging thing to write critically about a living community of which one is a part. It is even more difficult when this community is built on cherished spiritual ideals that many feel are inviolable. I have taken up the task of writing this short work primarily because of my great reverence for S. N. Goenka, but also because I feel that he has been misunderstood and misrepresented by many, including some of his own students. My hope is that a critical and informed perspective on the life of this great master, and the role he played in the dissemination of the Buddha's teachings in modernity, will prove helpful to anyone interested in those teachings.

My sense is that many will find this book strange. There is no genre in which it fits. Is it a hagiography of a great saint? A historical biography of an influential man? Is it a critique or a sympathetic account of the man at the center of the story? In carrying out research on Goenka and his organization over the past decade, and also in looking more broadly at a range of historical occurrences that developed in parallel with him, my sense is that to capture what has gone on requires us to write and think both within and above such categories. This means, however, that many will find this "nongenre" biography and collection of writings and teachings somewhat puzzling, perhaps even alienating. I encourage readers to investigate that puzzlement. This is where we may find S. N. Goenka as a man and S. N. Goenka as a community.

Since I am quite critical in the following pages of those who have chosen to overlook certain aspects of Goenka's life and legacy, I would be remiss if I were not to acknowledge that much has been deliberately overlooked in this book as well. While I try to show that Goenka was a complex person with a complex story, many of the more problematic issues of his identity, his mission, and his organization cannot be addressed in a short, schematic book such as this. These include issues of caste and untouchability in India; gender bias and conservatism; powerful strains of homophobia within the organization; cult dynamics and group behaviors; the specifics of meditative experiences induced on the courses Goenka taught; Goenka's personal relationships with individual students, as well as those individual students' roles in supporting his mission; many episodes and formative moments of Goenka's life that simply could not fit; and meta-level questions about ontologies and metaphysical commitments. These issues and many more must be addressed in other contexts, and I hope they will be.

May this work about my teacher be for the benefit of all beings.

aniccā vata saṅkhārā, uppādavayadhammino
uppajjitvā nirujjhanti, tesaṃ vūpasamo sukho

Karmic forces are indeed impermanent, certain to arise and pass away. Once they have arisen, they cease. Their cessation is happiness.

S. N. Goenka

Photo taken at the end of a special meditation course that U Ba Khin gave exclusively for the families of S. N. and Illaichidevi Goenka, Mother Sayama, and U Chit Tin (taken 1966–69). Courtesy of the Vipassana Research Institute.

Introduction

In a recent *New York Times* obituary in the "Overlooked No More" series, David Gelles provided readers with a picture of the renowned meditation master S. N. Goenka. Some aspects of the obituary coincide with the Goenka who appears in the pages of this book.[1] The title of the obituary was "S. N. Goenka, Who Brought Mindfulness to the West," and toward the beginning of the piece, Gelles attempted to capture what most today have come to see as an essential aspect of Goenka's identity. Gelles wrote, "Though his teachings were derived from Buddhist texts, Goenka kept the religiosity to a minimum." He went on to quote one of Goenka's well-worn ideas as it was presented in a speech delivered to the United Nations World Peace Summit in Davos, Switzerland, in 2000:

> "Rather than converting people from one organized religion to another organized religion," he said, "we should try to convert people from misery to happiness, from bondage to liberation, and from cruelty to compassion."

This is the Goenka with whom most people, particularly those in the West, have become familiar. He was a teacher of meditation who focused on ideas within the Buddha's teachings that appear amenable to "universal" values and goals. This allowed him to transcend organized religion and religious identities, and appeal to people from all walks of life.

Gelles is not the first to focus on this aspect of Goenka's identity in trying to encapsulate him for a modern global audience. Rather, he is drawing on a well-worn narrative, one that Goenka himself wrote with the help of his many Anglophone students. We might look briefly at a couple of prior depictions, prominent and easy to access digitally, that provide a basic consensus as to who Goenka was and his place in history.

The first piece appeared right after Goenka passed away, on September 29, 2013. It was written by Jay Michaelson, a journalist connected to the Insight Meditation Society (IMS) in western Massachusetts. Published in the *HuffPost* on September 30, Michaelson's piece was titled "S. N. Goenka: The Man Who Taught the World to Meditate." This wonderful title captures the important role Goenka played in the modern history of the mass dissemination of Asian meditation. In attempting to encapsulate Goenka in more particular terms, Michaelson wrote, "Basically a rationalist and a pragmatist, Goenka emphasized that meditation was not spirituality and not religion, but more like a technology—a set of tools for upgrading and optimizing the mind."[2]

A day after Michaelson's piece was published, another article—titled "S. N. Goenka, Pioneer of Secular Meditation Movement, Dies at 90"—appeared in the obituaries section of *Tricycle: A Buddhist Review*. In that article, the Harvard-trained scholar of modern Buddhist meditation, Erik Braun, wrote:

> Goenka's transformation of vipassana into a standalone movement has had a profound effect on general conceptions of Buddhist practice in the modern world. By presenting meditation as a universal art of living, Goenka enabled practice to further permeate societies as a secular technique, especially in Europe and North America. His later efforts, such as founding a research institute to study vipassana's

> social effects and, in 2002, touring 35 North American cities to spread the word about meditation, further reinforced the popular message that meditation is nonreligious. His practical presentation has influenced many, particularly in the West, to see vipassana as essentially about one's current life and how it is lived.[3]

In these two pieces we find the most basic elements of a core narrative of Goenka, one that has comc to dominate both popular and scholarly imaginations in recent years. It is a narrative that tends to emphasize one aspect of his identity, while overlooking many other aspects. The terminology of the "rationalist," the "pragmatist," "spirituality," "religion," "technology," the "secular," and the "nonreligious" holds within it value judgments that often go unnoticed, since many people take them for granted. Books upon books, debates upon debates, have attempted to unpack the way such terminology emerges from and gets deployed in particular historical, social, and material contexts. It is not my job to try to do that here.

For the purposes of this book, I would point to one fundamental asymmetry that is foundational to this one-sided core narrative. It is a perspective that takes Goenka as an important figure because of his influence "especially in Europe and America"—or in more problematic language, "the West." It is also a perspective that prioritizes the values most prized in some of the more dominant traditions of thought in those "societies," the rational or the pragmatic. In this story, what made Goenka's teaching of insight meditation (Hindi: *vipaśyanā*; Pali: *vipassanā*) important is that it came to bear on developments in "the West."

This asymmetry is at the heart of Gelles's article in the *New York Times*. Perhaps most telling is that nowhere in this piece is a single Asian voice found—aside from that of Goenka himself in his most

Anglophone appearance. This is one very powerful example of how, in an attempt to recognize a great man, a large part of who he was has indeed been overlooked.

The Goenka that is known and celebrated as a "rationalist," "secular," "nonreligious" teacher of meditation is only part—and a relatively small part—of who he was. This book attempts to provide readers with a more complete narrative of Goenka's life than the ones most commonly available to the global public today. Through his biography and the selections of his writings and oral teachings, it presents Goenka as a complex figure thoroughly rooted in traditional Indian, Burmese, Buddhist, and Hindu worldviews and value systems, even as he articulated his meditation teachings to global audiences in ways that stripped out—at least at the rhetorical level—many of his traditional commitments. As a public figure with audiences in multiple cultural contexts, he learned to speak in many languages and registers, figuratively and literally, to reach his listeners.

The biography draws primarily on Goenka's own autobiographical writings—many of them in Hindi—while at the same time situating those writings within a broader historical perspective than Goenka himself tended to present to his audiences. It is conventional in that it lays out Goenka's story in a linear narrative of key periods in his life, largely following his autobiography. It is unconventional in that it explicitly seeks to unsettle to some extent the standard narrative with which Goenka, his students, and others became and have become familiar. In doing so, it should also provide readers with an understanding of how Goenka himself, in developing his teaching tactics, participated in generating the one-sided story already discussed. It became a key tool for him in influencing a variety of audiences whom he hoped to reach.

I find it somewhat frustrating that I have to begin this story with the image of this one particular Goenka, only to go on to show that this image is formed in the eye of particular beholders. I would prefer to simply tell my story and let Goenka's many incarnations speak for themselves. But we live in a world in which the stories we tell cannot exit the web of conditioned arising. So that we might not continue to overlook Goenka—even in our explicit attempts to recognize him—we must deliberately seek a more symmetrical analysis. This means sometimes also deliberately displacing dominant narratives, even though such attempts may entrench those narratives further. This is a story of S. N. Goenka.

The Biography

CHAPTER 1

Son of Burma

SATYANĀRĀYAṆ (S. N.) GOENKA was born in the city of Mandalay, in the British colony of Burma (now modern Myanmar), on February 16, 1924.[4] He was one of nine children in a large family of Marwari traders with native connections to the Indian village of Churu, then part of the princely state of Bikaner in northwest India (now part of the state of Rajasthan). Goenka's father, Gopiram Goenka, worked with his brothers in the family business, a lucrative trading company trafficking primarily in Indian textiles. His mother, Kamaladevi, was a homemaker.

Nothing in the historical record indicates that there was anything out of the ordinary about Goenka's birth, but late in life he would infer to his close disciples that he believed himself to be a reincarnation of the Ledi Sayadaw, a renowned Burmese scholar-monk. The Sayadaw was a Buddhist meditation master from upper Burma, to whom Goenka looked as the fountainhead of his own lineage of meditation practice. The Sayadaw died some eight months before Goenka was born.[5]

As part of a close-knit immigrant community in colonial Burma, the Goenkas kept strong ties to their family traditions, maintaining associations with relatives in their native village and preserving the language, customs, and religious practices of their ancestors. S. N. Goenka in fact lived in his ancestral village of Churu from the age of three to five. At that time, his uncle—who eventually became his adoptive father—was constructing an ancestral *haveli*, a quadrangular mansion, for his grandparents.[6] However, the context for his most formative early years was British colonial Burma. As a second-generation Burmese of Indian origin, Goenka's connection to his ancestral motherland in his youth was largely through the religious, political, and literary imaginaries offered to him in his family life, local community, and formal education. The thought worlds with which these various contacts with India provided him were central to the formation of his identity as a young man. His religious, linguistic, and political sensibilities cannot be separated from this upbringing between cultural worlds in colonial Burma.[7]

In assessing the narrative arc of his own life, Goenka connected these Indian cultural sensibilities to a strong sense of his personal destiny. He was destined, by dint of his karmic connections to India, to return there and make it his *karmabhūmi*—the place where he would carry out his life's work. This karmic trajectory was constituted by his interaction with the Hindu devotionalism of his immediate and extended family, his deep concern for the political fate of India as a nation, and his eventual immersion in Burmese Buddhist meditation. We see elements of all these pieces of Goenka's identity in his own accounts of his early childhood.

Goenka grew up in a deeply conservative Hindu household and was strongly influenced by the devotional practices of his family members. His father was a devotee of the god Shiva, and his mother was a devotee of the god Krishna. He was therefore made to worship both of these deities. He regularly visited local temples with his family members and engaged in devotional singing, recitation, and prayers at home. Like most Hindus, he learned about religious ideals through narratives about the gods and goddesses and was encouraged to cultivate and embody the virtuous qualities they symbolized.

Goenka wrote particularly about his strong devotion to Krishna, and how, as a young child, he would experience intense emotions while reading religious stories out loud to his mother. At the age of seven, he would enact the roles of the characters in the stories, such as the mythical child Dhruv, crying along with his mother in devotion as she held him tightly in her lap. Deities and other mythical beings were brought to life in the religious literature that he read and loved. "I remained immersed in this devotion of emotional surrender for many years," he later wrote.[8]

As an adult, Goenka also regularly wrote and spoke of another early religious influence, that of his grandfather, Basesarlal Goenka (1859–1932). Known to the young Goenka as Baba, he had come to Burma in 1877, at the age of eighteen. He was the patriarch of the family and was his grandson's most direct tie to his ancestral identity. Goenka had a close relationship with his grandfather until he was eight years old, when Baba passed away. Goenka credited his grandfather with being a foundational, if inscrutable, influence on his later allegiance to the teachings of the Buddha, which led to an eventual repudiation of the rites and rituals of devotional Hinduism.

Some of his most prominent early memories of his grandfather were visits with him to the Mahamuni temple, a large and important Buddhist temple in Mandalay. While he had no memory of his grandfather participating in the Hindu devotionalism of the rest of his family, he vividly remembered sitting silently with him at the temple.[9] He associated these early experiences with his later connection to the meditative practices taught by the Buddha:

> When I joined my very first *vipaśyanā* course at the age of thirty-one, the atmosphere of silence and calm aroused the karmic forces (*saṃskār*) of my childhood, pulling them out of me like a magnet. The karmic perfections of my previous lives were surely with me, but it is also evident that *vipaśyanā* agreed with me as well as it did because of the influence of

the meritorious seed planted in my mind when sitting cross-legged and silent with Baba at the Mahamuni temple.[10]

In this way, Baba became, for Goenka, an early-life tie to the personality of the Buddha and a karmic tie to his ancestry in northern India. Goenka wrote in somewhat mystical terms about his gratitude to his grandfather for forging a trader's path into the lesser-known edges of the British empire:

> [When Baba] left home for the first time in his life—going out to seek a livelihood—he went to Calcutta (now Kolkata). Many people from Churu and its environs were living and working there. He also could have stayed there had he wanted to. But he felt some invisible force urging him to go further.[11]

Goenka felt that were it not for his grandfather's choice to settle in colonial Burma, he never would have come in contact with the meditative practices taught by the Buddha. These, Goenka believed, were preserved in their most authentic form by the traditional Buddhist lineages of Myanmar.

Aside from the trips into silence with his grandfather at the Mahamuni temple, the religious ideals presented to Goenka in his youth and later on were primarily those of his other family members. One important influence was his brother-in-law, Mahadev Nathani, the husband of his eldest sister. He was some twenty years older than Goenka and worked in the family shop. Goenka wrote of him:

> Even from a very young age, he powerfully influenced my thinking. I found his restrained lifestyle pleasing. He lived very simply.... He would eat plain food only once in twenty-four hours. He would wake up at four in the morning and

> walk to the Ayeyarwady (Irrawaddy) Ganga to bathe. He would return with some Ganga-water, and would drink it when he got thirsty. He did not sleep with my sister in the house, but instead slept in the family shop. He had one son and one daughter, and I heard him say many times that after the birth of one son and one daughter, one should live life like a forest hermit, observing faultless celibacy.[12]

While Goenka himself went on to have six sons, the ideal outlined here—the romantic image of the householder who lives like a forest hermit in the third stage of life, between household life and complete renunciation—would become his vision of an exemplary religious life.[13]

Mahadev Nathani was also something of a scholar. He was versed in Sanskrit and skilled at recitation and chanting. He had a powerful memory and could debate the meanings of traditional Hindu texts without even looking at physical copies of the texts under discussion. Goenka sought to emulate these qualities, and Mahadev Nathani taught him to chant verses of praise to the god Shiva. Goenka described being strongly influenced by the daily morning chanting of his brother-in-law:

> It was his resounding voice that was most captivating; its vibrations would give rise to a tingling in my heart. Some of his daily recitations made deep impressions on the surface of my heart that have lasted to this day.[14]

Later in life, when he went to India to teach the meditative practices he learned from his Buddhist teacher, Sayagyi U Ba Khin, Goenka would transfix his students with resounding chanting of Buddhist liturgical texts, which he used to create a powerful environment of purity and calm that would support his students' meditation practice. He also wrote and chanted *dohas* (couplets) in Hindi and Marwari that can sometimes be heard today in the mornings at the meditation centers he has built around the world. This early exposure to traditional Sanskrit chanting, through Mahadev Nathani, conditioned his approach to such practices.

Mahadev Nathani's staunch Hindu conservatism also contributed to Goenka's early conceptions of Buddhism, conceptions that became important later on as he developed his identity as a leader of the local Hindu community in Burma. He wrote of how Mahadev Nathani would criticize Goenka's grandfather for visiting the Mahamuni temple:

> He would at times speak about Baba, saying: "The influence of devotion to the Buddha on his thinking is dangerous. You must save your children from this." He believed that the Blessed Buddha was an incarnation of our Vishnu. So, there was no fault in maintaining a sense of faith toward him. But he thought that repeatedly visiting Buddha temples created the danger of getting involved with the Buddhist fold. He himself never went into any Buddha temple.[15]

This staunch conservatism was no doubt partly a symptom of the immigrant context. Surrounded by Buddhists in Mandalay, many of the Indian Hindu immigrants likely felt the need to stick stringently to their own traditions. But negative attitudes toward Buddhism also emerged from a broader set of narratives that had been developing for some time in India during British colonial rule. These narratives were formative for Goenka, and he came in contact with them primarily through his involvement in a social movement called the Arya Samaj ("Noble Society" or "Aryan Society"), starting at the age of fourteen. His exposure to this movement was in the form of a youth organization formed by a local priest, Mangaldevji Shastri:

> He aroused a new consciousness among the local teenagers and young men, organizing them into an association called the Arya Bal Sena ("Aryan Youth Army"). I was made its head, and we would gather every Sunday for intellectual discussions. We would also learn yogic postures and breathing exercises under the direction of Shastriji, as well as the martial art of wielding sticks and wooden swords. I loved it. He also very lovingly explained the doctrines of the Arya Samaj. I was very much impressed by the ideas of the fiercely intelligent Maharshi Dayananda Saraswati.[16]

Here Goenka described the hallmarks of the Arya Samaj's recruitment tactics.[17] Founded in 1875 by charismatic Hindu reformer Swami Dayananda Saraswati, the Arya Samaj was a key force in the project that many have called "cultural nationalism."[18] In India, such forms of nationalism developed in ideological distinction to the British colonial project, which might also be understood as a Christian colonial project. The Arya Samaj was an anticolonial organization designed to unify Indians under a common identity, language, and creed. It hoped to match the culturally destructive forces of British colonialism in India. Some of the key facets of Dayananda Saraswati's thought were the notion of a transcendent and nondual monotheistic ground of truth that has its basis in ancient Vedic scripture; a rejection of traditional Hindu caste ideology, with a particular focus on the problem of untouchability; a selective critique of the treatment of women in traditional Hinduism; and the notion of the ultimate unity of all Indian people under the umbrella of a single cultural identity. Part of this push involved the development of a uniform language register, a literary form of Sanskrit-derived Hindi.

At its heart, the Arya Samaj project was a fundamentalist project. It sought to ground Indian identity in a vision of an all-encompassing way of life, or Dharma. This Dharma was both ancient and scientific, beyond qualities but productive of a traditional Hindu society in accord with a Vedic tradition purified of immodest and unwarranted customs (to be found only in later scriptural sources). Though theoretically apolitical, these aspects of nationalist thinking very quickly became central to various forms of political nationalism in India. By the time Goenka came into contact with the Arya Samaj and its ideology, many of its ideas were thoroughly assimilated within a broader set of anticolonial nationalist ideas being advocated by Mahatma Gandhi's Indian National Congress.[19]

Goenka read Dayananda Saraswati's foundational treatise, *Light on the Meaning of Truth*, when he first came in contact with the Arya Samaj.[20] He was too young to fully understand the thrust of Dayananda Saraswati's big ideas at the time. Nonetheless, many of the concepts he was exposed to through his experiences with the Arya Bal Sena came to dominate his outlook, even later in life after he became a teacher of the meditative practices taught by the Buddha. While he was too immersed in his devotional practices to take on the idea of a God that was nondual and beyond qualities, he was drawn to the social and historical messages of the Arya Samaj.

Goenka appreciated Swami Dayananda Saraswati's method of assessing traditional Indian ideas and texts through intellectual critique, and to some extent he took on the Arya Samaj's critique of caste ideology and women's rights. For instance, on several occasions he attempted to have low-caste members of the community invested with a sacred thread—a ritual traditionally reserved for the higher castes—at the Arya Samaj temple.[21] He himself—to the dismay of his family members—chose not to undergo this coming-of-age initiation ritual, a mark of caste identity.[22] He also participated in attempts to "reconvert" or "purify" Indian Muslims.[23] He was an advocate for the education of women, including his own young bride-to-be, and pushed back against norms of child marriage within his community.[24] In his autobiographical writings, Goenka characterized himself as rebellious in this respect, even "rebellious by nature."[25] But it was rebellion in a profoundly conservative context. Because these activist engagements were dismally unsuccessful, he considered them to be youthful folly, and he remained quite conservative until the end of his life. Nonetheless, he would build on these early reformist sentiments later in life when he took on more radical ideas and practices that were not particularly popular among his more conservative family members.

One important aspect of the Arya Samaj's cultural nationalist narrative was a polemical critique of the non-Vedic Indian traditions, such as Buddhism and Jainism. The story went that such traditions contributed to the weakening of ancient Vedic culture—the essence of true Indian culture—and thereby powerfully contributed to the downfall of the Indian people (see chapter 9). The downfall reached its apex when the country was subjugated by Muslim invaders. This narrative gave strength to the kinds of arguments that Mahadev Nathani had made to Goenka in his youth about the dangers of falling in with the Burmese and their Buddhist ways.

The narrative was outlined in its starkest terms in the important nationalist treatise of Vinayak Damodar Savarkar, *Hindutva*, published in 1923.[26] (*Hindutva* can be translated as "Hinduness," but given the unfamiliarity of that term, I stick with the Sanskrit/Hindi *Hindutva* in this book—as did Savarkar in the title of his book.) Buddhism had not only diluted Vedic tradition and culture, it had set India on a path to political and military weakness.[27] The martial training enjoined by Goenka's Arya Bal Sena developed as a response to such narratives, and these organizational inflection points contributed to the expansion of more militant facets of the Indian independence movement. These ideas negatively colored Goenka's attitudes toward the teachings of the Buddha before he was directly exposed to Buddhist meditation practice. They also dominated his consciousness into his later life when he attempted to subvert them in presenting Buddhist meditation to his fellow Hindus in India (see chapters 9 and 10). Ironically, he would come to use the fundamentalist rhetoric of the Arya Samaj and Hindutva ideologies—the imaginary of a pure and perennial Dharma of an ideal ancient India—to reframe the teachings of the Buddha in the minds of his Indian students.

Goenka was keenly attuned to the politics of British colonial India and the independence movement from a young age. He attributed these interests to his grandfather who, with failing eyesight, would have his grandson read the newspaper to him every morning. Goenka took on his grandfather's Indian patriotism and his love and respect for Mahatma Gandhi, but the boy felt strongly as he came of age that Gandhi's nonviolence was not the most effective solution to the problem of the British colonial state. He read banned anticolonial literature and felt sympathy with advocates of violent revolution.[28] In his younger years, Goenka's participation in the political sphere was limited by his distance from the center of political activity in North India. What is more, he was part of a community of Marwari merchants who benefited from the British colonial setup. Still, he participated vicariously in the political life of India by closely following the news of various developments in the independence movement, and he assiduously studied Indian history and literature.

Though he only remained in school up to the tenth standard—completing his secondary school education and experiencing only three short days of higher education—Goenka loved to study and revered his teachers. He participated in two years of primary school in Churu before the age of five, where he learned basic Hindi and numbers. He then spent three years at a Marwari school in Mandalay, where he further studied Hindi and was exposed to Indian literature. From the third standard onward, Goenka studied at the Khalsa School, a school run by Indian Sikhs in Mandalay. At all of these schools, he was taught by Indian teachers, and the medium of study was Hindi. He had a deep love of the Hindi language and its literature. He wrote Hindi poetry—often with nationalist themes—and participated in a number of Hindi literature associations and gatherings.

Goenka wrote fondly about his primary and secondary school teachers, particularly his primary school teacher, Kalyan Dutt Dube. Dubeji, as Goenka respectfully referred to him, was responsible for encouraging his young student to cultivate public speaking skills, to value and respect social roles and family members, and to love India as a pluralistic nation. Dube also wrote plays, and Goenka enjoyed performing in them. He connected this early support from his primary school teacher to his later abilities as a Dharma teacher.

He also credited Dube with inspiring in him a love of literature. Dube introduced his young students to the devotional poetry of two important poets: Rahim (1556–1627), a Muslim by birth who became a devotee of Krishna; and Tulsidas (1532–1623), a devotee of Rama known for penning the famous *Ramcharitmanas*, an evocative poetic rendering of the story of the god-king Rama. Goenka came to draw on this literature in developing his devotional relationship to his own deity of choice, Krishna, but he also mined it for ideas about family ideals, social norms, equality among humans, and love of India. Dube helped him in this. Tulsidas's *Ramcharitmanas* in particular remained an important source for him throughout his life, though he would have to strip the text of many of its socially backward ideas to uncover the bits of "pure Dharma" that could be found in it.[29] In this way, Dube encouraged Goenka to develop a love of literature and also helped him to interpret it selectively, in a manner amenable to the social norms of the day. This approach to literature and interpretation would stay with him throughout his life. Of Dube, Goenka wrote:

> Because of the great kindness of that excellent teacher, Dubeji, I got a taste—at that young age—of the nectar that is devotion to parents, agreeable obedience to them, respect for my older brothers, and detached love toward my juniors. This was useful throughout life. That very valuable seed of Dharma, planted in the fertile ground of my young mind, became a very sweet fruit on the vine it produced.[30]

This quotation demonstrates that, though he could be rebellious on certain fronts, traditional conservative values ordered Goenka's approach to life. His was very much a family-focused life. This can be seen perhaps most clearly in his willingness to forgo higher education on the insistence of his father and other family members. In fact, he was lucky to make it through the final years of secondary school. His older brother, Babulal Goenka, had been taken out of school to work for the family business when he was fourteen. S. N. Goenka put in extra time and got himself a tutor so that he might skip a grade and pass the secondary school exams by the age of sixteen. After he had then convinced his father to enroll him in college in Rangoon (now Yangon), his other family members—fearing that more education might make him even more rebellious—insisted that he drop out and be put to work immediately in the family shop in Mandalay: "My college education was discontinued by force."[31] Though disappointed, he obeyed the order of his elders and withdrew from study after only three days of higher education.

Another sacrifice Goenka made in his youth involved his adoption by his paternal uncle, Dwarakdas Goenka. At the time, Dwarakdas was elderly and infirm, and he had no male children. So that he might have an heir, S. N. Goenka's father, Gopiram Goenka, gave up his son to allow his elder brother to adopt the boy. This occurred when S. N. Goenka was thirteen years old. A similar process had taken place for S. N. Goenka's eldest brother, Balkrishna Goenka, who had been adopted by Gopiram's eldest brother, Rameshvar Goenka, and taken to live with his new adoptive father in the city of Myitkyina in northern Burma.[32] While Dwarakdas lived in a joint family arrangement with his brother in Mandalay, Goenka still found the prospect of adoption distressing, since he was deeply attached to his birth mother:

> It was the year 1937, and I was thirteen years old. It is easy for a baby to be separated from its birth parents and adopted by someone else. But for me, at the age of thirteen, the very thought of it was unbearable. My older brother, Babulal, was about two years older than me, but we were like twins, always together. My birth mother and I had a strong attachment to one another. Her suffusive parental love was constant. Even at that young age, once or twice a year, unbearable migraine attacks would come over me. My mother would get very upset because of this. When I was in such states, she would have me lie down with my head in her lap, and she would massage my head for a while with fresh butter or almond oil. Her loving massage brought about miraculous results. Within a short time, a tingling sensation would start in my head, and it would spread through the entire body. This was, in a certain way, a foretaste of the future experience of *vipaśyanā* meditation, this feeling of my mother's touch of motherly affection. Because of this, no trace of pain would remain, and I would fall asleep with my head in my mother's lap. She would get up with tears of motherly affection on

> her face. It felt unbearable even to discuss being apart from my loving mother.[33]

This passage reveals how close Goenka was to his mother and also what a deep impression his early painful migraines left on him. As intimated here, his battle with migraines would eventually lead him to a meditative solution.

Despite this emotional difficulty, Goenka agreed to let his elderly uncle adopt him. Such arrangements were common in large Marwari merchant families and remain common today. These practices serve to maintain lines of inheritance and solidify business networks within these close-knit families and caste communities.[34] The sacrifice had to be made for the sake of the family and according to custom. While this was clearly a challenging process for the adolescent Goenka, he resolved the situation by recourse to an attitude of devotion to his elders:

> Listening to my father's words, charged with boundless faith and obligation toward his older brother, I could not oppose him in the slightest. Furthermore, I also saw how my uncle was like a deity, a person serene by nature. My aunt-mother was also always calm, the living image of a goddess. I never during my entire life heard her raise her voice while speaking. I also understood from my father that I would be able to stay close, and would not have to go far away like my brother Balkrishna. So, I accepted my father's decision.[35]

While Dwarakdas did in the end have his own son not long after he adopted Goenka, his adoptive son became the head of that wing of the family, even acting as a father figure to his young cousin-brother when his elderly uncle passed away some years later. In this way, Goenka learned from a very young age to put family first.

For him, a good life, a life of Dharma, could not easily be separated from the karmic bonds of obligation to family and community.

Like most in his community, Goenka began to establish his own family when he was quite young, not long after he left school and took up the family business. His marriage with the eldest daughter of a family friend of the same community—a man by the name of Balchand Makharia, who was a close neighbor—had been arranged many years earlier. When it came to marriage, Goenka was once again rebellious. He insisted that, unlike his two older brothers who had been married to child brides at the young age of fifteen, he would not be married until the age of eighteen. He was able to convince his family to allow this to happen based on the palm reading of an astrologer, who warned that he would face great difficulty in his eighteenth year and perhaps even die. Goenka claimed to have used this as a pretense to push back the date of his marriage for the sake of the young bride.[36]

But the stars turned out to be in his favor. He lived, and on June 21, 1942, the marriage rites of S. N Goenka and Illaichidevi Goenka were completed. He was eighteen years old, and she was twelve. They did not, however, settle simply into a householder's life in Mandalay. In a matter of weeks, when the Japanese marched to occupy Burma, Goenka was forced to flee the country with his family, crossing the border to India on foot and taking refuge in his ancestral village of Churu.[37]

CHAPTER 2

A Season in the Motherland

THE FIRST HINT of the Japanese threat in Burma came at the end of December 1941. The Japanese attacked Rangoon from the air. In the months that followed, hundreds of thousands of Indian Burmese trekked on foot to their ancestral motherland. About this "long land march" the historian Hugh Tinker wrote:

> There is no significant historical lesson to be learnt from the narrative which follows, except the lesson of human endurance.... Because the routes ran through largely uninhabited tracts of country, there was no relief organisation awaiting from Indian, non-official resources in the frontier zone. The refugees struggled on and on alone.... [T]he whole exodus took place overland, either via Arakan to Chittagong or via the Chindwin valley to Manipur, or—for the last stragglers—via the northern passes to Ledo and other termini in north Assam....When a camp census was carried out by the Indians Overseas Department of the Government of India, 393,735 "British Asiatics" were enumerated: though the department calculated that between 450,000 and 500,000 had arrived in India, many continuing straight on to their hometowns and villages without being checked on arrival.[38]

Goenka and his family were among the "last stragglers" of this long land march. They stayed in Burma until there was no other option but to leave. Indian communities in Burma were intimately tied in to the British colonial apparatus there. An invading Japanese force, hostile to Western powers, was a threat to these communities. Since more than half of the Indians living in colonial Burma at the time had in fact been born in India, and like the Goenkas maintained ties to their ancestral homes, a return to a safe British India seemed a natural solution.[39]

Goenka helped to lead a large group of his family members across the mountains to safety in India, and they arrived at a time of great political tension there.[40] The global strain of World War II had contributed to bringing the Indian independence movement to a head. In early August 1942, Mahatma Gandhi had called for the withdrawal of the British from India in his famous Quit India speech, in which he made a "do or die" pronouncement. At this politically precarious moment, Goenka found himself—for the first time as an adult—in his ancestral motherland, a country that up until then had existed more as an imaginary than a real place. He spent the years between 1942 and 1947 in India. He first took refuge in Churu for a year, then relocated to Cannanore (Kannur) in what is now Kerala, and subsequently went to Madras (Chennai) in what is now Tamil Nadu. His family had business interests in these areas of southern India.

Goenka's accounts of this time focused on his desire to participate in Indian politics.[41] He identified strongly with the independence movement, particularly its more radical elements, and wanted to find a way to get involved. An Indian of his generation could not have a public identity without in some way articulating oneself in relation to these important political developments. These desires, however, conflicted with his family responsibilities and the sensibilities of his community.

At that time, Churu was part of the princely state of Bikaner. It had been a British protectorate since 1818, and the leaders of the communities in this region supported British rule. By Goenka's account, there was virtually no revolutionary activity to be found there when he arrived in 1942. He felt pressure from the local community—eager to keep away from the politics of the independence movement—not to express his political views in public.[42] In the end, it appears that Goenka spent these years focusing primarily on building the family business networks in India. As it was while he was growing up in Burma, he had to participate in politics vicariously. But he made attempts to get involved and also engaged in literary activities that tied him to the nationalist project. After India achieved independence, when he returned to Burma, his involvement in politics became more explicit.

One event, which took place not long after Goenka arrived in India, stands out. He wrote about an attempt to get involved in the independence movement when he was sent on family business to the capital city of New Delhi, one of the centers of revolutionary activity:

> I did not know of and was not acquainted with anyone there. I had been in the country for less than six months. How might I come in contact with revolutionaries?
>
> Finally, after inquiring here and there, I came to know that a leading official of the Delhi Congress Committee stayed across from the *katras*[43] just past the clock tower in Chandni Chowk. His name was Ramchandra or something like that. I don't fully remember now. Seeking him out, I came to his place of business there on the first floor of a building. I met him and told him about why I had come. He first asked me to introduce myself, and I told him very truthfully that I had come from Burma and was very new to India. He then answered curtly, in a way that did not inspire enthusiasm: "There is no clear way forward. Gandhiji has given the order to 'do or die.' But he was arrested before he could announce

how to proceed. For this reason, we are not doing anything." I wanted to know about revolutionaries, particularly Jayaprakash Narayan, Ram Manohar Lohia, Aruna Asaf Ali, and other such people. I made clear my desire to know how to contact them. Laughing out loud, he said that if he knew how to reach them, then surely the government would be able to catch them too. I was quite disappointed. At the time I did not even consider that, even if he had known how to contact them, he probably would not have told me. It is possible that he thought I was a government spy! So, after two or three days wandering around in Delhi, I returned to Churu with my hopes dashed.[44]

In relaying this narrative, Goenka embedded himself in the historical moment of the Quit India movement. Though his attempt to get involved was unsuccessful, and he remained on the periphery of Indian politics, he was there. Of particular importance is Goenka's specific reference to Jayaprakash Narayan, Ram Manohar Lohia, and Aruna Asaf Ali. All of these actors were critical of Gandhi's program of nonviolence. While Goenka considered Gandhi to be a great saint and took on many of his social and political ideals, for the first half of his life he was strongly opposed to Gandhi's advocacy of nonviolent resistance (see chapter 9).

This political stance was heavily informed by the Hindutva narratives Goenka had adopted through his association with the Arya Samaj, and they colored his thinking until the end of his life. Even after he fully accepted the teachings of the Buddha and taught the total renunciation of action as the highest ideal of the spiritual life, he powerfully advocated the use of necessary force in the worldly sphere.[45]

This attitude toward political life was informed by Goenka's reading of Hindu scripture. As a devotee of Krishna, he was deeply immersed in the teachings of the Bhagavad Gita. On its face, the Gita advocates a devotional theism in support of necessary violence in the context of war.[46] While Gandhi and others developed interpretive approaches to the Gita that supported an absolute nonviolence, Goenka's more literal devotionalism led him to understand the Gita's take on Dharma or duty in a more concrete way. For Gandhi, the battle of the Gita was an internal one, a battle between good and evil that could only truly be fought within the self.[47] The kind of violence advocated by the Indian freedom fighters of the independence movement represented a victory for evil. Some of these ideas would seep into Goenka's thinking later in life (see chapter 10). But for the young Goenka, and many others like him, this approach to human duty did not fit the needs of the moment. Violence was justified in the context of a revolution for independence.

But Goenka's situation in Churu, along with his family and business obligations, kept him from participating in any real way in the independence movement. He did, however, continue to participate directly in the nationalist project through his ongoing study of and engagement with Hindi language and literature. After some time he moved to Kannur and then Chennai, where he was even further from the center of the nationalist movement. He lamented this fact:

> It was a wonderful place for me to make a living, but I had absolutely no opportunity to participate in social or political activities. So, merely able to express my inability to provide support in freeing Mother India from her shackles, I wrote poems—
>
> How might I free mother [India] from her shackles!
> The one hundred thousand difficulties of a shackled
> mother
> Overflow this pair of eyes . . .

> These verses were composed for my own enjoyment; who would I recite them for there? I had not come across any branch of the South India Association for the Spread of Hindi.[48]

In Churu, Goenka had participated in Hindi examinations through the Society for Hindi Literature, an organization devoted to developing Hindi into a standard national language. This organization, founded in 1910, was central in the project of developing a "pure" Hindi, differentiated from various local dialects and regional linguistic practices that may have taken on non-Indic influences.[49] Goenka was pleased, upon arriving in India, to take part in local gatherings of Hindi literati organized through a local Hindi-language academy in Churu. He wrote poems and performed them at such gatherings, and many of these poems had nationalist themes (see chapter 8). Goenka took pride in his mastery of Hindi. He tells the story of how, when he first arrived in India after the long land march, a well-known scholar of Sanskrit and Hindi literature, Paṇḍit Vidyadhar Shastri, praised his Hindi:

> I also used to take part in week-long literature conferences that took place there [in Churu]. . . . At one of these conferences, with little introduction, I recited one of my poems. A famous scholar from Bikaner, Paṇḍit Vidyadhar Shastri, had come to that conference. After the conference, he patted me on the back, and said: "It is surprising how, though living abroad, you speak and write such pure Hindi."[50]

Goenka's knowledge of Hindi, and his ability to speak publicly in an erudite Sanskritic register, was a major asset as he came of age and developed an identity as a public figure. This was important for him first as a young leader of the Hindu business community in postcolonial Burma and later as a teacher of Buddhist meditation in India. But it was also simply the language in which he felt the most comfortable. He and his brothers did very well in business in South India, and he could have stayed there, as his older brother Balkrishna did. But the call of his birthplace, and a community with which he was familiar, brought him back to Burma. He wrote:

> The land in Kerala is very beautiful, verdant year-round. The first time I saw it I was filled with delight. . . . The people are wonderful, the language lovely and sweet. Rich or poor, all the homes are neat and clean. . . . Everyone more or less wears the same cloths, whether they are wealthy or without resources. . . . But my life there felt colorless without Hindi-speaking friends. . . . Working tirelessly, I achieved success beyond expectation. . . . However, living among those wonderful people in that beautiful environment of unspoiled nature for approximately four years, my thoughts became vapid and dried up without access to any Hindi literature society. My mind was filled with delight, therefore, when I returned to Burma, the land of my birth. After some five years of separation, I returned to the loving lap of my mother[land].[51]

It is somewhat ironic that Goenka associated his return to Burma—and departure from his ancestral motherland, the supposed home of Hindi—with his desire for access to a community of Hindi-speaking literati. But it appears less ironic if we consider that in many ways the close-knit Hindu immigrant community in which Goenka was raised in colonial Burma perhaps fit the ideal India of his nationalist imaginary best. Though it was clearly a good place to do business, South India—with its Dravidian languages, its openness to English, and its particular regional history—was not the India that Goenka had come to know in his scriptural and literary encounters as a young man. He had to return to Burma to recover that India. It would not be until more than twenty years later that he would undertake to fully explore modern India in its true contours, this time with a very different agenda.

Though Goenka dwelled little on it in his accounts of this period, his family lost almost everything when the Japanese occupied Burma.[52] It must have taken much hard work, family cooperation, and diligent networking to rebuild the family's resources. This appears to be what consumed Goenka during his time in India as a young adult. He and his brothers found success by working tirelessly to develop their business in southern India, and Goenka was also a young father for the first time. By the time he returned to Burma, Illaichidevi Goenka had already given birth to two sons, Girdharilal and Banwarilal.

Returning to Burma in the wake of World War II, his family business revitalized, Goenka quickly established himself as a leader of the community there. He settled with his brother Babulal in a joint family home in Rangoon, the capital of the newly independent state of Burma. He forged strong connections with the budding independent government and expanded the family textile business into a thriving international trade group. Goenka included little in his autobiographical writings about the details of his business, but his wealth and proximity to some of the most powerful people in government gave him status and prestige in the high society of Rangoon.

With some like-minded friends, he established the All Burma Congress, an association of Indians living in Burma with interests in Indian nationalist politics. He helped to establish some fifty branches of this organization throughout Burma. In this capacity he came into direct contact with many leaders of the Indian government. He wrote in his autobiography about meeting Jawaharlal Nehru, the first prime minister of India, and discussing the future of India with him on a visit organized by the Congress around 1960.[53] He also established the Mahatma Gandhi Memorial Trust, which translated some of Gandhi's writings into Burmese for publication. Additionally, he helped to establish the All Burma Hindi Literature Association, which supported Hindi education in Burma. As part of this work, he was involved in establishing a government university for Hindi higher education and organized week-long Hindi literature conferences like the ones he had participated in while in Churu. He became the president of the Marwari Chamber of Commerce, and subsequently the Rangoon Chamber of Commerce, once he had reestablished his Burmese citizenship. Finally, because of his close connections with the new administration, he was asked by the finance minister, U Aung, to advise the government on matters connected with commerce. Goenka had done all of this before the age of twenty-five.[54]

In writing about his phenomenal success in business, the social sphere, and public life during this period, Goenka emphasized what an important role his Hindu faith played in his conceptualization of such success:

> [In our family shop in Mandalay,] there was always some image or another stuck on the rolls of fabric we sold. These stickers usually had on them images of the leaders of the independence struggle or images of the gods and goddesses that we worshipped. At one time I saw stuck to a roll of fabric a lovely image of the God Krishna, a deity I adored. With great love and faith, I removed the sticker. In accordance with whatever intelligence I was equipped with at that young age, I cut out a piece of cardboard the size of the sticker and

> stuck the image to it. I pasted a plastic protective cover over the image so that it would not get damaged. The picture was small enough that I could fit it into my shirt pocket.
>
> I remember well the deep faith and sense of attachment I held in my mind toward that image of God as an adolescent. My faith was so deep that for the next twenty years—whether I was in Burma, or India, or travelling abroad—I would put it in the pocket of whatever shirt I was wearing, keeping it close to my heart. I firmly believed that all the life success coming to me was by virtue of the grace of this Supreme God.[55]

This very concrete conception of devotion, and its cultivation in relation to a deity with a materially accessible form, shaped Goenka's religious life. At the same time, his exposure to other ways of conceptualizing God, such as those of the Arya Samaj, made him cognizant of a need for an ecumenical attitude when it came to the diversity of Hindu religious practice. Once he became known as a leader of the Hindu community in Rangoon, he would often be invited to give public talks on topics related to Indian religion and culture. In these contexts, he followed some of the tried and true ideas of modern Hindu pluralist inclusivism, which focused on common origins and the rhetoric of a common essence.[56] But at this point in time, after five years in India and even more exposure to cultural nationalist ideas about the bad influence of Buddhism and other *nāstika* or denier traditions—traditions that denied the validity of Vedic and Hindu ideas—Goenka had developed a strong distrust of Buddhism. It did not figure in his inclusivist approaches. He wrote much about this development, since his attachment to his Hindu identity led to a major internal conflict when he later came into direct contact with the meditative practices of Burmese Buddhism:

When I left Myanmar and came to India at the beginning of the war in 1942, I came to see many additional flaws in the teachings of the Buddha; the distrust that had developed in my youth increased. For instance, the Buddha was an extreme pessimist—[advocating the doctrine that human existence is misery]. This doctrine generated an atmosphere of hopelessness and despair in the country. In his teaching, all importance was given to the idea of the momentary transience of existence. In this philosophy of impermanence, no mention was made anywhere of the permanent, eternal, and constant. So, there was no aim, and no guidance offered on how to escape from this wheel of existence. His entire teaching was negative. Nowhere in it was there an affirmative teaching by which a person might hope for a brighter future. He was an advocate of indifference. So, his teachings may be fine and good for those who renounce household life, but they are entirely useless for householders. He was an ocean of compassion, and therefore he advocated complete nonviolence. Because of this, his teachings weakened our country. For example, the emperor Aśoka, who was brave in battle, broke his sword upon falling in with the teachings of the Buddha. He turned his back on war. This had harmful consequences and a negative impact. The country was repeatedly attacked by outsiders, and repeatedly we found ourselves shackled in subjugation. Because of the Buddha's teachings, the people's sense of enjoyment was destroyed, and life came to feel tasteless and futile. Everything was simply empty. No cheerfulness, joy, or enthusiasm remained among the people. This was extremely damaging for the country. As I continued to hear about and read about these ideas—and many other ideas like them—

> they continued to influence my thinking more and more deeply.[57]

We can see here how the Hindutva narrative of the failings of the Buddha and his teachings came to dominate Goenka's understanding of the Buddhist tradition so powerfully.[58] His time in India as a young adult helped to solidify this narrative to which he was exposed in his adolescence.

Living in Rangoon upon his return to Burma, with the teachings of the Buddha all around him in their local Burmese form, Goenka was able to respect his foreign Buddhist brothers from a distance. Things became more uncomfortable, however, when it came to confronting the question of the historical roots of the Buddhist tradition in relation to his own Hindu faith. Goenka wrote about how he found his Hindutva narrative challenged by Buddhist scholars in a number of contexts. One incident, which took place in the early 1950s, exemplified how Goenka's cultural nationalist historical narrative came into conflict with alternative narratives:

> In those days I would sometimes give talks on the occasion of Hindu festivals. On one such occasion, Swami Suryanandji of the Ramakrishna Mission Society arranged for me to give a talk on "The Quintessence of Hinduism."
>
> Because my talks were [always] in Hindi, the members of the audience would all be Hindi speakers. But on that day, I was surprised to see three or four Burmese friends—leading senior scholars of Burmese society—sitting in the front row.[59]

After the talk, Goenka learned that the event had been advertised in an English-language newspaper, without mention that the talk would be in Hindi.

> I apologized to my friends and invited them to eat with me at my home, telling them that during dinner I would give them a summary in English of what I had spoken about in my talk.
>
> . . . I explained to them that in the lecture I had said that the essence of Hindu Dharma is in the Vedas, the essence of the Vedas is in the Upanishads, the essence of the Upanishads is in the [Bhagavad] Gita, and the essence of the Gita is in the teaching on establishment of wisdom (*sthitaprajñatā*).[60] Then I explained the qualities of one who is established in wisdom. My friend U Ta Mya responded to this by saying that all of those qualities had been explained by the Buddha as qualities of an *arahant*, [a realized follower of the Buddha's teachings]. After hearing this, I displayed my ignorance by arguing that "after all, whatever the Blessed Buddha taught has been taken from our Gita." To this U Ta Mya replied that the Gita had in fact plagiarized the words of the Blessed Buddha in its description of the establishment of wisdom.[61]

A tense discussion ensued about the historical provenance of the Bhagavad Gita, Goenka insisting the text was five thousand years old, and U Ta Mya insisting that it had been composed many centuries after the Buddha lived. (The most recent scholarship on the text suggests that it was composed at least two hundred years after the Buddha lived.[62]) While the issue was diffused through the social graces of both parties, Goenka remained firm in his uninformed opinion: "I was not ready to retreat from my belief even a little."[63]

A similar encounter took place not long after this one, when a famous Indian Buddhist scholar-monk, Bhadant Anand Kausalyayan, visited Burma and stayed with Goenka at his home:

> Respected Bhadant Anand Kausalyananji visited Burma often and would stay as a guest in our house. We had received much assistance from him in our work promoting the Hindi language in Burma, and I was grateful for it. Performing the duties of a householder, I made sure to provide in every way for his hospitality. However, whenever he would begin a conversation about the Buddha's teachings, I would become uncomfortable. . . .
>
> Once we were having a conversation about the promotion of Hindi at my home. . . . U Ta Mya . . . was also present. Suddenly, he raised the topic [of our previous disagreement]. Anandji, taking his side, commented that it was in fact true that the Gita was composed well after the Buddha's time, and that it was influenced by the Buddha's teachings. It was, therefore, replete with the words of the Buddha. . . .
>
> I cannot describe the offense that I felt at this statement. I was more offended by this than I was when he said that it was a definite lie that Buddhism was the offspring of the Vedic tradition, but that it is true that today's Hinduism is the offspring of Buddhism. . . . I stayed silent, but they both understood that I was very unhappy. I felt that they must have been misled by the sectarian teachings of Buddhism.[64]

Goenka wrote that this encounter felt like a "deep affront to my Hindutva."[65] Though he remained friends with both of these scholars, he did not act on their scholarly challenges. He told how, after that incident, he only spoke once more with Bhadant Anand Kausalyayan about Buddhism. When the venerable monk's flight out of Rangoon was delayed, Goenka stayed with him during the two-hour wait. At that time, Bhadant Anand Kausalyayan encouraged Goenka to explore the teachings of the Buddha. And just before he left, he gave Goenka a Hindi translation of the *Dhamma-*

pada, a collection of foundational early teachings of the Buddha in pithy verses. Though Goenka graciously accepted the gift, he wrote that "it sat on my table for years, but I did not read even one page of that book. There was surely some error somewhere in the teachings of the Buddha that might lead me down a wrong path."[66]

We see here how Goenka's religious universe at this point in his life was a thoroughly bounded domain. He was completely immersed in his Hindu Dharma. He was able to keep it bounded in this way because he had a large family and tight-knit community of Burmese Indians in Rangoon who lived in a similarly bounded universe. The stringent maintenance of customs, traditions, and identities in these contexts helped to keep wealth within the community and build business networks that supported its prosperity and growth.

Despite his extraordinary success in business and his rich involvement in a range of social activities, things were not perfect in every sphere of Goenka's life. He struggled with bouts of anger at home, was intolerant of his children, and—perhaps most importantly for our story—began to suffer regularly from the migraines that had come upon him only intermittently in his early life.

About Goenka's anger, his sister, Ila Agrawal, wrote:

> Before *vipaśyanā*, my brother's nature was to get very angry at times. This was particularly the case when the children would bring home their report cards from the school exam results. Even if they did not fail, still they should have received a higher grade. Brother himself had always come very first in exams throughout his schooling. So, seeing the children with a low number, he would explode, [feeling that] the children were a disgrace. He would at times beat the children very badly. Once one of the children was so badly beaten that his cheek swelled up and his eyes became stuck

> shut. Fearing that the child might go blind, a doctor had to be called. Another time, he grabbed a different child by one foot and one hand and flung him down the cement stairs onto a cement terrace.[67]

While it was not out of the ordinary at that time and place for a father to discipline his children with force, this level of force is extreme by most measures. Goenka clearly struggled with his temper into adulthood and found fatherhood challenging. Later in life, he would often speak about his anger issues and how they disappeared after he began to practice vipaśyanā meditation. He used such transformations as benchmarks in the progress of meditation.

But he likely never would have come to meditation if it were not for another problem that reached a critical juncture when he was around the age of thirty:

> For as long as I can remember I had suffered from migraine headaches. In childhood, an attack would cripple me maybe once in a year or a year and a half. In youth, it escalated to two or three times in a year. By the time I was 25 years old, the intervals kept decreasing, till I suffered an attack every fortnight. The unbearable pain could not be contained by ordinary painkillers and the doctor would give morphine injections. This would alleviate the pain, but the side effects revealed themselves the next day when, upon waking up from the drug-induced stupor, nausea and nervous anxiety lingered throughout the day.
>
> . . . Another five years passed and the interval between the migraine attacks was reduced to every 8 to 10 days, and the morphine dose had to be increased. . . .
>
> [I sought treatment] under senior doctors in Switzerland, Germany, England and the U.S.A. . . . After months of chas-

> ing after relief, I returned home totally dejected. Migraine attacks now came weekly...[68]

In this state of defeat, Goenka became desperate for a solution. The solution that came would alter the course of his life in unthinkable ways.

CHAPTER 3

A Second Birth

IN HIS TEN-DAY vipaśyanā meditation courses, Goenka would tell the story of how he first came to practice this particular form of meditation. The story, as he told it, is therefore familiar to millions of people around the globe who have participated in his meditation courses over the past fifty years. (As we will see later on, videos of Goenka's talks were shown at retreats at meditation centers around the globe, which allowed for the mass dissemination of his teachings into the present to those who would never meet him.) Desperate to cure his migraines, he sought out a technique of stress reduction that would solve his "psychosomatic" problem. But in telling this story in his Dharma talks, Goenka provided little context for his listeners. Since his encounter with his meditation teacher, Sayagyi U Ba Khin, was perhaps the most important event in his life, we should understand who his teacher was and how he figured in the landscape of Burmese Buddhist meditation traditions.

U Ba Khin was born in 1899 in Rangoon. He therefore grew up and came of age during the height of British colonial influence in Burma. He was educated mostly at English-medium schools, first at a Methodist elementary school (1907–1914) and then at the prestigious St. Paul's High School.[69] This educational background exposed him to non-Burmese religious traditions and made him a capable communicator within English-speaking circles. His English education also set him apart from his own meditation teacher, the farmer Saya Thetgyi (1873–1945), and his teacher's teacher, the

Buddhist scholar-monk Ledi Sayadaw (1846–1923). Both of these teachers were bound to Burmese-speaking contexts or had to use translators to communicate beyond them.

As his parents had passed away before he completed high school, U Ba Khin did not go on to higher studies and instead entered the workforce, working first for a local newspaper and then as a clerk in the Office of the Accountant General of Burma in 1917. He passed the Indian colonial government accountancy exams in 1926 and worked his way up to a position of deputy supervisor in the Office of the Auditor General by 1934. Being the only Burmese in an office primarily made up of Indian civil servants, U Ba Khin was promoted to the position of special supervisor when Burma established its own accountancy department, and at the beginning of 1941 another promotion made him an accountant officer for the Railways' Board. Finally, on the day of Burma's independence in 1948, U Ba Khin became the first accountant general of an independent Burma.[70]

U Ba Khin was a hard worker and strict disciplinarian, both in his work as the accountant general and in his capacity as a meditation teacher. He was at times heard yelling at his meditation students when they did not strictly follow their prescribed course of practice. Many thought him too strict, but his close disciples understood his strictness to be an expression of his loving-kindness. The quality most discussed by his students in defining him was industriousness. It was said that he never left a task unfinished at the end of a day of work. In matters of meditation, he was similar. He would push his students to their limits so that they might break through and attain the goals of meditation practice.

U Ba Khin's first encounter with meditation occurred somewhat late in life, in 1937, at the age of thirty-eight. After briefly learning a simple technique of breath meditation during a chance encounter at the house of an acquaintance, he resolved immediately to go on retreat at the meditation center of the lay meditation teacher Saya

Thetgyi, not far from Rangoon. Some years earlier, Saya Thetgyi had been charged by the meditation master Ledi Sayadaw with teaching meditation to six thousand laymen. This development was part of a broader social movement in which traditional forms of monastic meditation were made accessible to the lay community.[71] Saya Thetgyi was one of the first lay teachers authorized to teach during this time.

Like Saya Thetgyi, U Ba Khin was a rare example of a lay meditation teacher. There is little in the historical record about U Ba Khin's formal meditation practice between 1937 and 1941. But we do know that he began teaching meditation in 1941, after a chance encounter with the great meditator monk, the Webu Sayadaw. On a work trip in his capacity as an officer of the Railways' Board, he found himself waylaid in the village of Kyaukse where the sayadaw—rumored to be an *arhat*—lived. In an encounter with him, U Ba Khin impressed him so much by his powerful presence that the sayadaw encouraged him to immediately begin teaching meditation.[72] On that same day, U Ba Khin taught his work assistant a basic form of breath meditation. The incitement from the great monk, along with continued visits to Saya Thetgyi and his rise to the post of accountant general, set the stage for U Ba Khin's career as a meditation teacher.

U Ba Khin began formally teaching meditation in 1951, at the Office of the Accountant General. U Ko Lay, his close disciple and biographer, described the founding of the Vipassana Research Association on the full moon day of Waso, July 18, 1951, as the beginning of this endeavor:

> Sayagyi and his close disciples studied, explored, investigated, and innovated—by using the approaches of scientific research, assessing whether [their method] conforms with the *Path of Purification*[73] and whether or not it is precise and complete with respect to the 37 factors of enlightenment.

From such researches, the right method of practice that can be carried out in a short period based on the threefold training—of morality, concentration and meditative wisdom—was discovered. From this, by practicing according to these methods, it was seen that the vibrational force of wisdom (*vijjādhāt'*) arises as soon as one attains correct insight knowledge (*vipassanāñāṇa*), which can eradicate craving and mental defilements. This supernormal power of *vijjādhāt'* enacts the cleaning of defilements rooted in the aggregates. So, Sayagyi was able to prove in practice that people with karmic perfections are able to attain happiness, both in body and mind, along with the peace and happiness of nirvana.

Apart from having the experience of seeing the true nature of the supernormal power of the *vijjādhāt'*, the method to maintain this power was also discovered according to the research. Further, as soon as one practices to reach real insight knowledge, at the same time the nature of destructive forces is discovered. Thus, the methods to protect and prevent from them were recorded as per the research. These records are written in a very systematic way. They are complicated and profound matters, [and] not all the records are allowed to be read....

At the time that Sayagyi became the Accountant General, half of the high-ranking Indian officers were still left [in the office]. Sayagyi taught the Dhamma not only to the local Buddhist staff, but also to these officers.... [N]ot only the staff in his office, but their family members and relatives got interested in learning meditation from Sayagyi. Then, the shrine room at the top floor of Account General's office was not large enough to fit all of them. It was therefore considered necessary to have a meditation center large enough for the staff and their family members.[74]

This account relates the context of the founding of Sayagyi U Ba Khin's International Meditation Centre (IMC), where Goenka first learned vipaśyanā. Several aspects of this description help us to understand what Goenka was getting involved in when he decided to take part in an intensive retreat at Sayagyi U Ba Khin's center.

First, U Ba Khin is here characterized as an experimentalist and an innovator. His method of meditation, though drawn from his training with his teacher, was really his own. Second, his method of practice is characterized as "the right method of practice that can be carried out in a short period." This was a key element of U Ba Khin's approach. He claimed to be able to bring people to high states of meditative accomplishment in very short periods of time.[75] The particulars of how he was able to do this are hinted at when U Ko Lay refers to Sayagyi's ability not only to arouse "the supernormal power of the vibrational force of wisdom" in his students but also to "protect" his students from "destructive forces," supernormal agents that might become barriers to progress in meditation. These descriptions reveal how U Ba Khin's teaching methods were embedded in a context in which meditation was conceptualized as a battle of "forces" (*dhāt'*; Pali: *dhātu*). The goal of meditation was to remove bad forces from within oneself and allow good forces to enter. In Burmese tradition, these forces are conceptualized as supernormal agents—agents of the Dharma or agents seeking to thwart the Dharma—that a powerful teacher can harness in teaching contexts. This conceptual framework is shared with the Burmese *weizzā* (wisdom/wizardry; Pāli: *vijjā*; Sanskrit: *vidyā*) tradition, a complex spectrum of spiritual practices that includes esoteric traditions of alchemy and healing.[76] In the context of U Ba Khin's teachings, the practice of *vipassanā* comes to be the supreme *weizzā*, a power-wisdom that allows the teacher to utilize supernormal agents of the Dharma and banish evil forces that prevent the progress of individual meditators.

What is not explicitly mentioned in U Ko Lay's description, however, is U Ba Khin's notoriety as a healer. While U Ba Khin taught vipassanā as a path to the highest goal of Buddhist practice, nirvana, his popularity as a teacher in mid-twentieth-century Rangoon may have been primarily due to his powerful ability to heal the worldly ailments of many of those who came to him to learn meditation. While his formal writings and teachings do not emphasize this aspect of what he was doing, his oral teachings reveal that he took pride in his healing powers and put much emphasis on them to draw in students.[77] It was precisely U Ba Khin's reputation as a healer that drew Goenka to him when the latter was desperate to find a remedy for his excruciating migraine attacks.

Note that, in the preceding description, U Ko Lay narrated how the International Meditation Centre was founded as the outgrowth of a work association directly affiliated with the government office over which U Ba Khin presided. This means that the establishment of the center was the direct result of a postcolonial project of public and state-sponsored Buddhism. Such a project mirrored and participated in a social imaginary of the intimate connection between state authority and spiritual authority that goes back to the basic thought structures of early Indian Buddhism. Moreover, many of the staff of U Ba Khin's office were Indians and non-Buddhists. Since he considered it his job to teach meditation to all those in his employ, he was obliged to find approaches to teaching that could accommodate those of other traditions. It is in these unique circumstances that we find the seed of a tradition of vipaśyanā meditation that might become both public and non-Buddhist.

On October 23, 1952—only a few years before Goenka came in contact with his teacher, and in preparation for the founding of the International Meditation Centre—U Ba Khin put out the following notice:

Towards Peace of Mankind

My Dear Brothers & Sisters,

...I propose to specialise in giving courses of meditation to men of all religions without interfering with their religious faith.

Each candidate will have to undergo a course of meditation for 10 days at the International Meditation Centre which will be opened on or about the 2nd of December 1952.

Christians may contact Mr. A. N. David, Deputy Accountant General, and Hindus Mr. S. Venkataraman Superintendent, for further particulars or registration.[78]

U Ba Khin
President
Vipassana Research Association

Goenka's first encounter with U Ba Khin occurred in the context of this ecumenical project. It was precisely U Ba Khin's policy of noninterference with his students' individual religious faiths that made it possible for Goenka, the staunch Hindu with an ax to grind with the Buddha, to consider taking part in a course on Buddhist meditation to find relief from his migraines.

It was U Chan Htoon, the first attorney general of independent Burma—and eventually a judge on its supreme court—who urged Goenka to learn meditation.[79] Goenka told how U Chan Htoon suggested that his migraines were likely "psychosomatic" or the result of "mental stress."[80] As such, a course in meditation might bring a cure. Though Goenka was hesitant, he allowed his friend to arrange a meeting between himself and U Ba Khin. He had two meetings with U Ba Khin before finally taking part in a ten-day course of meditation at the International Meditation Centre. The first meeting took place at U Ba Khin's home and the second at his meditation center.

Goenka's narrative of these two meetings foregrounded two primary facets of his relationship to meditation, aspects of his identity that came to dominate his religious life and teachings. The first meeting laid the doctrinal foundations for his acceptance of a practice that was associated with a religious tradition different from his own. The second led to an experience that convinced him that there was something special about U Ba Khin and his meditation center.

Initially Goenka was hesitant to meet with U Ba Khin because of his own concerns about becoming involved with Buddhism. However, so as not to offend U Chan Htoon, he met U Ba Khin at his home. In telling about this first meeting, Goenka usually emphasized two things: (1) how Sayagyi U Ba Khin refused to teach him meditation as a treatment for his migraines, and (2) how Sayagyi U Ba Khin skillfully convinced him that learning meditation did not involve converting to Buddhism.

According to Goenka, U Ba Khin at first refused to take him as a student because he wanted to stress the soteriological aspect of meditation. U Ba Khin said:

> This is a very high spiritual wisdom. It is the ancient technique of *vipattanā* (*vipassanā*), the highest spiritual wisdom of your country. It should not be devalued by using it to treat a physical disease. So, I am unable to teach you this wisdom.[81]

In Goenka's own narrative, he was surprised that U Ba Khin was so staunchly devoted to his high soteriological path that he would turn away an important person such as himself as a student. But Goenka also related how the conversation immediately reversed course. U Ba Khin went on to say:

> If you want to set up a sugar mill, you do so to obtain sugar, not for molasses, correct? Molasses will certainly be derived, but as a byproduct. Your aim will remain the manufacture of sugar, correct? Similarly, if you adopt this highly developed knowledge for its spiritual achievements, the mind will get purified. And a mind free of defilements will naturally be free from stress. As a result, a migraine may disappear; this result will be automatically achieved as a byproduct.[82]

Despite the ease he felt in U Ba Khin's presence, Goenka remained hesitant, primarily because of his aversion to Buddhism. Because of U Ba Khin's previous experiences with non-Buddhists, he had a tried and true way to assuage Goenka's concerns. He took recourse to Buddhist doctrine:

> You are a leader of the Hindus here. In your Hindu Dharma is there any opposition to *sīla*, to good conduct? . . . Tell me, does your Hindu Dharma have any objection to *samādhi* [one-pointed focus to control the mind]? . . . Does your Hindu Dharma have any opposition to *paññā* [meditative wisdom that removes mental defilements]?[83]

Goenka found nothing to object to in these practices. Rather, he found a wealth of examples in his trove of religious knowledge that made him think that such practices might be amenable to his Hindu values. When Sayagyi finally said, "That's it. That's all that we teach here in *vipassanā*," Goenka found a doctrinal foundation that allowed him to open his heart to the possibility of learning meditation from U Ba Khin. Upon returning home, Goenka decided that "*sīla, samādhi, paññā*—these three are also found in our Dharma."[84]

Primed by this discussion on doctrine, Goenka's second encounter with his teacher was a key experiential turning point on his path to meditation. Concerned about the amenities at the meditation center—particularly whether he would be able to maintain a vegetarian diet—he visited the center on the weekend following his first meeting with U Ba Khin:

> As I got out of the car, I saw Sayagyi sitting with a few disciples some ten footsteps away on a two-foot-tall wooden platform with a simple bamboo hut on it. I folded my hands in respectful greeting, and he called out to me lovingly: "Come, Goenka."
>
> (Some thirty years later I came to know what he said about me at the time to one of the disciples sitting with him. He said: "This is an individual endowed with abundant meritorious perfections. If he takes *vipaśyanā*, his life will be transformed.")[85]

This parenthetical aside in Goenka's narrative—which happens to be omitted from the only English translation of this story—is fundamental to his retrospective conception of this important moment in his spiritual trajectory. It also hints at a particular feature of U Ba Khin's persona and pedagogy. In the cult that developed around Sayagyi U Ba Khin, he was understood to be a very special person with unique powers and unusual access to the forces of the Dharma. His closest disciples, including Goenka, considered him to be a bodhisattva, one who takes a vow to stay in the cycle of existence and eventually become a fully enlightened teaching buddha. And he was not understood to be just any bodhisattva, but the being who would eventually become the next fully enlightened teaching buddha in cosmic history, the buddha Maitreya.[86]

U Ba Khin's ability to bring people to the early stages of enlightenment quickly was, therefore, attributed to his great collection of karmic perfections (*pāramitā/pāramī*). He also made sure that he only took students who had a developed stock of karmic perfections, so they might quickly attain the first stages of enlightenment or powerfully develop their karmic perfections as he was doing. To determine whether his students were worthy of his teachings, he had several disciples with psychic powers who would look into the students' past lives to assess their karmic capacities. One of these disciples was U Ba Khin's close confidant and coteacher, Daw Mya Thwin, or Mother Sayama, whom we will meet shortly. The earlier parenthetical comment indicates that U Ba Khin had positively assessed Goenka's stock of karmic perfections—and his disciples were talking about Goenka's great karmic promise—before he ever attended a meditation retreat.

Apparently Goenka knew none of this when he first visited the meditation center. Rather, it was a set of explicit experiences there that pulled him to the center. After paying his respects to U Ba Khin and telling the teacher that he found no fault with his doctrinal arguments and was interested in possibly attending a meditation course, Goenka was invited for a meal:

> [Sayagyi] said, "Now it is meal time, so come, let us all eat together. You will like our food." Then he called out, "Sayama, get a plate for our guest as well."
>
> ... He invited me to sit by him in the dining hall. Sitting near him, I began to feel a coolness and peace beyond words. Sitting there, I looked out at the ashram, and sensed a quiet peace all around.... Suddenly, another wave of coolness and peace came wafting in. A smiling woman about my age came in. This was Sayama, Sayagyi's chief disciple. I would later come to address her as Mother Sayama. Sayagyi introduced me to her and asked her to serve me food. After serving Sayagyi, she served me potato curry and rice....
>
> [After eating and getting a tour of the center,] I respectfully

bid farewell to Sayagyi, took leave of him, and returned home. The start of the course was some two or three months away. I was surprised to see that for that many days I did not suffer a migraine attack. Without even having learned meditation, my mind would again and again become concentrated inward, and a very pleasant experience would be there.

Days passed in anticipation of the beginning of the course. The draw toward the pleasant peace that I had sensed there was strong, and though firm in my resolve to go, I became anxious now and again. Have I made a wrong decision? The practice of morality, concentration, and meditative wisdom is good, but will I not somehow become a Buddhist? Will I not become a denialist and ruin my future?[87] Will I not damage my trajectory in the afterlife? The coating of the old karmic forces on the mind made me hesitate. On the other hand, I would remember Sayagyi. Remembering the meditation center and the experience of pleasant peace there, my mind would again become confident. . . .

Finally, the time of the course was near. Two days before it was to start, a very intense migraine headache came on. Someone said: "The forces of Dharma are giving you a warning to prevent you from getting involved in Buddhist Dharma." But I was not deterred at all by this statement. On the auspicious day of September 1st, 1955, my destiny arose, and I arrived at the meditation center.[88]

We see in Goenka's account a clear conflict of religious identity. In the end, however, a number of direct experiences come to trump this attachment to identity. First, his encounter with the "coolness and peace" of his teachers, U Ba Khin and Sayama, is palpable in his memory. It is noteworthy here that the community of practitioners at the International Meditation Centre often characterized the experience of emerging from the state of nirvana in similar terms. Second, Goenka found himself free of migraines for several months after visiting the meditation center and was able to access an experience of inward meditative bliss even though he had not yet learned meditation. These powerful experiences—particularly the absence of migraines—appear to have affected him enough that he was willing to put aside the doubts about religious identity that continued to assail him. The reliance on "direct experience"—in the face of various intellectual or theoretical storms—became a hallmark of Goenka's own teaching approach later on.

The final part of this narrative is of interest because it speaks implicitly to some of the more esoteric aspects of U Ba Khin's teaching methods. Goenka described the onset of a migraine attack just before his first meditation retreat with U Ba Khin. The teacher's account of his second meeting with Goenka puts Goenka's narrative in a different light. It also provides us with a more explicit understanding of how U Ba Khin's work as a healer was directly tied up with his methods of teaching vipassanā meditation. During a ten-day meditation course in the early 1960s, U Ba Khin told the following story to his Burmese students:

> Māra really exists.... I believe what the Buddha said. Here too, we have disturbances.... [Because of this, meditators] offer themselves to the teacher.[89] So, the teacher owns the meditators that have offered themselves, and it makes him more effective in protecting them. But for a meditator who has less willingness to offer his body to a teacher, how can a teacher protect him? Protection of a person is not hanging around hand in hand beside him. Protection is given by good

deities who have karmic perfections with me in the cycle of existence. Therefore, if a meditator has less willingness to take protection, the deities know. . . .

[People] come and meditate here. Among them is a high-ranked person. . . . Why does this person pay much respect to me? He had migraine headaches since he was seven. At the age of twenty-seven, it became serious. Every ten days, he regularly suffered terrible migraine headaches. . . . So, he came to me to meditate. I told him that he would have to eat and stay like us without going anywhere. He is a Hindu and they have a caste system. He did not want to eat food from here. But he had no choice. He came here in July. Before, there was no meditation retreat during the rainy season. . . . So, I told him to come back in September for meditation. He offered his body to me. He accepted himself as Sayagyi's disciple. As soon as he did so, his headache was gone. But there was another point to consider. He ate a meal with potato curry from here, too. Because of faith, his headache was gone. So, practice with faith.

Then, he felt flippantly that his headache was gone. On the first Friday of September, the meditation retreat was going to start, but he did not appear. He did not enroll in the list either. Here, we were going to start on Friday. He suffered a headache, as seriously as before, the Wednesday prior. How? He broke his promise, right? Therefore, I guess that the guardian deities who gave protection in favor of me did not protect him anymore. So, he suffered a headache like before. Such diseases are not because of material changes, but because of *dhātu* [nonhuman forces]. Later, he meditated here and he was completely free from headaches. So, he pays much respect to me. . . . That Hindu man got

> migraines because [supernormal beings] teased him by riding on his shoulders. So, he got headaches. By the power of *mettā* [loving-kindness] from a noble person, such a disease can be cured. No need for medication.[90]

The final words in this rich account reveal that the work of healing was perhaps not as marginal to U Ba Khin's teaching as indicated in Goenka's narrative of the initial encounter. What is more, the work of healing is explicitly attributed here to the power of the teacher, while less emphasis is given to the process of meditation. To understand Goenka's formation as both a practitioner and teacher of vipassanā/vipaśyanā, we must see how his encounter with meditation can't be separated from a direct experience of faith healing and a strong devotional bond to a powerful teacher, a teacher he would eventually come to consider a special bodhisattva.

Goenka's initial encounters with his teacher were the beginning of a long, close relationship, one that became formally constituted when he finally participated in a ten-day meditation retreat. In describing his first retreat, Goenka once again put a strong emphasis on how the specifics of his meditative experiences opened his mind and brought him to fully embrace the teachings of the Buddha. Though he encountered difficulties at first and almost quit the course, he decided to stay thanks to the encouraging words of a fellow meditator. In a short time, he found himself immersed in a deep exploration of the nature of reality. Of his first retreat, he wrote:

> My progress surpassed all expectations. When *vipaśyanā* was given after two days, the experience was truly extraordinary. The entire body melted into a mass of subatomic particles, with varied movements and sensations. This inner world was totally unknown to me. That there was a constant flow

> of varied sensations throughout the body was something that I could have never even conceived of. I felt as if I had entered a mysterious land. . . .
>
> The days passed. I remained immersed in meditation and I came across many unusual experiences. The inert body became enlivened, with no solidity anywhere; only wavelets, wavelets, everywhere. The entire spinal cord turned into a mass of wavelets, thousands of openings on what appeared to be the skull burst into wavelets, and then from the top of the head a fountain erupted. By the end of the course it felt as if tons of weight had been lifted off me. I felt so light, as if the gravitational pull of the earth was no more and I was ready to fly in the air.[91]

Descriptions of this sort—with a strong emphasis on the direct experience of the impermanence of sensations in the body—came to characterize the substance of much of Goenka's later teachings. He clearly found these early experiences compelling, and they became a foundational impetus for him to fully explore the teachings of the Buddha in both theory and practice. Not only were his migraines completely gone after his first course of vipaśyanā with Sayagyi U Ba Khin and Mother Sayama, but he had found his true calling. He went on to devote his entire life to the practice, study, and teaching of the Buddha's teachings.

Later on, Goenka came to refer to his initiation into the practice of vipaśyanā as a "second birth." Playing on the traditional brahminical metaphor of a bird that gets born twice, he wrote:

> In the first birth, I came out of my mother's womb. In the second, I got to break the shell of ignorance at Sayagyi U Ba Khin's vipaśyanā meditation center on Inya Myaing Road. . . . This was my actual birth. It is just like when a bird takes

> birth from its mother's belly in the form of an egg. Its real birth is when it breaks the shell of the egg and emerges from it. For this reason we refer to it as twice-born.[92] . . . In the same way, when I broke the shell of ignorance and emerged from it through the practice of vipaśyanā—thanks to the benevolence of my teacher—at that time my second birth occurred. It was a real birth. With my good fortune, I became a twice-born.[93]

Goenka characterized this second birth as a major turning point in his life, a moment when his destiny arose before him, and insisted it was the result of the grace of his teacher. In other words, Goenka felt that his earlier misguided devotionalism had now found a worthy object in the person of Sayagyi U Ba Khin. The powerful wisdom of vipaśyanā—which had allowed Goenka to see directly into the nature of reality and realize experientially what his ancient Indian traditions regarded as the highest goal of the spiritual life—had been given to him by this charismatic Burmese Buddhist civil servant.

One final aspect of Goenka's narrative of this moment must be noted. It is a facet of his identity that became central, later in life, to his own conception of his mission to spread vipaśyanā meditation around the world. On many occasions, Goenka pointed out that the year he took his second birth coincided with the lead-up to the twenty-five hundredth anniversary year of the death of the Buddha, according to traditional Theravada Buddhist reckonings. According to such a chronology, this anniversary also marked a halfway point in the five-thousand-year period during which the Buddha's teachings (*sāsana*) will remain in the world.

To commemorate this event, the newly independent Burmese government sponsored a large council between 1954 and 1956 to bring together monks from various Buddhist countries and to authenticate the Pali Buddhist scriptures, which are considered some of the oldest and most historically authentic representations of the Buddha's teachings to have been preserved. This council was understood to be the sixth in a series of such councils that have taken place in the history of Theravada Buddhism.

Some Buddhists in Myanmar believe that this anniversary of the Buddha's death marked a cosmic turning point for his teachings in the world, a moment that would bring about a massive resurgence of the practice of authentic Buddhist meditative wisdom. Goenka explicitly associated this moment with his own introduction to vipaśyanā, and this idea became foundational to his sense of identity throughout his career as a meditation teacher:

> This council was being held at the time when the first period of 2,500 years of the Buddha's teaching (*sāsana*) was ending, and the 2,500 years of the second period was beginning. After my first meditation course, Sayagyi U Ba Khin told me about an ancient belief that the second period of the Buddha *sāsana* would begin with the expansion of the meditative wisdom of *vipaśyanā*.[94] He said that *vipaśyanā* meditation would not only spread there in Burma, but that it would return to the country in which it originated, India, and then spread throughout the world. It was a coincidence that I received this invaluable gem in that important year when the two periods of the teaching converged—one ending and the other beginning. But it was a supremely fortunate moment for me.[95]

CHAPTER 4

Training Grounds

ON APRIL 27, 1958, the Indian Hindu guru Maharishi Mahesh Yogi arrived in Rangoon. This was the first stop of his first trip outside India to spread his newly minted meditation technique, Transcendental Meditation (TM®), to the world.[96] S. N. Goenka picked him up at the airport, and the Goenka family hosted him during his stay in Rangoon. The Maharishi recounted his visit to Rangoon as follows:

> The first country out of India was Burma—Rangoon. One businessman did this whole thing. He was the only one man who received me at the airport, and about ten days I stayed in Rangoon. I initiated about 200 people. Just one talk was enough to keep me engaged for 24 hours, like that. And when I was about to leave, the whole airport was flooded with all kinds of Burmese: government officials, military people in their dress, police, and the monks—monks of various orders, Burmese Buddhist monks . . .[97]

In many ways, this moment was a key turning point in the history of the modern dissemination of Asian contemplative traditions to a global public. The Maharishi would soon become a world-famous meditation teacher, and the scientific study of the health effects of TM would become foundational for a range of later developments that brought Asian contemplative traditions into the mainstream of

Western medical culture.[98] (A decade later, Goenka would also come to play a more direct role in this process.) It is another apparent coincidence that Goenka and his family were key participants in this moment. Many members of Goenka's large family were some of the first outside India to be initiated into the Maharishi's mantra meditation.

When the Maharishi came to Rangoon in the late 1950s, Goenka was still quite new to meditation and deep in the process of integrating his powerful experiences at U Ba Khin's meditation center with his identity as a leader of the Hindu community. He had begun an in-depth study of the Buddha's teachings—after all those years, he finally picked up the copy of the *Dhammapada* that Bhadant Anand Kausalyayan had given him—and he regularly visited and made donations to the International Meditation Centre. At the same time, he remained a fixture of the Indian expatriate community in Rangoon, and his family was still strongly devoted to traditional Hindu religious practices. He developed his identity as a practitioner of vipaśyanā meditation in this in-between space of religious identity.

To do so comfortably, he relied strongly on Sayagyi U Ba Khin's claim that one could practice the Buddha's teachings "without interfering with... religious faith."[99] This is a negotiation that Goenka would be involved in for the rest of his life, and it became even more explicit when he himself began to disseminate the teachings of the Buddha in India.

It was also around this time that groups of Europeans and Americans began to trickle into the International Meditation Centre to learn meditation from U Ba Khin, assisted by Mother Sayama. In the context of this postcolonial cosmopolitan globalism, Goenka found himself engaging in broader conversations about the relationship of ancient Indian religious traditions to other traditions. One tool he used to navigate this in-between space of religious identity was a perennialist perspective of a common ultimate truth.

This approach was, of course, merely an extension of conversations that had been developing for more than a century within the colonial context. However, although Goenka often used the rhetoric of perennialism to negotiate identity politics among competing religious narratives, his direct and powerful meditative experiences ultimately held primacy for him, convincing him that vipaśyanā took practitioners most effectively to the ultimate spiritual goal.

Several anecdotes, each of which captures a different aspect of Goenka's situation in this historical moment, evince this process of integration. The first is from the diary of John Hislop, who visited the International Meditation Centre and practiced meditation with Sayagyi U Ba Khin and Mother Sayama in May 1960. Hislop's stay at the center coincided with a five-day stay by the monk Webu Sayadaw.[100] In his diary, Hislop—who went on to become one of the most important American disciples of the famous Indian guru Sathya Sai Baba[101]—discussed his own perennialist perspective on the practice of meditation and recounted a conversation with Goenka after one of Webu Sayadaw's talks:

> There are more things in existence than can be readily seen, and to me one of the most extraordinary is the existence of quite independent paths to freedom. There is the mighty example of the Buddha. There is the achievement of Lao Tse of China, there is Ramana Maharshi, there is Maharishi and Guru Dev, there is Krishnamurti[102] (another tremendous solitary achievement) and no doubt many other quite divergent yet successful paths. I am convinced they exist, but I do not comprehend the fact and its significance....
>
> After the discourse, I was talking with Mr. Goenka—the wealthy Indo-Burmese manufacturer. He said that in the discourse, electric-like currents coursed up and down his body and were still continuing. He said that when he

> met Maharishi in India, Maharishi gave him a flower and briefly touched his hand. At the touch, waves of vibrations coursed through his body and he said to himself, "Here is a powerful yogi." Neither Goenka nor I can see any conflict between the Dhamma of the Buddha and Maharishi's meditation. Neither could Maharishi when Goenka explained the technique—Maharishi said, "Same goal."[103]

Here Goenka is depicted as an admiring devotee, in awe of the Maharishi's yogic prowess. He is also eager to discuss his own extraordinary meditative experiences. Perhaps most importantly, we see someone who is motivated to find common ground between the practices that the Buddha taught and the practices of traditional Hindu yoga and meditation.

In Goenka's own retrospective accounts of the Maharishi Mahesh Yogi, a slightly different perspective emerges. In telling his story of the Maharishi's visit to Rangoon, he made sure to point out that he hosted the great meditation teacher primarily for the sake of his family, so that they might be initiated into a form of meditation that was acceptable for them as Hindus. He noted that though they had seen a great positive change in him as a result of his practice of vipaśyanā, "no member of my family was yet ready to go to a vipaśyanā course."[104] Goenka went on to describe one particular conversation with the Maharishi about meditation:

> While he was staying in Rangoon, Maharishiji went with me to meet my respected teacher, Sayagyi U Ba Khin. They had a conversation about what was taught there [at the International Meditation Centre]. He also listened [when I told him about] my experiences in meditative practice. I told him how the entire physical body became animated with consciousness, and how there was no trace of solidity anywhere.

> [I noted], however, that this state did not remain constant, but that it would remain during meditation and for quite some time afterward. And in between [periods of meditation] as well, when the mind would turn inward, there would be this kind of experience. Hearing this, Maharishiji said: "This is indeed the final stage of meditation. There is nothing more beyond this. This is the state without object. Having reached this state, all objects of meditation are removed, and only consciousness upon consciousness, only bliss upon bliss [remains]. Why has your teacher not informed you that you have attained the final stage of meditation?" What answer could I give? I knew very well that in vipaśyanā there are many stages beyond this. Many of my guru-brothers and guru-sisters had attained them, and many were in the process of attaining them. So what could I say to him? But I myself understood well that there were various additional steps on the path to liberation from existence. . . . The final goal is indeed a state without object. There are no two minds about it. However, how could the state that I was experiencing be said to be without object? In that state, the sensations that arise as a result of the association of mind and body are being experienced. . . . The stage that is actually beyond existence, beyond the world [of phenomena] is above this [stage]. It is where body and mind are transcended and cease. . . . But the teachings of the Blessed Buddha had disappeared in India. India's very ancient—and in those days widespread—wisdom of *vipaśyanā* and the entire literature describing it had completely disappeared. Therefore, . . .[105] the identification of the various intermediary stages of practice had been forgotten.[106]

Goenka appears to use this account of his encounter with the Maharishi to underline the Maharishi's ignorance and to point up his own knowledge of the path of meditation. In this perspective, the contemplative traditions of modern India had lost the true knowledge of vipaśyanā, the complete map of the universally accessible stages leading to liberatory wisdom.

It is hard to know how much of this account is colored by Goenka's retrospective stance. He wrote it late in life. Hislop's account certainly suggests that the narrative may be overdetermined by interests and attitudes of a later time.[107] One thing is clear, however. Goenka was at work to bring his experience with meditation into his family and public life. He was eager for his family members to embrace vipaśyanā, but he knew that most of them were not yet open to doing so. He was eager for the Hindu community to understand how meditative practices, such as those he had learned from U Ba Khin, were the best way to fully enact the religious ideals of their traditions. Yet the cultural barriers that stood between the Indian expatriate community and the local Burmese community were strong. By publicly supporting the Maharishi and getting his family members involved in the practice of TM, Goenka could show his continued connection to the Hindu community while advancing his interests in the practical contemplative aspects of the religion.

Another revealing anecdote from the Maharishi's time in Rangoon shows how Goenka participated in this project, while at the same time carrying on with the criticism evident in the earlier account. Goenka wrote:

> The Maharishiji's beneficence is boundless in that he oriented not just our family in Rangoon to the path of meditation, but countless other Indians there. One remarkable incident occurred: Though I was completely satisfied with the [practice of the] wisdom of vipaśyanā, I was myself [unwittingly] drawn into mantra meditation. It happened that when the Maharishiji had formally initiated the entire

> family into mantra, only my wife Illaichidevi was left. When she was ready to be initiated, Maharishiji said: "We should not give her a mantra by herself. A husband and wife should take a mantra together." When I asked him why that would be necessary, since he himself had said that I had reached the final goal of meditation, he said that I need not take a mantra with her, but that I should merely remain seated with her [during the initiation]. I assented to this. Normally, he would whisper when giving a mantra to a meditator. But in this case, he gave the mantra in a slightly louder voice, so that I would also hear it. As we exited the guesthouse and came to our bedroom, I saw that without any effort the mantra had begun to reverberate throughout my body. When I sat [to meditate], I sat continuously for three hours, [the mantra reverberating] without a break. In this way, without taking the mantra, I got initiated. My vipaśyanā was never forsaken, but by experiencing mantra, I came to understand clearly the difference between the two practices.[108]

This passage reveals, again, that Goenka's take on the Maharishi's mantra meditation was critical and polemical. But it also suggests that at this early stage in his meditative career, Goenka was less exclusive in his attitudes about other meditation traditions, even though he later on strongly dissuaded his disciples from practicing more than one type of meditation. In this narrative, Goenka gets to have it both ways. In his capacity as a master of hospitality, he hosted the Maharishi. Yet he was initiated into mantra against his will as an aloof vipaśyanā meditator with superior knowledge. He was grateful that the Maharishi's incomplete teachings could serve as a stepping-stone for his family members, but for him the involuntary initiation served merely to help him experience directly the shallowness of those teachings.

I dwell at length on this moment because it captures a transitional period in Goenka's life. Perhaps most importantly, it captures him caught between his enthusiasm for a new avocation of vipaśyanā meditation and his established identity as a leader of the Hindu community. The challenges he faced in developing an identity as a Hindu advocate for the meditative teachings of the Buddha is perhaps most explicitly evidenced in his negotiations with his family members. His attempts to get them involved in the practice of vipaśyanā and to alter their attitudes about religious practice more generally were a central component of this transitional process.

For this reason, the story about the eagerness of Goenka's own wife to be initiated by the Maharishi stands out. Illaichidevi Goenka would later become S. N. Goenka's constant companion on most of the vipaśyanā meditation courses he taught throughout his lifetime, coming to be referred to as Mataji, or "respected mother," by his disciples. But in the late 1950s and early 1960s, Goenka had to struggle to convince her and his other family members that his new path of religious practice was amenable to their Hindu values.

There was another issue that may have contributed to Illaichidevi's hesitation to fully support her husband's new spiritual endeavors. It came out in a story from S. N. Goenka's childhood, told by his sister, Ila Agrawal:

> There was a period of worry whenever my brother joined a ten-day *vipaśyanā* course. I had heard from my mother now and again about a time when my mother and father had taken their two sons, Babulal and S.N. Goenka (*pū. Gurujī*), with them to stay in the family home in our ancestral village of Churu. Mother was busy with her household duties and the two boys were playing at the threshold of the haveli. At that time, a well-known wandering ascetic (*sanyāsī*) came to the door and called out: "Alms-food, please." Mother

> brought some alms-food in a pot and came out of the haveli. When she was offering the food to the saint, he questioned her: "Mother, whose children are these?" Mother replied naturally: "They are both my sons, Maharaj." Gesturing in the direction of S. N. Goenka (*Gurujī*), he said: "Mother, this son of yours will go on to bring benefit to the world. Entrust him to me, and I will make him into a worthy vessel." Mother became afraid, corralled the two boys, and brought them inside. Later on, others also made such prophecies. For this reason, my sister-in-law [Illaichidevi] and my mother naturally worried that somehow this meditation might influence [Goenka] to become a renunciant monk.[109]

This anecdote explains why Illaichidevi and other members of the family were generally wary of spiritual paths that might prioritize renunciation, perhaps most paradigmatically embodied in the Buddha's monastic vows. This concern was surely inspired by the family-oriented Hindu social model in which the Goenka family participated. Sayagyi U Ba Khin's model of meditation practice and his personal example—as a householder meditator, successful in the worldly sphere—became a helpful touchstone for Goenka in his attempts to convince his family members that they need not fear that he might become a renunciant.

Goenka was still working with his wife on this issue as late as 1970, when he began teaching vipaśyanā meditation in India. By this time, Illaichidevi had participated in ten-day courses at the International Meditation Centre and had been practicing vipaśyanā meditation for some years. In a letter to her dated September 5, 1970, Goenka writes to her of teaching young female meditators from her ancestral area of Rajasthan. He holds up the example of his teacher Mother Sayama and her husband, U Chit Tin, to emphasize the possibility of making serious progress on the path of meditation while carrying out the duties of a householder. Goenka referred to his students as his "sons" and "daughters" in meditation, just as he referred to his own teacher as his "Dharma father":

> All of these daughters would have been very happy to see you, and you would have very much enjoyed meeting them. It pleases them that people can practice meditation without leaving the responsibilities of household life and becoming wandering ascetics. Just as Mother Sayama and U Chit Tin carry out their household responsibilities while also remaining engaged in meditation, you also—when you come to India—will continue to take care of the family while at the same time distributing the *prasād* of the Dharma[110] to sons and daughters such as these. This is the particularity of the Blessed One's path of meditation.[111]

During fourteen years of studying meditation with Sayagyi U Ba Khin, Mother Sayama, and others at the International Meditation Centre in Burma, Goenka slowly integrated these distinct religious and cultural worlds that his new identity encompassed. His experiences with his family's staunch Hindu conservatism indicate that this integration was a continual and deliberate negotiation.

During this time, Goenka became more and more immersed in the practice of vipaśyanā. He studied the teachings of the Buddha in Hindi translation and began to learn Pali, the ancient Indian language of the Theravada scriptures. He participated in many meditation retreats at the International Meditation Centre, encouraged friends and family to participate, and assisted U Ba Khin whenever Indians came to the center to practice. He also hosted many visitors from abroad at his home and always took those interested in meditation to meet his teacher.

At some point in this process, it became clear that U Ba Khin was training Goenka to teach.[112] U Ba Khin had, for some time after establishing his meditation center, nursed the idea that he might someday teach meditation beyond the borders of Burma. He had a particular desire to teach in "the West." This desire was sparked by his experiences teaching quite a few foreign visitors, which gave him a strong sense that people in the rest of the world were ready and eager to take up the teachings of the Buddha.[113] He articulated this desire in a letter to one of his American students, John Coleman, dated April 24, 1969:

> My life ambition has been to teach Buddha Dhamma in the West. After 30 years of research work and trials, with successes and failures, I have reached a stage at which I may consider myself well-established to teach Buddha Dhamma in practice to the people of the world interested to work for the goal of Buddhism. I have made attempts since 1966 to get a pass-port to go abroad for this very purpose but have not so far been successful.[114]

U Ba Khin's desire was thwarted by the political situation in Burma. After the 1962 military coup, which involved a takeover of the democratically elected government by General Ne Win and the nationalization of all industry, it became very difficult for Burmese nationals to leave the country. U Ba Khin did travel briefly to Europe in 1963 in his capacity as a government official, but he never got the chance to teach meditation there. Some of his foreign students did, in a few instances, offer introductory courses on Buddhism after their experiences with him in Burma, and U Ba Khin encouraged those who could not come to Burma to make contact with such people and learn the basics of meditation.[115]

But U Ba Khin's teaching methods relied heavily on the context of the bounded space of his meditation center, a closely monitored and individual course of training, and his and his assistants' ability to harness supernormal forces to push students to states of attainment. To be able to properly spread the "Buddha Dhamma in practice" abroad, he would need to somehow replicate those conditions. Through a series of meditative experiments, he came up with a unique metaphysical solution to this dilemma. In an authorization letter that was sent to six American and European students in April 1969, U Ba Khin wrote:

> My recent experiments in giving courses of Buddhist Meditation to disciples outside of Burma by distant control were quite satisfactory and most encouraging. The chances of my going abroad to teach Buddhist Meditation are still very remote. So I have decided to conduct courses of Meditation by distant control for those who had taken lessons from me in Rangoon and who are now eager to have a refresher course...
>
> I have also decided to give the following disciples the necessary authorization to conduct courses of Buddhist Meditation (Anapana and Vipassana) on my behalf for new students interested in Buddhist Meditation as soon as I find them competent to do so after refresher courses.[116]

U Ba Khin went on to list the names of six of his Western students: Leon Wright, United States; Robert Hover, United States; Ruth Denison, United States (to teach women only); Forella Landie, Canada (to teach women only); John Earl Coleman, United Kingdom; and Jan Van Amersfoort, The Netherlands. Out of these six, three took up U Ba Khin's charge. Hover, an aerospace engineer, did so eagerly; Coleman, a retired CIA agent, did so with reluctance; and Denison, a Hollywood movement artist, began teaching U Ba Khin's Buddha Dhamma in America, Australia, and Europe in the years that followed. On June 20, 1969, not long after this letter of authorization was written to his Western students, U Ba Khin also formally authorized S. N. Goenka to become his deputy in spreading the teachings in India.[117] In a certificate of authorization, U Ba Khin wrote:

> This is to certify that Satyanarayan Goenka, of No. 77, Shwebontha Street, Rangoon, has been practicing Buddhist Meditation under my guidance from September 1955 to date and that he has made a good study of the fundamentals of the theory of Buddhism.... I consider him to be well established to teach Buddhist Meditation abroad and I accordingly authorise him to teach Buddhist Meditation on my behalf...[118]

In fact, a series of events a few years earlier marked Goenka's first formal engagement in this missionary project. In January and April 1967, Goenka and U Ba Khin traveled to Mandalay and then Maymyo (Pyin Oo Lwin) in Upper Burma to conduct courses for the Indian community there. U Ko Lay, who was present during these courses, recounted Goenka's role:

> In 1967... I got the message: Sayagyi [U Ba Khin] is coming up to Mandalay to give a course. Out of the blue. He had never given a course outside of his center.... The course was given [with the help of Goenkaji] to only Hindu Hindu, the Indian Indian population.... The second day, there was some trouble. Some Hindu leaders came to see him [Goenka] and there was some talk in Hindi. But we found out later that the Hindu leaders and Hindu people from Mandalay were so angry with Goenkaji, that he became a teacher of Buddhist meditation. At that time, he hadn't started. He was

> just helping the teaching in Rangoon center. . . . [since] 1965 means ten years he has been working with Sayagyi in Rangoon only, helping the Indian community there. But mainly people didn't know anything about it. Then when they came up here, and when they found that Goenkaji was helping in giving courses, then they felt dissatisfied and came to see him. . . . They blame him, they accuse him of disloyalty and all that sort of thing. So, he just discharged them, making an arrangement for a meeting with them that evening in their community. . . There he explained them about this Dhamma, in Hindi, in that place. Afterward, after that talk, there was no more protest from the Mandalay crowd at all. . . . That course ended very successfully.[119]

U Ko Lay described these two courses in Upper Burma as "field training" for Goenka. A part of this training was the daily recitation of Pali protective chants (*paritta*). U Ko Lay specifically remembers U Ba Khin and Goenka reciting the *Mangalasutta* every morning in preparation for the day's meditation.[120] In this narrative, U Ba Khin was not only training Goenka to face the opposing forces of entrenched religious identities among his Indian brethren. He was also training him to ritually sanctify the bounded space of temporary meditation camps to create a protective "cover" to shield meditation students from destructive supernormal forces.

Through a combination of his technique of "distant control" and the ritual sanctification of meditation spaces, U Ba Khin could provide his students with the means to teach his methods to others in the least hospitable of circumstances outside Burma. This was the model of teaching that Goenka, and the American and European students selected by U Ba Khin to teach abroad, came to enact from 1969 onward.

In describing his unique method of distant control, U Ba Khin used the metaphor of radio waves. By way of experiment, he had discovered how to extend his psychic influence in a targeted way to his students anywhere around the globe. His students could likewise "tune in" to this influence at prescribed times and get the support of his "thought waves charged with Nibbana Dhatu" and his *mettā* (Sanskrit/Hindi: *maitrī*), or "loving-kindness." Access to these psychic forces also entailed the support of powerful guardian deities karmically associated with U Ba Khin. In his authorization letter to his American and European students, he wrote:

> Whenever you find it necessary to get over any difficulty, you will just transmit your thought to me at my seat in the Shrine room of the I. M. C. for a while and then take to a short or long session of Anicca [impermanence] meditation as may be necessary.[121]

As we saw in chapter 3, U Ba Khin explained to his students that people can be healed by "the power of mettā from a noble person." U Ba Khin's work of distant control involved his capacity to deploy such powers remotely in the service of his students, to support their meditation and their work of teaching meditation to others around the globe.[122] For Goenka and other close disciples of Sayagyi U Ba Khin, his ability to do this work—and the great force of his mettā—was directly tied to his status as a special bodhisattva, the being working to become the future buddha Maitreya.

In 1969, when Goenka got word that his mother was suffering from a mental disturbance in India, he was certain that the only solution to her problem was a course of vipaśyanā meditation. His parents had been living in India for some years, and his mother had become disturbed about the political situation in Burma and the challenges her son was facing there after the nationalization of industry as a result of the 1962 military coup.[123] The news of his mother's illness became the catalyst for a trip to India from which he would not return—at least not for many years. Goenka immediately applied for a visa to travel to India. Though such visas were difficult to obtain in Burma in those days, he was able to procure one with the help of a friend, U Thi Han, the minister of foreign affairs. With a plan to teach a few courses in India and then return to Burma, Goenka set off under the force of U Ba Khin's strong encouragement. Goenka wrote: "Gurudev gave me the assurance that, 'Not you, but I will be carrying out this work.'"[124] As an emissary of the future buddha—a vessel for his powerful mettā—Goenka was to bring the teachings of the historical Buddha back to the land of their origin, back to India.

CHAPTER 5

Leaving Home

In 1958, U Ba Khin's American disciple, Dr. Leon Wright, wrote him a long-overdue letter about returning to the United States after practicing meditation at the International Meditation Centre in Rangoon. In the letter, he wrote of challenges he faced upon his return home:

> It has been most strange: whether walking or privately meditating I call readily into being the purifying flux and warmth of change—of Anicca. Gurugyi, I owe this all to you....
>
> Surely you will recall your constant warning to me of the eternal conflict of forces. Indeed, ... clear to America, according to the letter of your prediction, even unto now I have struggled against—but have never failed to recognize—the opposition of conflicting forces whose purpose is to defeat positive spiritual endeavour. You have given me the clearest awareness of this I've ever had. Upon arriving in America in December, we ran into a hurricane—the kind of extreme physical disturbance you predicted I would meet. From that point on, it has been a matter of an almost constant succession of reverses, conflicts, disappointments; the evil forces have sought to break me.[125]

This communication reveals the outlook U Ba Khin and his disciples had toward the project of spreading the practical teachings of the Buddha in contexts where local forces may or may not have been amenable to "positive spiritual endeavor." They conceptualized such missionary work as a metaphysical battle between Dharma forces and anti-Dharma forces, one that might also be evidenced by attendant phenomena in the physical world. The forces at work in America in the late 1950s appear to have been somewhat hostile to the Dharma.

When S. N. Goenka set off for India on June 22, 1969, U Ba Khin made a prediction along similar lines:

> Sayagyi [U Ba Khin] had said that on my arrival in India, nature would give a sign of my future success. I travelled by air from Yangon (Rangoon) and, as it happened, when I descended from the plane in Calcutta, there was an earth tremor. The next day I read in the newspapers that it had affected a large area of northern India. To me it was as if the country was thrilled to regain the long-lost jewel of the Dhamma.[126]

In spite of such remarkable assurances along the way, which kept him tied to his life's mission, Goenka faced many challenges in India. Unlike Wright, he was bringing the teachings of the Buddha not to barbarian lands but to the land of their origin. Still, he encountered many conflicting forces particular to India, especially in his first decade of teaching vipaśyanā in India. In this process, he also confronted powerful moments of doubt about his path as a meditation teacher.

Goenka taught vipaśyanā for the first time as U Ba Khin's formal proxy on July 3, 1969, not long after arriving in India. Already in this debut meditation course, a conflict arose. He had come to teach vipaśyanā to his mother, but many of his family members in India were against it. His brothers and their families had recently become devotees of the Ananda Marga, a religious group founded in 1955 and dedicated to personal spiritual development and social service.[127] The brothers did not want their mother getting involved in vipaśyanā, so she was hesitant to participate:

> The atmosphere was filled with disappointment and frustration. I thought that I would have to return to Myanmar without success....
>
> One evening I sat to meditate in this frame of mind. The meditation was very strong. Just a short while before its end, I found that dense clouds had gathered inside and there was total darkness in all directions. The atmosphere around was filled with doubts and tension but, when I examined the state of my mind, I found that it was not affected at all. Instead, it was firmly established in equanimity. Suddenly my mind was filled with a strong resolve: "What is to be will be. I am dedicated to Dhamma. Let Dhamma do as Dhamma wishes. If I am a worthy vessel of Dhamma and if I have a sufficient store of previous *pāramitā*, the darkness will dissipate. If it does not, I shall accept my unworthiness and return to Myanmar after meeting my family and friends."
>
> As soon as I made this resolve, I felt strong mettā toward my brothers who were deeply involved in Anand Marg: "May they be happy. May they be successful." My mind was suffused with these emotions. Suddenly the darkness started to dissolve and within a few seconds was gone. In its place a stream of joy arose and enthusiasm started to overflow. No trace of despair remained anywhere.[128]

When Goenka arose from his meditation, the grandson of a friend from Burma, Vijay Adukia, was waiting to meet him. He had found a site in Mumbai where Goenka could conduct a ten-day meditation course. Adukia's enthusiasm to organize and participate in the course, along with that of an old associate from Burma, Kantibhai G. Shah, created the impetus Goenka needed to get his mother and father to participate in this first course. Though there was some hesitation—primarily associated with the need to continue daily Hindu ritual practices—once Goenka's father agreed to participate in the course, the path was cleared for his mother to participate as well.[129] Thirteen people, including Goenka's parents, participated in the first course he taught in India, at the Panchayati Wadi Dharmshala in Bombay (now Mumbai).

After this initial offering, the path opened up for Goenka to teach more courses. His brothers—particularly his older brother Balkrishna Goenka—became more supportive, and friends and family members spread the word about his courses.[130] Goenka noted that he was surprised at how quickly things developed, attributing this catalyzation of his mission primarily to the blessings of his teacher: "It was by the greatness of Dharma and the blessings of Sayagyi U Ba Khin that there were no difficulties."[131] In retrospect, he also attributed the ease with which his teachings spread to karma, and to the prophecy about the second 2,500-year period of revival of the Buddha's teachings in which U Ba Khin had so strongly believed:

> When I came to India, I was really wonderstruck when I saw what was happening.... Now, in the courses, people started coming. Unknown people. And from every sect, from every community—unbelievable.... How is it they were coming? What miracle?
>
> ... Slowly it became clearer and clearer. People come to the courses and when I come in contact with them, when I see many of them—meet them, discuss with them, talk with them—something inside starts feeling that this person is known to me, known to me from a long time ago: "This

> person is known to me; yes, known to me, for so many lives. This person must have been meditating in Vipassana with me. Now the time has come. This person already has the seed of Vipassana, the seed of Dhamma. Now the time has ripened for this person to grow in Dhamma. And not only help himself or herself, but to help others—there is a potentiality for them not only to help themselves, but to help others also."[132]

For Goenka, these natural karmic connections were clear evidence of his prophetic destiny:

> This was the prophecy not only of my teacher but also that of saints thousands of years ago. For me, his blessings and this confident prophecy were like nourishing provisions sustaining me on my journey.[133]

Goenka quickly made connections, and soon he was teaching meditation all over the country. Between 1969 and 1980, he taught more than two hundred meditation courses across the Indian subcontinent, from Chennai to the Himalayas, from Gujarat to Kolkata. During this time, he also established three large meditation centers—one in the hills of Maharashtra, one in Hyderabad, and one in Jaipur. Goenka had the good fortune of being financially supported by his family, particularly his elder brother Balkrishna. Because of this support, he was able to travel freely and teach meditation at no cost. Goenka wrote little about his own meditation practice during this time, but it was surely a transformative period for him as he came to confront a wide range of new people from various communities and traditions. It was a period of education, adaptation, and network building.

The initial and ongoing conflict with his family was a microcosm of challenges that he would go on to face while trying to spread the

Buddha's meditation teachings. The prejudices toward Buddhism that he himself had grown up with and nursed for much of his life were even stronger in India than they had been in his Hindu community in Burma. Therefore, he had to engage in a public relations campaign, actively courting the approval of a variety of communities and their leaders. He had to show that what he was teaching—the practices he considered to be the core teachings of the historical Buddha—was socially relevant in India and amenable to those who identified as Hindu. He also made attempts to connect with Jain, Buddhist, and Christian communities.

This campaign was a long and hard-fought process. In what remains of this chapter, we will focus on a series of encounters, dialogues, exchanges, and conflicts that Goenka had with other teachers and communities as he developed his mission during his first decade of teaching vipaśyanā in India. Through these engagements, we see Goenka negotiate the various "conflicting forces" particular to the Indian religious landscape. This process of negotiation is what transformed Goenka into the teacher he would become in the decades that followed.

Mahatma Gandhi and Swami Vivekananda

Goenka used several practical and rhetorical strategies throughout his mission in India to draw in his fellow Indians. Two anecdotes from his first years of teaching reveal these strategies at work. They show Goenka arguing the case that vipaśyanā is actually aligned and compatible with the legacy of certain saintly figures revered by Hindu Indians—in this case, Mahatma Gandhi and Swami Vivekananda. They also show how Goenka cherished perennialist assumptions about the universal and timeless nature of Indian spiritual wisdom while at the same time feeling that he himself had privileged access to and understanding of such wisdom through his teachers in Burma. For Goenka, the Buddha's teachings were the clearest and most incisive form of that wisdom.

In March 1972, Goenka conducted a meditation course at the Sewagram Ashram founded by Mahatma Gandhi. About twelve close associates of Gandhi took part in the course.

> The course was successful. On the tenth day, many among them attained the stage of [knowledge of] dissolution (*bhaṅg avasthā*)....The meditators were very happy, and so was I.
>
> One of them, Shri Annasaheb Sahasrabuddhe, said to me: "Now I understand what Bapu [Gandhi] was doing." When I asked what he meant, he told me that in the evenings Gandhi would organize prayer meetings, in which sometimes thousands of people would participate. [During these gatherings,] Bapu would sit cross-legged on a platform and remain seated with his eyes closed. The sea of people would sing the "Ram Dhun" [a devotional song to Ram],...and along with the well-known tune, they would clap their hands. In this context, Mahatma Gandhi would remain seated, silent and with eyes closed.[134]

According to Goenka, when this disciple asked Gandhi why he did not participate in the singing and clapping, Gandhi explained:

> "I am working at a higher level than this, and so I remain engaged in that [work]." Hearing this made us more curious, and so we asked him: "What kind of higher work are you doing?" He replied: "I am seeing God....There can be, and there are, different opinions about whether or not a personal God that has a form truly exists. But there can be no difference of opinion on the fact that 'God is Truth.' It is this God, in the form of Truth, that I am seeing....When

> I sit with eyes closed, I introspect such that my awareness moves in a single flow from head to feet and a deep peace is attained, much bliss is experienced. I become immersed in this. For me, this is seeing God. I sometimes come to important worldly decisions in this state, and they are always correct." It was in this connection that Annasaheb said to me: "Now I understand that he [Gandhi] was doing *vipaśyanā* itself, because on the eighth and ninth days [of the course] we also began to experience this kind of flow of awareness."[135]

Goenka assessed this account by recourse to his own meditative experiences and the doctrinal frameworks of U Ba Khin:

> It is clear that the Mahatmaji was experiencing the state of dissolution, which he took to be God in the form of truth, a God without attributes or form. It seems that it has become prevalent in India today to take this blissful consciousness arising throughout the body as [the manifestation of] a permanent, eternal, and fixed God, without attributes or form. Normally, it is not easy to attain this state. It can take years to reach it. *Vipaśyanā* is a simple method of the sort that takes a meditator to this state very quickly. My respected teacher Sayagyi U Ba Khin used to say that a person who has done *vipaśyanā* in previous lives and was able to maintain the awareness of impermanence of sensations at the time of death in their last life—whether it was a birth as a deity or a human—can begin to experience this flow within the body on their own, without any [meditation] practice or [meditation] guidance. Perhaps something of this sort happened in the case of Mahatma Gandhi! I can't say anything with certainty.[136]

Goenka's religious and national identity, like that of most Indians, was tied to Gandhi's great legacy. In fact, this allegiance to Gandhian tradition pushed Goenka to orient his teaching of vipaśyanā toward particular social agendas, as we will see later. However, this narrative affirms Gandhi's saintliness in a particular way: Gandhi himself was practicing vipaśyanā without realizing it. Embedded in this anecdote is a critique of Gandhi's theology. He experienced high states of spiritual wisdom but misidentified them because of his Hindu context. While he was not definitive, Goenka could explain Gandhi's experiences—and his great saintly power—by recourse to a theory of rebirth. At some point in a past life Gandhi had likely accessed the meditative wisdom of impermanence found in the teachings of the Buddha. On the one hand, we see here the notion of a perennial wisdom to which many in the world might be privy. On the other hand, this wisdom can be entered and properly recognized only in particular contexts and by particular people.

Goenka laid bare the more critical side of this equation in another telling anecdote, this one about the memory of the great Hindu missionary yogi Swami Vivekananda (1863–1902), an early global emissary of Indian spiritual wisdom:

> I always had much reverence for Swami Vivekanandaji. . . .
>
> Some years ago, while organizing a *vipaśyanā* camp in South India, I went on a pilgrimage to Kanyakumari with some of my family members. . . .
>
> This is the shore from which Swami Vivekananda went out to a rocky island, where he remained immersed in meditation for three days. . . . We also meditated blissfully in that sanctified location for a few hours.
>
> While meditating, a very strong Dharma intention arose in

> my mind: "In the distant past, the beneficent teachings of the Buddha and the wisdom of *vipaśyanā* spread to other countries, carried on the waves of the great oceans—the Indian Ocean, the Bay of Bengal, and Arabian Sea—by intrepid renunciant monks who were messengers of the Dharma. In the more recent past, another important spiritual lineage of India was spread to distant countries by Swami Vivekanandaji. In the same way, may the wisdom of *vipaśyanā*, which brings welfare to all people, once again spread out in four directions, to six continents. May the suffering humans of those places be quenched by the stream of nectar of the True Dharma and freed from the suffering of wandering through existence."[137]

After vowing to emulate Vivekananda's path-forging travels in America—without which Goenka's own mission would likely never have been possible—Goenka went on to discuss Vivekananda's spiritual practice:

> I was pleased to discover that Vivekanandaji had spent some of his last days meditating under the Bodhi tree in Bodh Gaya. We do not know what kind of meditation he practiced while on Vivekananda Island or under the Bodhi tree. But it is quite clear that it was not *vipaśyanā*, since at that time *vipaśyanā* had not yet returned to India. India was entirely oblivious of its priceless heritage.
>
> Alas! If a saintly person of the likes of Vivekanandaji—clear-sighted and of powerful intelligence—had obtained the ancient Indian wisdom of *vipaśyanā* and the original words of the Buddha, there would have been untold beneficial results.[138]

Here the limits of Goenka's perennialism can be seen more explicitly. Whatever wisdom Swami Vivekananda had, and whatever he practiced, must have been distinct from—and inferior to—the ultimate wisdom realized through the practice of vipaśyanā. According to Goenka, such wisdom was unknown to India in modernity until he himself brought it from Burma in 1969.

Again, such accounts are retrospective, written by Goenka late in his life. Still, these attitudes appear to have been central to his outlook for much of his mission. What comes out perhaps most clearly in these narratives is just how important it was for Goenka to connect himself with the legacy of people like Gandhi and Vivekananda. In carrying out his work of refamiliarizing the country of India with the teachings of the Buddha, tying his identity to these great sons of the nation served Goenka well. Such associations helped him gain public approval for his mission.

This work to gain such approval manifested in a number of ways. Goenka sought the imprimatur of religious leaders and teachers, and he modified his use of language to suit his Indian audience. After his first course in Mumbai, he began traveling across the country, teaching at least one course every month and often more than that. In the year 1969 alone—after arriving in India in late June—he taught nine ten-day vipaśyanā courses in places as far-flung as Chennai, Sarnath, New Delhi, Kolkata, and Tadepalligudem. And he maintained the pace. With the encouragement and distant control of Sayagyi U Ba Khin and Mother Sayama in Burma, Goenka remained in India and taught course after course of vipaśyanā meditation. Through this process, he came to know India like never before. India was now his karmabhūmi, his sphere of action. And act he did—with great enthusiasm.

Seekers, Hippies, and Indian Buddhists

Starting around 1970, less than two years into his effort to return vipaśyanā to its homeland, the landscape of Goenka's mission was altered by an encounter with a new demographic: Western travelers to India in search of Buddhist meditation teachings. In April of that year, he taught his first course in Bodh Gaya, the place of the historical Buddha's enlightenment. Writing to his wife in Burma not long after the course, Goenka briefly described it:

> The course in Buddhagayā was quite magnificent. First because the holy land there has been powered up in the past by the meditative force of the Blessed Buddha, and second because of the blessing of our respected teacher, the people who sat the course were of such great merit that they understood thoroughly the mystery of the Dharma. For this reason, the merit of that course was indeed very great. By the power of that merit, all of the members of our family will be benefited. And your benefit is also certain.[139]

Up to this point, Goenka had primarily taught Indians from Hindu communities with which he was more familiar, and he had taught primarily in Hindi. But Bodh Gaya was a point of attraction for Americans and Europeans interested in Buddhism, and suddenly Goenka found himself coming in contact with large groups of young hippies, children of the flowering counterculture in the West. In his autobiography, Goenka particularly notes the role of the famous psychonaut—the Harvard psychology professor turned Hindu guru Ram Dass—in raising awareness of his teachings among American and European hippies: "...The American Baba Ram Dass came to the course in Bodh Gaya and, after taking part in it, was very pleased. He did a few courses and, pleased with them, returned to his country. After that, many of his disciples began coming to the courses."[140] Not long after this, many foreigners—not just disciples of Ram Dass—began attending Goenka's courses, and he began teaching in English (see chapter 15).

While Ram Dass was a known entity on the New Age scene, a number of other young Americans who participated in Goenka's first course in Bodh Gaya were not. But many of them would go on to become influential in the landscape of American meditation traditions. Joseph Goldstein, Sharon Salzberg, Daniel Goleman, Mirabai Bush, and Wes Nisker—all of whom were involved in popularizing meditation in America—attended this course.[141] We will return to Goldstein and Salzberg in particular, but perhaps most important in terms of understanding Goenka's sense of identity in this moment is the fact that Goenka's old friend, the Indian Buddhist meditation master Munindra Barua (Anagarika Munindra), helped to organize the course, encouraged his students to participate in it, and participated in it himself.[142]

Munindra's participation was a defining moment for Goenka because his presence in Bodh Gaya brought to the surface questions about Goenka's identity as the single true revivor in India of the Buddha's pure teachings preserved in Burma. Munindra was a Bengali Buddhist who had spent nine years in Burma, from 1957 to 1966, studying ancient Pali Buddhist texts and learning meditation from a number of monastic teachers, most notably the Mahasi Sayadaw. Goenka was Munindra's sponsor during that time, and the two knew each other well. But Goenka was not yet a teacher then. He had introduced Munindra to U Ba Khin, and Munindra had hoped to learn meditation from the latter. But U Ba Khin declined to teach him, since Munindra was already the student of a monastic teacher, and it was U Ba Khin's policy not to teach those who were already students of other teachers. Apparently, U Ba Khin wanted to avoid the controversy that could arise from the comparison of practice lineages.[143]

In private, U Ba Khin was quite critical of many other local traditions of meditation. In particular, he criticized those who—like the great Mahasi Sayadaw—claimed that stages of enlightenment could be attained without the force of deep states of meditative concentration (samādhi). He even wrote a small booklet outlining his prowess in teaching absorption meditation, or *jhāna*.[144] But he himself used unorthodox methods to push his students to enlightenment without them attaining such states of concentrated absorption. He did so by harnessing the psychic force of his own concentrated states, those of the guardian deities associated with him by dint of his powerful karmic merit, and those of his advanced students and coteachers such as Mother Sayama. So U Ba Khin's real criticism appears to have been that most other teachers did not have the ability to harness the supernormal forces to which he had access. Goenka's sense of identity as a teacher also seems to have derived from the idea that he was the purveyor of a singularly pure stream of supernormal power made accessible to him by his teacher and by dint of his own karmic merit.

These critical issues came up when Munindra helped Goenka organize his first course in Bodh Gaya. U Ba Khin, however, encouraged Goenka not to follow his own policy of only teaching students who did not already have another teacher, because the controversies between meditation traditions that U Ba Khin had to negotiate in Burma were not prevalent in India. With that obstacle cleared, Munindra helped organize the course and himself participated as Goenka's student. In a letter to U Ba Khin upon completing the course, he wrote the following:

> You will be glad to know that we had the opportunity to organize a ten-day Vipassana meditation course at the most sacred place of Buddhagaya and it was started on the 19th of April. It was conducted by my *Dhamma-mitta* and *Kalyana-*

> *mitta* Shri Satya Narayanji Goenka, who is one of your competent and devout disciples.... I myself took advantage of participating in this seminar and have been greatly benefited by this Vipassana course. In such a short time, the technique helped to open up the new dimension of understanding that it was surprising.... I experienced sleepless nights with mind inward, observing *anicca*—the continuous change of my corporeal body. Body became so sensitive and alive that some times with the very contact of objects of sense doors I felt and observed the whole body like bubbles in the water appearing and disappearing when I was deeply aware and mindful.
>
> During this ten-day course, my *Dhamma-mitta* Shri Goenkaji used to give a talk on Dhamma every evening to all the *yogis*. All talks were on different aspects of Buddha Dhamma—related to the practice and true to the point and meaning in accordance with the teaching. The talks were so inspiring, encouraging and ennobling that since my return from Burma I had no opportunity to hear such good *Dhamma-desana* anywhere in India. I had no idea that my friend was so well conversant with and such a good exponent of Dhamma in its true spirit both in theory and practice. I feel so happy and fortunate myself that I took part in it.[145]

On the one hand, this is a statement of approval from a master of Buddhist meditation who had been teaching Burmese vipaśyanā in India for three years before Goenka's arrival in 1969. On the other hand—and this is how Goenka and his disciples retrospectively narrate this moment—it was an acknowledgment of the particular efficacy of U Ba Khin's, and thereby Goenka's, method of practice.[146] This acknowledgment allowed Goenka to affirm his sense of identity as the single true agent of the prophecy of revival, since Munindra could now be brought under his and U Ba Khin's powerful umbrella. U Ba Khin helped to solidify this idea in a letter to Goenka a few months after the Bodh Gaya course, some five months before his passing: "When we come to realise that YOU are the first to revive Vipassana meditation in India after a lapse of over 2000 years to give practical and concrete results, we cannot help feeling that we are doing a very great work to pay the debt of gratitude to Buddha."[147] While some of the issues around these questions of identity would resurface in other contexts, Goenka and Munindra remained lifelong friends, and Munindra spent the last years of his life living at Goenka's main meditation center in Igatpuri, Maharashtra.

Dialogues with Contemporary Spiritual Teachers

Another key moment in Goenka's early years of teaching, one that radically shifted certain aspects of his teaching focus, took place in March 1972, after the course at Gandhi's Sewagram Ashram mentioned earlier. After the course, Goenka was taken to meet Vinayak Narahari "Vinoba" Bhave (1895–1982), the famed social activist and close associate of Gandhi. Bhave challenged Goenka, saying that the latter's teaching of vipaśyanā could only be relevant in India if it could be shown to improve the lot of low-caste children and hardened criminals. While security rules within prisons in India made it difficult to get approval for residential courses in prisons, Bhave immediately arranged for Goenka to teach meditation to teenagers at the Samanvay School in Bodh Gaya. The school was one of Bhave's projects, and it primarily served the Mushahar community, a downtrodden group that takes its name from the practice of eating mice and rats. The story goes that Goenka was able to train the unruly children of this community, removing some of their bad habits—particularly bad language—and proving to Bhave that vipaśyanā was relevant as a socially transformative practice. Later on, with the help of one of his students, Ram Singh—who was the home secretary of Rajasthan at the time—Goenka was able to give vipaśyanā courses in prisons, beginning with a course in the Central Jail of Jaipur in Rajasthan State in 1975. Some years later, in the 1990s, meditation courses were arranged in one of the largest jails in India, Tihar Jail, where a permanent vipaśyanā meditation center was eventually established. This pioneering marriage of Gandhian social theory and the contemplative practices of the Buddhist tradition set the stage for what has today become a global idea—that the meditative teachings of the Buddha are powerful tools for social engagement and self-improvement.

In 1974, Goenka met the young Dalai Lama. He remembered talking with him through the night about meditation—"all about technique." The Dalai Lama was amazed to know that Goenka could bring his students to a state of lucid concentration, in which they saw a light, in just a few days.[148] In Tibetan tradition, the state of seeing the luminosity of the mind's pure state (*gsal ba*) is a high stage of meditation. It appears that in this conversation Goenka equated the counterpart sign of classical Theravada meditation, which is a mark of progress in preliminary concentration meditation, with the gsal ba of Tibetan tradition.[149] Goenka recounted that he told the Dalai Lama, "You better send a few of your lamas and let them experience it. If I am wrong, I will rectify it. I don't teach them that they must see light. It is merely a sign, a milestone on a long path, not the final goal."[150]

Goenka went on to explain how the Dalai Lama "sent three lamas to my next course in Sarnath. All three of them saw light, and they were so happy." After this, the Dalai Lama organized a large course at the Tibetan Library in Dharamshala, where a large number of Tibetan Buddhist monks and a smaller number of laymen participated. One American participant in this course described it as follows:

> It was a very unusual ten-day Goenka retreat. There were about a hundred spaces available, and most of them, about eighty of them, were taken up by monks and nuns. So you had all these like heavy tantric lamas... And later I found out that these are actually quite famous rinpoches of various sorts. So it was interesting. It was interesting to hear what the Tibetan monks had to say about Goenka. They considered him a tantric master.[151]

This particular assessment of Goenka by accomplished masters of the Tibetan Buddhist tradition is intriguing, and it is perhaps a reminder of the roots of Goenka's teaching methods and their place at one end of a spectrum of the weizzā traditions of Myanmar (discussed in chapter 3). The tantric traditions of India and Tibet show some family resemblances with these weizzā traditions: all are esoteric traditions, emphasizing the necessity of initiation and access to the karmic potency of an enlightened tantric master. Perhaps most important, it is within the sphere of tantric tradition that a householder who is also a meditation master finds a place in Tibetan Buddhist thought. That Goenka was a householder—who brought his wife along with him on his meditation retreats—and yet could bring monastics to deep states of meditative wisdom in a short time fit well with the category of "tantric master" in these traditions.

Another encounter in Goenka's early years had an effect on how he framed his teaching. In 1973, he met the famous dissident prodigy of the Theosophical Society, Jiddu Krishnamurti.[152] Krishnamurti was an influential figure in his time and remains deeply respected among Goenka's disciples into the present.[153] One of Goenka's students, who was instrumental in helping him build his meditation tradition into a national and global institution in the 1980s and 1990s, once told me that Krishnamurti was "the closest to a modern-day Buddha that I have seen in my life." Krishnamurti was well known for his iconoclasm and his criticism of any "system" or "technique" of spiritual practice.

In his teaching of vipaśyanā, both in his early years and into later life, Goenka often referred to it as a "technique" of meditation in English-language contexts. As Goenka told the story, Krishnamurti was critical of this way of talking about meditation practice when the two met. However, Goenka was able to convince him that such language was merely a manner of speaking:

> His teaching is nothing but *vipaśyanā*. [He was] a very saintly person, a very wonderful person. But difficulty he has in his experience in India, where so many types of meditations are going on, so many techniques are going on. And he was disgusted to see all that. So he kept on denouncing: "All the techniques are harmful." . . .
>
> Then a meeting was arranged between Krishnamurti and myself. And I told him that "if I am making any mistake please correct me. You are an elderly person, more experienced,"—and a saintly person—his vibrations were very good. So he said: "Alright, what are you teaching?" [I said:] "The first day I teach this." [He said:] "No technique, this is not a technique." And the second day, third day, tenth day. [He said:] "No technique, this is not a technique. People can practice, nothing wrong." . . . He accepted everything. . . . And after that I heard that, some of his very close disciples, he started asking them to observe respiration.[154]

Here, again, Goenka employed what we might at this point recognize as a well-worn rhetorical tactic. He interacted with this great saintly person with sincere deference, received his approval, and in the end came to influence him in a reversal of the normal order of things. Whether this is in fact an accurate representation of the two teachers' meeting remains a question; at least into the late seventies, Krishnamurti spoke critically against vipaśyanā meditation as a "system."[155] But one thing is clear: Krishnamurti's critique appears to have influenced the way Goenka talked about his own teachings to his more serious students. Goenka's forceful statement on one of his long retreats in 1989 revealed this influence:

> If one is still involved in the sectarian beliefs, dogmas, faiths, one cannot progress on the path of Dhamma. For such a person it is just a technique. One comes to a course to learn a technique from a technician.... How can such a person make a deep operation of the mind and take out the deep-rooted complexes? Because this person takes it only as a technique.[156]

Krishnamurti's critique of gurus and the problematic power relationships that are entailed in traditional guru-disciple relationships in India also led Goenka to downplay his role as a Guru (with a capital G). In many ways, this public de-emphasis masked the very traditional guru-disciple relationship he had with his own teacher and likewise perpetuated with his closest students.

As a final dialogical inflection point from Goenka's early years in India, we might briefly touch on his engagement—from 1974 onward—with some important leaders of the Jain community in India. Early on, a number of Jains became interested in Goenka's teachings. Because of the close similarities between the Jain and Buddhist traditions, which emerged from a common milieu of religious practice in early India, quite a few Jains took seriously to vipaśyanā early in Goenka's mission. Some of his closest helpers were Jains, and they came to believe that Goenka was bringing the long-lost, true Jain method of burning off karmic impurities that the founder of Jainism, Mahavira, had taught. In 1974, Goenka was introduced to an influential Jain reformer, Acharya Tulsi, who invited him to teach courses to Jain monks and nuns at his ashram in western Rajasthan. This made Goenka even more popular among the Jain community. But it also led one of Tulsi's students, Acharya Mahapragya, to feel the need to clearly delineate what was unique to the Jain path. In this process, Mahapragya developed a new tradition of meditation, which drew in part on Goenka's teachings, and called it Preksha Dhyan, or "the Meditation of Perception."[157]

This series of exchanges during Goenka's first years in India represents a small selection of the many interactions he had as he developed his mission and his public relations campaign. Goenka remained constantly active during this time, teaching meditation courses at makeshift camps and ashrams around the country; engaging in dialogue with other spiritual teachers; bringing his teachings into public contexts such as schools, prisons, and police academies; and eventually beginning to establish permanent meditation centers.

In 1973, Goenka visited the land that was to become his main meditation center, Dhamma Giri, and approved it as a suitable site. By 1974, a number of his students were living and meditating on the land, and by 1975 the first formal meditation course—an inaugural short course—was held there. Another piece of land, which was to become Dhamma Khetta, was donated in Hyderabad, and the first course there took place in September 1976. By the end of 1978, a third meditation center, Dhamma Thali, had been established in Jaipur.[158] Goenka was also writing prolifically during this time. He established a monthly Hindi-language newsletter, *Vipaśyanā*, in July 1971 and used this venue as a site to establish his doctrinal and personal credentials (see, for example, chapter 11). He also published a definitive introductory book on vipaśyanā in Hindi in 1976.[159] Though he had originally planned to teach only in Hindi, as noted earlier he began teaching courses in both English and Hindi by popular demand starting in 1970 (see chapter 15). By 1980 Goenka had taught some two hundred meditation courses in virtually every region of the Indian subcontinent and had begun to teach abroad as well.

Two Defining Moments of Conflict[160]

As indicated in the last chapter, during these early years of his mission, Goenka was not the only one of U Ba Khin's students working to bring the practices to a global audience. Three of U Ba Khin's American students—Robert Hover, John Coleman, and Ruth Denison—took up the call of his authorization letters.[161] Though Goenka did not know these foreign students of U Ba Khin well, when streams of young foreigners came to his courses, he directed them to make contact with his Western guru-brothers and guru-sister.

Robert Hover was the first of these three to begin teaching formally, in the autumn of 1971, and he did so with energy and enthusiasm. Between the years 1971 and 1980, he traveled widely to teach in North America, Australia, New Zealand, and India. He was also responsible for establishing the *Vipassana Newsletter*, an English-language quarterly inspired by Goenka's Hindi-language *Vipaśyanā* newsletter, in 1974. Further, he was an early proponent for the scientific study of meditation, since he himself was a chemical engineer. John Coleman, a retired CIA agent, was a bit more reluctant to teach. He capitulated, however, to some of Goenka's students, who harangued him at his home in the United Kingdom in the early seventies and requested him to begin offering courses there. As a result of this pressure, he slowly began to teach course after course, eventually teaching globally—in Great Britain, continental Europe, North America, Thailand, and Japan. He also became the president of the International Meditation Centre in the United Kingdom once it was established in the late seventies. Ruth Denison did not begin teaching until she found herself on a meditation course with Robert Hover in 1974 in Germany, and he encouraged her to take on a teaching role. Both Hover and Coleman traveled to India in the early seventies to meditate with Goenka and, in Hover's case, to teach alongside him. In this way, they came to form a small global team of teachers, working together to spread the teachings of U Ba Khin.

U Ba Khin passed away in January 1971, less than two years after he made his formal call for his foreign students to begin their global mission. Upon his death, his students looked to Mother Sayama as his successor and as a psychic channel to him in the gross material realm. While Goenka encouraged his American and European students to make contact with Hover, Coleman, and Denison and to organize courses upon returning to their home countries, he also sent his students to Burma for more advanced guidance from Mother Sayama. She was assisted by her husband, U Chit Tin, and a few of U Ba Khin's other Burmese students, such as U Tint Yee and U Ba Po.

This global collaboration was in place through the spring of 1977, and communities of meditation practitioners devoted to practicing vipaśyanā "in the tradition of Sayagyi U Ba Khin" sprang up in Northern and Southern California, Massachusetts, the United Kingdom, Australia, and all over India. But trouble was afoot. We see the first public signs of it in the summer 1974 edition of the English-language *Vipassana Newsletter*, originally established in California by Robert Hover. The issue included a notice for a thirty-day meditation course to be taught in California by Joseph Goldstein:

Seek and Find

> A 30-day sati-patanna [*sic*] course will be taught by Joseph Goldstein between September 4 and October 4. The course will be limited to 40 people and will be held in a Sierra mountain camp. A $20 deposit will insure you a place in the course. Send it to Robert Fraser, Box 278, Lagunitas, Ca 94938. Also anyone who would like to cook for the first half of the course contact Robert.[162]

Goldstein, as noted earlier, was a student of Anagarika Munindra and one of the young Americans who had participated in Goenka's first course in Bodh Gaya in 1970. In the years leading up to the "30-day sati-patanna" retreat in California in 1974, Goldstein had spent much of his time in India participating in Goenka's meditations courses while remaining connected to Munindra.[163] During this time, he came to be recognized as a leader among the small community of Western meditators there, and it appeared to some other students at the time that Goenka was grooming Goldstein to become a meditation teacher in his lineage. Goldstein was known to give Dharma talks regularly to small groups who were part of the community of Goenka's students in Dalhousie, an enclave for practitioners at the time.[164]

After Goldstein taught the advertised course in California, questions about his perceived status as an heir to Goenka's teachings began to emerge within communities of meditators involved in Goenka's mission in India. Some felt that Goldstein's teaching and practice approach on this first course in America did not adhere to the strict contours of Goenka's approach. This development brought to the surface the differences between the practice approaches of Goldstein's first teacher, Anagarika Munindra, and Goenka.

In Goldstein's retrospective account of this moment, he notes that in 1973 or early 1974 he and Goenka had "something of a split" over personal matters as well as stylistic differences relating to the practice.[165] This initial split appears to have remained private, but when it manifested publicly in Goldstein's choice to teach on his own in the wide open spiritual terrain of a budding New Age North America, it contributed to a developing tension within the various communities of practitioners connected to Goenka, Munindra, and Hover in both North America and India.

In particular, it brought up the question of what constitutes *sati-paṭṭhāna*, or "the foundations of mindfulness" (spelled incorrectly as *sati-patanna* in the quoted notice). Munindra and his primary Burmese teacher, the Mahasi Sayadaw, drew quite explicitly on *The Great Discourse on the Foundations of Mindfulness* (*Mahāsatipaṭṭhāna-sutta*), an important discourse of the Buddha outlining four foundations of mindfulness: mindfulness of the body (*kāya*); mindfulness of sensations and feelings (*vedanā*); mindfulness of mental states (*citta*); and mindfulness of mental contents (*dhamma*).[166] While U Ba Khin's teaching approach—streamlined by Goenka—can also be understood as a teaching on the foundations of mindfulness, he never emphasized this important traditional source in his teachings. Rather, U Ba Khin and Goenka focused primarily on establishing an awareness of sensations and feelings, suggesting that all four foundations of mindfulness develop together.[167] Mahasi and his students put a stronger emphasis in their preliminary teachings on the practice of mindfulness of activities and mental states by way of discursive noting, and they sought to more clearly delineate the practical distinctions between establishing each of the four foundations.[168]

Goldstein's emphasis on the foundations of mindfulness in his first American retreat diverged in this respect from Goenka's approach. The teachings of the young American—encapsulated in his pioneering book *The Experience of Insight*—wove together classical analyses on the four foundations of mindfulness inspired by Munindra and the forceful, body-oriented approach of Goenka's vipaśyanā.[169] Though there is no explicit public record of the developing tension of this moment, we find echoes of it in one of Goenka's Dharma talks, given on a course in Varanasi in December 1974, just a month after Goldstein's "sati-patanna course":

> [There is] a big confusion in the minds of Western students with these words of *satipaṭṭhāna* and *vipaśyanā*. Awareness of walking, walking, walking, awareness of eating, eating, eating is taken up by many students as *satipaṭṭhāna*. And awareness of sensation, subtle sensations in the body, is taken up as *vipaśyanā,* which has created a lot of confusion.
>
> The word *sati* means "awareness." *Paṭṭhāna* means "getting strongly established." And *sati* is, the awareness is, really strongly established when there is *paññā* with it, wisdom with it. Otherwise, it remains in the field of samādhi (concentration) only, *samatha* (calming) only. You can be just aware; but without wisdom, without *paññā*, you cannot get established in Dhamma. So the whole discourse of Buddha, called *Satipaṭṭhāna-sutta, or Mahāsatipaṭṭhāna-sutta*, is for training the mind for both: awareness and wisdom. Awareness and wisdom. *Sati-sampajāna, sati sapaññā*: wisdom, awareness; wisdom, awareness.
>
> Because of not understanding the real purpose, those students who have started developing wisdom by experiencing subtler realities, many times, out of just... out of their inquisitiveness, some new practice—that means something new what's going on in other schools—they start practicing with these grosser objects of the grosser activities of the body. Nothing wrong. But what's wrong is, by forgetting

> all about the subtler realities, they get themselves so much engrossed in these gross activities of the body that they start losing all the subtle sensations. The entire body gets once again blocked up. Although the poor teacher—the guide who gives this, this so-called *satipaṭṭhāna*—says very clearly that you have to go [to] the subtler stages, but because of this not understanding the whole basic theory behind Buddha's teaching of practice, they again make themselves, their minds, so blunt—though aware, but aware of the grosser things—that for them it becomes a big thing to go to the subtler stages of the body and mind.[170]

This discussion of "confusion in the minds of Western students" is almost certainly a veiled reference to Joseph Goldstein.[171] Goenka here drew a soft line between his own approach and "what's going on in other schools," but this moment marks the beginning of a contraction of his ecumenical openness.

It is noteworthy that the notice for Goldstein's first course in America appeared in the international *Vipassana Newsletter*—the English-language quarterly established by Robert Hover—which later on came to be an exclusive forum for those practicing "in the tradition of Sayagyi U Ba Khin." This lineage-oriented phrase appeared for the first time on the cover of the fall 1975 newsletter about a year after Goldstein taught his "sati-patanna" course. In the pages of this same issue, two notices marked an additional exacerbation of the subtle tensions that had surfaced in the wake of that course.

The first notice announced that "A year-round Vipassana Meditation Retreat Center has been established in western Massachusetts . . . the Insight Meditation Center of New England."[172] The notice went on to provide some details about the center:

> The center will be exclusively devoted to the practice of Insight Meditation in the Theravada Buddhist Traditions. . . . Mr. Hover's course will officially open the center on August 28, and he will conduct another retreat there in January. There are tentative plans for retreats in the spring to be conducted by Mrs. Denison and Mr. Coleman. This fall there will be courses led by teachers of other Vipassana Meditation practices.

This notice is in fact the first public record of the establishment of what soon came to be called the Insight Meditation Society. U Ba Khin's American students—with Robert Hover as a principal senior authorizing presence—played an important role in the establishment of this center.

Though the first line presents a conservative approach to traditional Buddhist meditation, binding the center's mission to teaching "Insight Meditation in the Theravada Buddhist traditions," the plural "traditions" indicates an ecumenical openness. While the establishment of the center was clearly associated with and spearheaded by the members of U Ba Khin's global team—particularly Robert Hover—it also would become a space for "other Vipassana Meditation practices." The fact that this nonspecific binary—that of the teachers in U Ba Khin's lineage and teachers of "other" practices—was set out in the first public announcement of the center is telling. This key distinction would soon become one of the primary reasons for a parting of ways between U Ba Khin's Asian students and many of the students in America.

But before we get to that key moment, one additional notice in this issue of the *Vipassana Newsletter* deserves comment. A short article on the very last page, just next to the previous notice, was titled "Mrs. Denison Brings New Aspect." This article briefly described Ruth Denison's first course taught in America, explaining that "[t]he routine of the course was quite different from what many of us knew before. The whole day, from early morning into the night, we remained together meditating as a group, eating together, and even walking together during breaks."[173]

Denison's creative and unique model of teaching—which departed from the models of Hover and Coleman, who had both trained with Goenka in India—raised hackles in Asia. At the same time, the establishment of a meditation center in America that would not be exclusively dedicated to teaching meditation "in the tradition of Sayagyi U Ba Khin" troubled both Mother Sayama in Burma and Goenka in India. Robert Hover did indeed teach the official inaugural course at the Insight Meditation Society—which ended up being established in Barre, Massachusetts—and this course was advertised in the fall 1975 issue of the *Vipassana Newsletter*. Further, all three of U Ba Khin's American students taught courses there in 1976 and 1977 as proxies of U Ba Khin.

But this state of affairs did not last long. The tensions that had been building between the American and Asian communities of U Ba Khin's students since Joseph Goldstein's first course in America came to a head and appeared in the open in the *Vipassana Newsletter* of May 1977. A notice in that newsletter read:

> We have received word through Mother Sayama in Rangoon that Robert Hover and Ruth Denison are no longer recognized as teachers in the Sayagyi U Ba Khin Tradition. Their course schedules will no longer be published in this newsletter.[174]

It is evident here that Mother Sayama in Burma was calling the shots as to who was included under the U Ba Khin umbrella. But Goenka participated in this process along with her. We have already seen that Goenka had a critical view of some of the developments in America. That his critical take also came to bear on the fate of Hover and Denison becomes apparent in light of an influential retrospective narrative of the beginning of the Insight Meditation Society. In this narrative, the Society's putative founders become the young Joseph Goldstein, Sharon Salzberg, and Jack Kornfield. As noted above, Goldstein and Salzberg were students of both Goenka and Munindra, and they also studied with another of Munindra's students, Dipa Ma (Nani Bala Barua). This narrative can be found in the public record in the words of Jack Kornfield, and it explains how Goenka's previous tacit criticism of the "big confusion in the minds of Western students" transformed into a formal rejection of the eclectic teaching model supported by his various once-were students at the founding moment of the Insight Meditation Society. Kornfield relates how Goenka not only refused an invitation to teach at the Insight Meditation Society at that time but also made clear in a letter that the center's organizers were misguided because they were "mixing techniques," creating an opening for evil forces and diluting the pure stream of the Dharma handed down by U Ba Khin.[175]

In this narrative, Robert Hover is virtually erased from the history of the establishment of the Insight Meditation Society, and Ruth Denison becomes an emblem for the eclectic and creative ecumenism of American Buddhism.[176] In a virtually unknown alternate narrative, Mother Sayama and Goenka were strongly tied to a teaching model in which they were working as a channel of their guru—a particularly powerful bodhisattva—and therefore could not abide the dilution of that channel by Westerners without a proper understanding of the supernormal mechanics at work in their model.

It is remarkable that at this moment John Coleman remained in the U Ba Khin fold with Mother Sayama's sanction. He was able to do this because he subserviently pledged himself to her, considering her to be in large part responsible for his attainment of a "quiet mind" at the International Meditation Centre in Rangoon in 1958.[177]

This fissure marked the formal end of the association between the U Ba Khin lineage and the Insight Meditation Society, but it did not solve all the problems at play among U Ba Khin's global team. The diminished team carried on with its work—Goenka in India, John Coleman based in the United Kingdom, and Mother Sayama and U Chit Tin in Burma. Goenka kept up his pace, and the community grew fast. But a new development altered the balance of things when, in 1978, Mother Sayama and U Chit Tin were granted permission to leave Burma and begin teaching abroad. This development occurred in part because general elections satisfactory to the military coalition in Burma had been held in 1974, and the country was opening up a bit. Their first trip brought them to the United Kingdom and India.

Their initial goal was to establish a meditation center in the United Kingdom, but Goenka had also requested Sayama's help in solving some of the problems he was facing in developing his centers in India. Apparently, nonhuman forces unsupportive of the teaching of Dharma were wreaking havoc at his main meditation center, Dhamma Giri, as well as at his center in Jaipur, Dhamma Thali. Due to this "conflict of forces," construction projects languished at Dhamma Giri, and nightly howling haunted the wilderness around Dhamma Thali. Goenka called in Sayama—who was known to have powerful supernormal abilities—to help banish these destructive forces from the premises.

Mother Sayama's first trip outside of Burma was celebrated in the Hindi-language *Vipaśyanā* newsletter: "Happy Arrival: Gurudev Goenkaji's Dharma-mother, 'Mother Sayama,' will be stopping in India on her way from Burma to London. For the benefit of meditators, she will stay at Dhamma Giri until the end of this month."[178] The phrase "Dharma-mother" makes clear that Mother Sayama was understood to be Goenka's own teacher. In another notice, we find a call for meditators to come to Dhamma Giri so they might "get the benefit of the presence of the embodiment of Dharma, Mother Sayama."[179]

But Mother Sayama's presence in India and on the global scene led to a shift in the cultural balance that had been established in the first decade of Goenka's mission. First that balance was unsettled by American creativity, and now it was unsettled by the true face of Goenka's Burmese past arriving in India. In India, Goenka had carefully crafted an image of vipaśyanā that was amenable to Hindu tradition and fully separate from a Buddhist identity of the sort that U Ba Khin and Mother Sayama maintained. This worked well at a distance, and it even worked fine for the most part outside of India. But it created a problem for Goenka in the Indian context.

The conflict that developed between Mother Sayama and Goenka was complex, and many factors were involved. In the retrospective narratives of Goenka's students, it was a conflict about money. Mother Sayama and U Chit Tin, like U Ba Khin before them, proposed to develop a meditation center in the United Kingdom that would function by asking students to pay fees for food and center maintenance. Goenka, on the other hand, developed a model in which all aspects of the center were run by donation only. This was one source of conflict, but there was more.

After a flurry of coordinated activity between Goenka, Mother Sayama, U Chit Tin, and John Coleman between 1978 and 1981, and just as several meditation centers exclusively dedicated to teaching insight meditation "in the tradition of Sayagyi U Ba Khin" were being established in the United States, France, Australia, and the United Kingdom, the following notice appeared in the English-language edition of the *Vipassana Newsletter* of autumn 1981:

A Notice of Change

Certain recent developments seem to Goenka-ji to be unacceptable, since they go contrary to his understanding of Dhamma and of the Teachings of Sayagyi U Ba Khin. Therefore he has regretfully decided henceforth to work separately.

In accordance with this decision, the Vipassana Newsletter will in future carry information about courses and other activities of Goenka-ji only.

Those wishing to receive information about courses to be taught by Mother Sayama, Saya U Chit Tin, and John Coleman may contact Splatts House, Heddington near Calne, Wiltshire SN11 OPE, England.

In his teaching, Goenka-ji will continue to hold firm to the following Dhamma principles, which were always cherished by Sayagyi U Ba Khin:

1. that Centres and courses must be supported solely by the donations of grateful old students (dana);
2. that Teachers must not receive any remuneration for teaching Dhamma, nor use it as a means for personal gain;
3. that all emphasis in the Teaching be placed on the Eightfold Noble Path of Sila, Samadhi, and Panna, which is practical, rational, logical, and producing tangible, here-and-now, concrete beneficial results that can be verified objectively;
4. that students should take refuge in Dhamma, and not in any personality; that they should be encouraged to develop their own insight, and try to rely on it;
5. that Dhamma should be presented in a way that is non-sectarian, and that it should be taken not as a religion but as an ideal way of life.[180]

In narrating the conflict between Goenka and Mother Sayama, virtually every student of Goenka I have spoken with emphasizes only the first two points on this list. (Goenka ordered all of his close students never to speak publicly about the conflict.) These two points appear to tacitly suggest that Mother Sayama, U Chit Tin, and John Coleman were in some measure immoral with respect to their financial practices.

However, the quick response from Mother Sayama, U Chit Tin, and John Coleman suggests that the real crux of the issue may have been more about religious identity. In "A Notice of Clarification" published in a newly minted *Vipassana Newsletter* of the International Meditation Center of the United Kingdom, Coleman wrote in response to the original notice:

> ... [T]he principles enunciated in the article are not considered to be completely in keeping with the Buddha Dhamma, or the principles always cherished by Sayagyi U Ba Khin, who was Buddhist by birth, faith and practice.
>
> It is felt that to present the Buddha Dhamma only as an ideal way of life would be directly contradictory to all of Sayagyi U Ba Khin's faith and beliefs ...[181]

In making this point, Coleman characterizes the teaching approach laid out by Goenka in his notice as "*adhammavada*—wrong view."

It appears from this exchange that points 3 through 5 in Goenka's "Notice of Change" were the issues that stood at the center of the conflict. In light of history, it is certainly clear that these are the ones that had the most impact on how Goenka's teachings came to be presented to a global public. These points read like a manifesto for modern secular meditation, and they were central to how he presented the tradition to his non-Buddhist students in particular. Points 3 and 4 became primary in his presentation to the West, and points 4 and 5 became dominant in his presentation to Indians, for reasons particular to these distinct cultural contexts.

In retrospectively narrating this conflict in 2008, however, Goenka himself provided a confounding counterpoint to the rhetorical position laid out in his list from nearly thirty years earlier. In this account, he described in quite different terms how his conflict with Mother Sayama came to a head during his second "world tour" to spread vipaśyanā outside of India in 1981:

> I was on a world tour to conduct courses. When I reached Japan, an important person [Mother Sayama] spread the rumour by phone that revered Sayagyi U Ba Khin had withdrawn his blessing and support to me; and that he would not even give *mettā* to me in courses. This message made everyone nervous. I too felt that if this is true, I should not conduct any more courses. I felt that all courses in Japan and elsewhere should be cancelled and I should return home. We were staying in Dhamma daughter Sachiko's home. This unpleasant news had been spread by what seemed to be a reliable source. According to this news, since I was no longer a teacher in the tradition of Sayagyi U Ba Khin, Sachiko could have told us to leave but she didn't.
>
> John Beary proposed to all the assembled meditators that the next course should not be cancelled. This message may have been spread out of ill will. He suggested that the course should be held and if *mettā* is found to be weak, then the remaining courses could be cancelled. The course was conducted and it was very successful. Everyone said that the *mettā* was even stronger than before. . . . Because of the success of this course, everyone including me was convinced that Sayagyi's *mettā* and blessing were definitely with me.[182]

This story generates a powerful dissonance when read alongside the "Notice of Change" and the classically Buddhist modernist statements made in it. Points 3 through 5 of that notice strongly emphasize that the teaching is "practical, rational, logical, . . . producing . . . beneficial results that can be verified objectively" (point 3); "that students should take refuge in the Dhamma, not in any personality" (point 4); and "that Dhamma . . . should be taken not as a religion" (point 5). Yet in this account of Goenka's own approach to dealing with one of the most consequential moments in his life as a teacher of vipaśyanā meditation—an account that involved a number of his closest disciples who are today leaders of the community he built—we see an entirely subjective process, virtually impossible to verify objectively, being used to validate the entire foundation of a religious mission. What is more, this process explicitly relies on and involves the direct influence of the personality of a great guru, a great bodhisattva, and a dead one at that.

This key historical moment was the forge in which S. N. Goenka's true identity as a meditation teacher was fashioned, and the dynamics at play here and in the ouster of Hover and Denison form the fulcrum of a range of issues that come to serve as major fault lines in modern Buddhist meditation traditions and global secularized insight and mindfulness practices. A "conflict of forces" became manifest in these moments at the level of cultural differences and issues of religious and personal identity. After pushing into exile his American guru-siblings and many of his students, Goenka had to turn his back on his Burmese Dharma-mother in order to fully step out on his own and become the truly global teacher he felt destined to become.

CHAPTER 6

Preparing Fields, Spreading Seeds

THERE IS A STORY about Sayagyi U Ba Khin that I have heard told repeatedly among disciples of S. N. Goenka. U Ba Khin was known to chant protective verses, mantras, and discourses attributed to the Buddha. He considered this to be one of his primary occupations as a meditation teacher (and bodhisattva). In his diary, he kept detailed lists of the number of recitations he did every day, along with lists of other meritorious actions.[183] He would also sometimes recite verses of his own. The story goes that U Ba Khin liked to recite one particular mantra in Pali that went something like "... May I not come into contact with the ignorant / May I encounter only wise, saintly people / until I attain *nibbāna*." This mantric verse emerged from a vow he had taken: "May only ripened people with very good *pāramīs* (virtues) from the past come to me to take Dhamma, and may these people later take the torch of Dhamma, and spread it 'round the world." Being a devout student of U Ba Khin and wanting to emulate him, S. N. Goenka learned the mantra and would go around reciting it. One day U Ba Khin heard him reciting it and rebuked him: "These words are not for you!" he said. "You are to give seeds of Dhamma to a very large number of people."[184]

Whenever I have heard this story, it has been related as an explanation for why S. N. Goenka was a teacher surpassing all others and yet did not explicitly teach advanced stages of meditation to his students. It, therefore, presents a retrospective explanation of what became the defining characteristic of Goenka's mission, particularly after he parted ways with Robert Hover, Ruth Denison, John Coleman, Mother Sayama, U Chit Tin, and others at the International Meditation Centre in Rangoon. According to this story, by dint of his great collection of karmic merit—which surpassed that of his guru-brothers and guru-sisters, even the woman he called his Dharma-mother—Goenka was destined to teach to the global masses in large numbers. He was to give them the seed of Dharma rather than focus on bringing karmically developed practitioners to stages of enlightened attainment.

How does this story help us to understand who Goenka was—or who he considered himself to be—as a master and teacher of meditation? I have already noted that U Ba Khin's close disciples understood U Ba Khin to be a special bodhisattva, an emanation of the next buddha, Maitreya. Within this cosmology, some of U Ba Khin's disciples were thought to be vow-takers. That is, they were believed to have taken vows in past lives not to attain nirvana in their current lives, but instead to remain in the cycle of rebirth so they might cultivate karmic merit. Eventually, they would become enlightened disciples under U Ba Khin when he attained enlightenment as Maitreya. In his later years, Goenka explained to his close disciples that he, along with them, would be reborn at a time in the distant future under a future buddha, and all of them would attain enlightenment together as a group.

This outlook was a part of Goenka's identity as a meditation teacher from early on. However, since the belief about U Ba Khin's identity as a special bodhisattva was doctrinally controversial, it could not become an aspect of Goenka's public identity. Yet the very public story about Goenka's special status as a purveyor of the "seeds of Dhamma" makes much more sense when we understand this esoteric aspect of U Ba Khin's identity and when we take into account the associated long-term cosmological vision that informed Goenka's sense of his mission.

This outlook became even more salient, and more loaded, when Goenka parted ways with Mother Sayama. Although a brief initial period in India had seen Goenka try to emulate U Ba Khin's teaching style—bringing as many people as possible, as quickly as possible, to at least the first stage of enlightenment—when this proved difficult, it was attributed to the challenges presented by teaching contexts outside of Burma, as well as to Goenka's particular role. Ultimately, it became Goenka's job to simply introduce students to the teachings. Those who got serious about meditation could travel to Burma for the more intimate and vibrationally supportive atmosphere of the International Meditation Centre. Such students could work directly with Mother Sayama, whose psychic powers were known to help create that particularly supportive atmosphere.

Once Goenka made his break from Mother Sayama and U Chit Tin, this arrangement came to an end. As a consequence, the narrative of Goenka being destined to "give seeds of Dhamma to a very large number of people" became more prominent. In the end, it came to serve as the defining mantra of his mission and the organization he went on to build. At the same time, this emphasis took off the table the possibility that those coming to learn meditation from Goenka might actually attain the stages of enlightenment that were the final goal of practice.[185]

In chapter 5 we encountered the idea of "the seed of *vipassanā*, the seed of Dhamma." Goenka spoke about it on every ten-day meditation course he taught, and it is recapitulated even now on the many courses at meditation centers around the globe that continue to use video and audio recordings of his teachings to guide students in meditation. On the tenth day of his ten-day course, Goenka explains how, when he began teaching meditation in India, he felt convinced that many whom he met "already ha[d] the seed of *vipassanā*, the seed of Dhamma. Now the time has ripened for this person to grow in Dhamma. And not only help himself or herself, but to help others—there is a potentiality for them not only to help themselves, but to help others also."[186] This potentiality was predicated, however, on the existence of another demographic: "I also see that there are people who have come just to take the seed of Dhamma. They have done some very wholesome deed, some very good karma, and the ripening of that deed has helped them to get a seed of Dhamma."[187]

In this taxonomy of karmic types, one group is omitted: those who have the potentiality to attain enlightenment or awakening in this very life. This omission stands out when we consider that, aside from Goenka, most of the other teachers selected by U Ba Khin to spread his teachings globally were confirmed to be attainers.[188] That is, U Ba Khin had tested them and confirmed that they had attained at least the first stage of enlightenment according to early Buddhist tradition, the stage of stream-entry. This does not appear to be the case for Goenka: there is no evidence that he was ever confirmed to be an attainer. This identity—as one who will remain in the cycle of rebirth "to help others" rather than "only to help oneself"—forms the foundation of his mission and the organizational structures that he built to enact it globally.

The narrative of Goenka as a purveyor of seeds achieved—and continues to achieve—a number of things. It set Goenka apart as an especially powerful teacher of a particular kind. It likewise served to explain why most if not all of Goenka's students were unable to attain stages of enlightenment under his guidance. Additionally, it justified why Goenka did not need to teach particular practices that were part of the repertoire of classical Theravada meditation, as well as why he never focused on teaching technical aspects of the higher stages of meditation. Finally, it became a justification for his break from Mother Sayama and others at the International Meditation Centre, though the break was rarely discussed publicly.

Parallel Identities

Not long after the split with Mother Sayama, Goenka founded meditation centers in North America, Australia, and France. These centers were exclusively devoted to distributing his teachings. By the end of the 1990s, he had established some forty permanent meditation centers around the world, including in England, Japan, Myanmar, Nepal, New Zealand, Taiwan, Thailand, Spain, Sri Lanka, and Switzerland. By the time of his death in 2013, Goenka (with the help of his students) had established at least 120 more centers, extending to every corner of the globe. In addition to these permanent meditation centers, Goenka made it a priority to make his teachings available at temporary camps wherever it was not possible to establish a permanent center.[189]

This breathtaking spread was possible precisely because Goenka focused his energies primarily on building a large-scale global distribution system—and a network of devoted volunteers to facilitate its maintenance. He wanted an organization that could deliver to as many people as possible, in as many places as possible, the seeds of the Buddha's teachings in the form of his vipaśyanā meditation. For the most part, these meditation centers ran bimonthly, ten-day meditation retreats and were maintained entirely on the donations of past students.

To an observer of his life during this time, Goenka as a person appears to recede into the horizon of his identity as a *viśvaguru*, a "world teacher" or "global teacher." We have already seen how his public relations campaign during the early years in India, and his interaction with a variety of personalities and communities, conditioned the parameters of his rhetorical tactics and teaching approach. His institution-building and his attempts to ensure that his teachings could be accessible to an ever larger audience were an extension of this campaign. To carry it out globally, Goenka relied on his ability to speak to different audiences in different registers and to curate an identity palatable to a global audience. Because of the necessity of this multiregister presentation, he came to rely even more heavily on a perennialist rhetoric that allowed people to hear what they wanted in his teachings. As a by-product, Goenka's more personal commitments were gradually effaced in public representations. This effacement was most obvious in English-language contexts, accessible primarily to his globalized non-Indian audience. Many of Goenka's more personal commitments were retained when he spoke to or wrote for Hindi-speaking audiences.

Two parallel identities came into being in the latter decades of Goenka's life and teaching—a global Goenka who taught a universal secular technique of meditation amenable to all social contexts, and an Indian Goenka who taught a public nonsectarian Dharma amenable to the politics of Indian pluralism. Both of these identities—and the space between them where the historical Goenka might actually be located—have their roots in a cultic Goenka, a devotee of U Ba Khin dedicated to serving his teacher. More particularly, he was dedicated to serving as a powerful channel for his teacher's *vijjādhātu* or *weizzādhāt*, the psychic force of the wisdom of vipaśyanā made available to Goenka and his students by the grace of U Ba Khin and his enlightened nonhuman guides.

These parallel identities—or rather, the ongoing overlay of identities that came to constitute Goenka's fragmented presentation of himself to the world—came about through a series of institutional developments.

Foundations of Mindfulness

The process began with Goenka advancing a new exegetical agenda. In December 1981, not long after his break with the International Meditation Centre, he began to teach a new kind of meditation course, one in which he presented a comprehensive analysis of the *The Great Discourse on the Foundations of Mindfulness*. This development was first announced in an issue of the *Vipaśyanā* newsletter:

> *Mahāsati Paṭṭhāna* [*sic*] *Sutta*: For the sake of the awakening of some select old meditators [those who have previously participated in ten-day courses], Respected Guru Goenkaji will present explanations of the Blessed Buddha's famous discourse connected with *vipaśyanā*, "*The Great Discourse on the Foundations of Mindfulness*," from the 16th to the 23rd of December, 1981. It is compulsory that those meditators participate in course number 204 (5–16 December, 1981). Those old meditators who want to get the benefit of this [opportunity] should please send a letter to the registrar of the [Vipaśyanā International] Academy.[190]

In these new courses, Goenka attempted to show how the practice he taught could be reconciled with this well-known traditional text. This performance allowed him to individuate himself from his Burmese counterparts and to push back against criticisms directed at his teaching approach by some of his Western students and the more traditional lineages of Burmese monastic vipassanā. In this way, Goenka was also able to set himself up as a true *paṇḍita*, or learned scholar—with a core text and commentarial tradition—for his Indian and global publics.

The satipaṭṭhāna course soon became a formal requirement for those who wanted to be considered serious students of meditation within Goenka's community. It is important to note once again that *The Great Discourse on the Foundations of Mindfulness* was not central to the meditation teachings of any of Goenka's predecessors in his Burmese lineage.[191] It became a focus and a tool for building authority only under the pressures of a particular historical moment. We saw the beginnings of this process earlier, when Goenka implicitly responded to Joseph Goldstein's teaching of a satipaṭṭhāna course in America in 1974. But now Goenka put this exegetical project at the center of his institution- and community-building projects.

In retrospect, it appears somewhat confounding that Goenka felt the need to do this. As we have seen, the meditation practice that he taught is very much a practice of establishing the four foundations of mindful awareness. But it does not easily fit into the structure of *The Great Discourse on the Foundations of Mindfulness*, which is a complicated hybrid text with a murky textual history.[192] The practices Goenka inherited from U Ba Khin fit more appropriately with approaches to meditation outlined in texts such as *The Discourse on Mindfulness of Breathing* (*Ānāpānasati Sutta*) or *The Discourse on the Analysis of the Elements* (*Dhātuvibhaṅga Sutta*).[193] But these texts, being less famous, did not have the popular currency of *The Great Discourse on the Foundations of Mindfulness*.

Goenka tacitly acknowledged the tension of his choice even at the outset of his satipaṭṭhāna courses. In introducing students to a new theoretical framework for interpreting the practices to which they had been introduced previously, he emphasized the subsidiary role of theoretical knowledge:

> Understand, the technique remains the same. Your practice remains the same. But the course is a special course in the sense that you will try to understand the words of the Enlightened One, the Buddha, with reference to the technique.[194]

For Goenka, the technique he taught was manifestly true by dint of experience, and there was no doubt that it encompassed what the Buddha taught. Any legitimate Buddhist scripture would necessarily contain it. From this perspective, one can only understand the words of the Buddha—in this particular case, the words found in *The Great Discourse on the Foundations of Mindfulness*—once one has experienced directly the technique to which Goenka had privileged access.

In setting up for his students such a relationship to theoretical knowledge—exemplified by and embodied in Buddhist scripture—Goenka distinctly played down the importance of textual learning:

> These seven days we will make use of this particular *sutta* [discourse]. Later on it is not necessary that every student must study the entire Tipiṭaka [canon of scripture], all the words of [the] Buddha. [It is] not necessary. If someone finds time to go through all that, wonderful. Every word, as I say, is like nectar. . . . But yet I say, it is not necessary.[195]

Since Goenka positioned textual learning and theoretical knowledge as largely unnecessary even at the outset of his effort to interpret Buddhist sutras, it appears that the development of the satipaṭṭhāna course was less about giving students access to the theoretical models elucidated in Buddhist scripture and more about Goenka establishing his authority as a man of learning. This particular performance of the mastery of scripture allowed him not only to prove that his teachings had scriptural warrant but also to critique other traditions with different interpretations of the famous scripture. This project became a key component in the development of an organization dedicated to spreading the seeds of the Buddha's teachings.

Community as Institution: Channeling the Pure Stream of Dharma

In early 1982, just after he taught his first satipaṭṭhāna course, Goenka announced another institutional development that would have a lasting impact on the organizational structures, teaching models, and practice emphases of Goenka and his community of students. He would begin to train and appoint assistant teachers to teach under him—"ripened old meditators, both Indian and foreign," to engage in the work of Dharma service.[196]

This project was laid out explicitly in a formal announcement in the *Vipaśyanā* newsletter:

> The Spread of *Vipaśyanā*: Over the past one or two years, Respected Guru Goenkaji has remained so busy organizing Vipaśyanā courses that he has not had a break to engage in other necessary duties. The schedule until the end of the coming October is [likewise] packed with one [course] after another so that there will be no break during that time [either]. The reason for all of this is that there is not just demand for *vipaśyanā* in India. [The demand] has also grown so much throughout the world that it cannot be fulfilled. This is direct proof of the immediate benefit of the True Dharma for meditators. For this reason, Goenkaji has been training some people over the past few years to teach *vipaśyanā*. During last winter's courses, he appointed as Assistant Teachers eight from among those in training....
>
> Some of them have already begun the work of teaching. Mr. Bill Hart's first course, in which old and new meditators got full benefit, took place in Bodhgaya at the "Burmese Buddhist Monastery" from the 10th to the 20th of March. The course was completed very successfully....
>
> In all of these Assistant Teacher (AT) courses, [students] listen to Goenkaji's discourses on tapes, and [they] listen to the various necessary daily instructions given by him throughout the course on tapes as well. In this way, with the

> presence and guidance of the Assistant Teachers, all new and old meditators get the full Dharma-benefit. This has become clear from the success of this last course [conducted by Mr. Bill Hart]. So, those desiring to take courses should, without hesitation, participate in these courses and get the benefit.[197]

The popularity of the practice was seen as "direct proof" of its beneficial efficacy and authenticity. The number of courses taught, the number of people coming to individual courses, the development of new meditation centers, and the sense of "benefit" expressed by students became the primary benchmarks for the success of Goenka's mission. Missionary success and its concomitant demands had brought the need for more institutional infrastructure, as well as more warm bodies to do the work of spreading the teachings. The assistant teacher model was developed to serve this need. It seems clear, however, that Goenka did not feel that his students were yet competent to teach the Dharma themselves. His experiences with students who had gone on to teach against his judgment had perhaps made him wary of giving other students too much license as individuals. This led to the novel solution of using tape-recorded instructions and talks to structure the meditation courses. This technological innovation allowed Goenka to harness the zeal of his close disciples and provide more and more courses as demand increased while remaining the only actual teaching authority within the institution he was building.

Given that the announcement encouraged people to participate "without hesitation" since they could still get the "full benefit" of a course, there was clearly some trepidation about these developments in the community. In later years, the organization would insist that the use of tape recordings and assistants worked well for all course participants, even those learning meditation for the first time. It has become a refrain in courses taught to the present day that participating in such a course is just like "taking a course directly with Goenka-ji."

Looking back from our time—a digital era in which it is commonplace to see meditation being taught through online courses, apps, YouTube videos, and podcasts—Goenka's decision to use audio and audiovisual materials as a standard method of teaching is remarkable. That moment marked the beginning of unprecedented mass dissemination of meditation aided by the development of these portable technologies. In the ensuing decades, Goenka's English-language instructions and discourses were translated into dozens of languages and used by assistants at centers around the globe.[198] This development prefigured and created the possibility for the digitally mediated spread of mindfulness meditation that has become a mainstream part of global wellness culture, Buddhism, and spirituality both within and outside of traditional practice contexts. At the same time, in the context of Goenka's organization, the early 1980s also marked the beginning of an institutional formation in which a single teacher was able to ensure that no other individual might subsume his role.

In assessing this institutional development, it is helpful to think back to the early days of Goenka's mission, when he was still connected with the other members of U Ba Khin's global team. We have seen how Goenka, from the beginning of his time in India, thought of himself and his fellow students as mere agents of his teachers' will. This process was palpable for him as he taught his courses under the distant control of his teachers and felt himself filled with and protected by their mettā. The "radio waves" of this powerful force coursed through him when he taught—even after U Ba Khin had passed away—and he perceived himself as simply a channel for the flow of U Ba Khin's transmission of Dharma.

The primary difference in the new setup that Goenka created was that his assistants were given much less leeway to act on their own, particularly outside India. While initially it appeared that Goenka intended for his assistants to become teachers in their own right, carrying out scriptural recitations and teaching the Dharma from the Dharma seat on their own in evening discourses, by 1996 he had made it clear that this would never be the case. Instead, he built a large organization of assistants who would forever remain his proxies.[199] The organization thus became one made up entirely of assistants, proxies, and administrators, each a node for the mettā flowing from U Ba Khin, through Goenka, and into the ritual format of worldwide meditation courses.

Goenka and his community developed this teaching model to serve the needs of a particular historical moment, and it continues to be enacted today at Goenka's meditation centers around the world. It has at its foundation the notion of a tiered psychic channel originating in the person of the bodhisattva who will become the next fully enlightened buddha, Maitreya. It is indeed remarkable that this phenomenally successful model, which has shaped global secular mindfulness as much as almost anything, is in fact based on the idea that a late and little-known Burmese lay teacher is the next future buddha.

Publishing for an Indian and Global Public

Around the same time that the assistant teacher program was getting off the ground and Goenka launched his course on *The Great Discourse on the Foundations of Mindfulness*, the *Vipaśyanā* newsletter began serial publication (in Hindi) of summaries of oral discourses of Goenka's ten-day vipaśyanā courses.[200] These summaries—produced by Ram Singh, one of Goenka's first assistants and an influential politician from the state of Rajasthan—transposed the oral tradition of Goenka's elegant Dharma talks into a simple and accessible Hindi-language literary form.[201] The objective of creating such summaries was for meditators to have short, readable reminders of Goenka's teachings for inspiration in their daily lives. The project also provided those who had already learned the basics of meditation a literary source for the teachings. Not long after this, Hindi translations of the liturgy that Goenka chanted in the course of his standard ten-day retreats were also published serially in the newsletter.[202]

These publications began a process of making available the "essence" of the meditative teachings in a variety of literary forms that stripped out a large part of the substantive practical and doctrinal content of the broader historical tradition of the Buddha's teachings. In this way, meditation students were provided with reading material that might keep them occupied and provide them a sense of engaging with the tradition intellectually. At the same time, this material was largely redundant and therefore uncontroversial, and it served to solidify Goenka's interpretation of the teachings of the Buddha as an alternative to providing meditation students with direct access to the historical teachings. This process was the literary parallel of the assistant teacher program in that it further simplified an already simplified set of doctrinal concepts and stripped out much of the nuance and context of U Ba Khin's original teachings, as well as the teachings of the Buddha.

The *Vipaśyanā* newsletter was the initial forum for these writings, but by the mid-1980s another idea had developed: Goenka and his followers would found a research institute for the study of vipaśyanā in traditional religious texts and in daily life. So, in 1985, the Vipassana Research Institute was born.

The first public signs of this development appeared in the July 1984 *Vipaśyanā* newsletter:

Vipaśyanā Research Activity: The Sayaji U Ba Khin Memorial Trust has decided that scientific research into Vipaśyanā meditation should be undertaken on its behalf. There are many topics of research, such as:

1. Freedom from addiction through *vipaśyanā*
2. Freedom from illness through *vipaśyanā*
3. Improvement of bodily and social deportment through *vipaśyanā*
4. Improvement of individual and social deportment through *vipaśyanā*
5. The enhanced benefit of Nature Cure when combined with *vipaśyanā*
6. The enhanced benefit of *yoga* practice when combined with *vipaśyanā*
7. Improvement in modern education when combined with *vipaśyanā*
8. The comprehensive translation of the Buddha's teachings as well as the teachings of other Dharma texts on the basis of [insights gleaned from] *vipaśyanā* practice[203]

This announcement signaled the development of S. N. Goenka's interest in a new research agenda, one in line with developments beginning to make waves in North America. The seminal research of scholar-practitioners such as Daniel Goleman and Jack Kornfield—the former a student of Goenka and the latter a one-time student of U Ba Khin—had set the stage for the development of "mindfulness" for medical and self-help purposes in North America. This project was perhaps most consequentially developed by the now-famous Jon Kabat-Zinn—a student of Robert Hover and others at the Insight Meditation Society.[204] Kabat-Zinn's Stress Reduction Clinic had begun to publish scientific studies on mindfulness/

awareness meditation beginning in the early 1980s, and the results presented in those studies had a powerful effect on the development of globalized secular meditation.[205]

It appears that at this time Goenka and his community felt the need to participate more directly in such developments. However, the actual goal in the founding of the Vipassana Research Institute was not really serious scientific research on the effects of meditation on addiction, health, and education. Since he himself had been instrumental in bringing together meditation and self-improvement programs under the pressure of social activist Vinoba Bhave (see chapter 5), Goenka was already convinced that the teachings were efficacious as therapeutic mechanisms. He had brought meditation to schools and prisons in India, and such programs would be developed further into large-scale projects in the decades that followed. His teachings came to be used in police training, in business contexts, and in a number of other institutional settings. The efficacy of meditation was evident to him through his own experience with his teacher and the many students he had helped to heal and improve themselves in various ways. Rather than being an instrument to prove what was already self-evident, the Vipassana Research Institute solved an organizational dilemma while at the same time serving as an authority-building mechanism.

The central logic behind the establishment of the institute was laid out in an announcement in the *Vipaśyanā* newsletter in July 1985:

> The "Vipassana Research Institute" has been established particularly for the sake of disseminating literature connected with Vipaśyanā meditation. Before this, such work was done by the "Sayaji U Ba Khin Memorial Trust." But the Trust's purpose is primarily to promote the practical aspect of meditation. It is not appropriate that it should be involved in business dealings. Since there has arisen a demand for liter-

> ature from all sectors, in order to carry out the business of publication in accordance with the order of [our] Respected Teacher, the aforementioned trust has been established. Its purpose will be to make literature available at an appropriate price without making any profit. If there is ever any profit, it will be used for the promotion of Dharma.[206]

This announcement highlights what was and is the main priority of Goenka and his organization: to spread Goenka's teachings of vipaśyanā meditation far and wide and to give the seed of Dharma in the form of those teachings to as many people in the world as possible. It also tacitly points to the real driving force behind the establishment of a research institute. A research institute can act as a publishing house, participate in the business of selling books, and remain exempt from taxes if its goal is research and not profit.

At the same time, to obtain the formal status of a research institute, the organization would have to carry out actual research and provide educational facilities. The Vipassana Research Institute was born of these necessities. Under such onus, a Pali studies program was developed in connection with Bombay University, several seminars were held on vipaśyanā and health, and Goenka began writing about the importance of textual learning for the practice of meditation.[207] Research and educational programs had to be carried out so that a tax-exempt press could continue to churn out missionary materials free of encumbrance.

One project that could be carried out without impinging too much on the primary focus of conducting as many meditation courses as possible—and which could likewise be conceptualized by all as a powerfully meritorious work of good karma—was the transliteration of traditional Burmese Theravada Buddhist texts into non-Burmese scripts and the publication of the Theravada Buddhist canon in a new Indian edition. Goenka spearheaded a reproduction of the Burmese version of the Pali canon and made it the primary project of the Vipassana Research Institute to publish this version in an Indian edition.

The institute did eventually produce an elegant Indian transliteration of the 1956 Burmese version of the Pali canon and its commentaries. It also made the texts available in a searchable electronic format. However, it has produced virtually nothing that might be understood as original peer-reviewed research for three decades now.[208] This lackluster attitude toward research reflects the organization's ambivalence about diverting resources and attention from its core mission of spreading vipaśyanā meditation. This ambivalence showed up even in the instititute's most cherished projects, such as the publication of a new edition of the Pali scriptures.

The Vipassana Research Institute's work on publishing the Burmese version of the Pali canon helped to solidify the community's identity as a singularly pure purveyor of the Buddha's teachings. It also helped to underwrite the tradition's authority. In an exposition of the institute's Indian edition of the canon in the early 1990s, we find the following:

> V.R.I. has entered the entire Pali canon [and commentaries]...on computer in Devanagari and is preparing to publish [it] simultaneously...not only for its own research purposes, but for the use of various educational and research institutions in India and abroad....Clearly, the research work is best done by those with direct experience of the Buddha's teaching.[209]

There is a tension here between making the canon available for all researchers around the world and suggesting that most researchers are not really qualified to do such research work. The experience-oriented outlook of Goenka and his close disciples was foundationally anti-intellectual, and this final statement really means that the only way to truly understand the Buddha's words—and therefore the only way to be able to responsibly interpret and translate them—is to practice vipaśyanā as taught by S. N. Goenka in the tradition of Sayagyi U Ba Khin. This attitude toward research into traditional textual sources rendered serious research unnecessary at best and certain to be misguided at worst. However, a project of publishing and comprehensively studying the canon served to lend authority to the internal narrative of the tradition while at the same time calling into question the interpretations of anyone outside it—those not fully committed to Goenka, his community, and his mission.

In this way, the Vipassana Research Institute was a powerful tool in Goenka's missionary toolbox. It gave him a publishing mouthpiece through which to distribute simplified versions of his teachings, and it enabled the community to invoke the rhetoric of science and historical scholarship, thereby justifying why Goenka's teachings are historically correct and should be adopted by as many people as possible around the world. As an accredited research institute, this platform also allowed Goenka to set himself up even more forcefully than before as an authentic global authority on and purveyor of pure Dharma. This is a key facet of the emergence of both Goenka the Indian paṇḍita and Goenka the global authority on the history of the Buddha's teachings.

The Art of Living: Translating a Global Goenka into English and Beyond

In 1987, a strategic rendering of Goenka's teachings was published in English under the title *The Art of Living*. The title of this book is a direct translation of the subtitle of Goenka's first introductory book for a Hindi-speaking public, *Jīvan Jīne kī Kalā*, which was published for the first time in 1976 (see chapter 18). It is instructive to point out, however, that though the titles of these two books are the same, they are quite distinct in terms of their content, structure, and cultural register. What is more, though Goenka was heavily involved in the writing of *The Art of Living*, the actual author of the book was one of his Canadian students—and one of his first appointed assistant teachers—William Hart. This book became *the* English-language source for introducing a global audience to Goenka's teachings, and to date it has been translated into dozens of different languages. In contrast, Goenka's *Jīvan Jīne kī Kalā* has never been translated into English or any non-Indian language.

In comparing these two introductory books, one can discern the creation of two overlapping yet distinct registers of communication and identity for Goenka. While there is, of course, much overlap in the presentations, the sophistication of Goenka's traditional Sanskritic language is blunted and the metaphysical assumptions behind his framework of practice are stripped down in William Hart's simple English. This makes it difficult to discern the cultural peculiarities of the teachings, even as Hart wields Pali words and performs knowledge of scriptural tradition. It is, in fact, quite difficult to see Hart's maneuvers precisely because modern Buddhist readers have been spoon-fed on books such as these—translations of Asian Buddhist texts that strongly orient themselves toward global audiences without making clear that they are doing so—for nearly fifty years now.

We can discern the distinctions in the two registers by comparing two representative passages from *The Art of Living* and *Jīvan Jīne kī Kalā*. In the first chapter of the *The Art of Living*, we find the following:

> The Buddha did not teach any religion or philosophy or system of belief. He called his teaching *Dhamma*, that is, "law," the law of nature. He had no interest in dogma or idle speculation. Instead he offered a universal, practical

> solution for a universal problem. "Now as before," he said, "I teach about suffering and the eradication of suffering." He refused even to discuss anything which did not lead to liberation from misery.[210]

And in the eighteenth chapter of *Jīvan Jīne kī Kalā*, Goenka describes how this "law of nature" or Dharma works:

> Once we recognize that truth itself is the creator and maintain a detached faith in it, then, when we practice to see the Dharma, we become liberated from suffering to the extent that we are able to see the Dharma—that is, see the truth. In that state, we come into harmony with the infinite subtle realities of nature. Because these realities of nature are bound by their own laws, they begin to protect us automatically. When we take it on, Dharma automatically protects us. This is the law of Dharma. When our minds are entangled in bad qualities, and they generate vibrations of impure mental activity, they come into harmony with the impure vibrations that pervade the entire universe and, as a result, proliferate suffering. In quite the same way, when our minds are pure because they are free of bad qualities, when they are full of good qualities and begin to give rise to vibrations of good mental activity, then the pure, Dharma-constituted, virtuous vibrations of virtuous deities and brahmas—among the seen and unseen living beings in this infinite universe—come to meet us. They provide us strength, amplify our happiness, and protect us. This is the law, the order of things. It can be experienced directly.[211]

While the discrepancy may be easy to gloss over in a casual perusal of such writings, a discriminating reader will observe here that the universal "law of nature" described in *The Art of Living* is something quite different from *Jīvan Jīne kī Kalā*'s "infinite subtle realities of nature" that are "entangled" with our mental qualities as well as nonhuman agents. Although overlapping use of language via translation largely masks the difference, these two passages invoke two wholly distinct metaphysical systems. It is also worth noting that, for Goenka's Hindi-speaking audience, traces of U Ba Khin's system—in which good and bad *dhāt'*, or "forces," were conceptualized as agents that might enter into or be removed from a meditation practitioner—are obliquely retained. For his English-speaking public, however, this system is almost entirely effaced.

While this complicated dance of language and cultural presentation was part of Goenka's way of carrying out his mission from the beginning of his time in India, certain features of the pattern became more and more entrenched once his teachings were strategically translated under the influence of his non-Indian students. The publication of *The Art of Living* and its use as a primary tool to introduce beginners to the basic concepts behind Goenka's practice of meditation in global contexts mark the full-blown institutional emergence of the global Goenka—the Goenka most people know today.

Goenka's Dharma Returns to Myanmar

In 1991, Goenka was finally able to return to Myanmar, the land of his birth. Having become a well-known teacher of Burmese insight meditation, he did so as a guest of the government, and the occasion revealed just how much Goenka's Indian and global identities brought him to recast the Burmese Buddhist origins of his teachings. In relating the story of this initial return trip—the first of quite a few in the last decades of his life—Goenka described how he conveyed his message of nonsectarian, universal Dharma to a group of Burmese Buddhist monks:

> I said that the Blessed Buddha had never taught Buddhist Dharma. Rather, he taught Dharma, which is for everyone. In Burmese also, they use the word *Ṭayā* for Dharma. "*Ṭayā nā thauṃ mai*" means "I will listen to the Dharma." "*Ṭayā ṭhāiṃ mai*" means "I will sit in the practice of meditation." Never does one speak of a Buddhist *Ṭayā*. "Buddhism" has been imposed on us. We don't need to do such a thing. The word "Buddhist" should be removed. The scholars of Myanmar assessed this interpretation against the teachings of the Buddha, and finally they were pleased that my talk was so true. In this way, the restriction that had been placed on me [to travel to Myanmar] was removed, and it became easy for the work of the spread of Dharma to develop. The blessing of the order of monks in Myanmar was attained, and it was a wonderful thing that the path was open for me to travel freely to my mother country. The monks of Myanmar accepted that the Blessed Buddha never taught "Buddhist Dharma," and that he taught Dharma, which is for everyone.

Goenka's "Buddhafied" Hindutva Dharma came home to Myanmar in its most global and universal form. At that moment, as Goenka narrated it, the Burmese monastic community learned a lesson about sectarianism from this great global lay teacher, an Indo-Burmese son of the nation returned. This lesson opened the door for the spread of Dharma in Myanmar. This narrative reverses the story of Goenka's original mission. Rather than exporting the priceless heritage of Burma to the rest of the world, he reimported that commodity in an even purer form than the form in which he received it.

It is difficult not to hear echoes in this account of Goenka's traumatic moment of conflict with his Dharma-mother Sayama and the "Notice of Change" that he issued tacitly criticizing her for adherence to Buddhist religious dogma. However, in this quite different historical moment, Goenka found himself in a new kind of position, fully formed as a teacher. He had become internationally recognized and was welcomed in Myanmar as the government's guest. Not long after this event, Goenka established his first meditation center in Myanmar: Dhamma Joti, or "Light of Dhamma," was established in Rangoon in 1993, not far from the International Meditation Centre. Today, there are twenty-three meditation centers across Myanmar dedicated exclusively to disseminating Goenka's vipaśyanā.

The Controversy over Concentration and Insight

There has been little discussion in this book about the particularities of Goenka's meditation methods. In chapters 3 and 5, we saw that U Ba Khin's model of practice was unique, innovative, and critical of others in the landscape of early twentieth-century Burma, and that Goenka's repackaging of U Ba Khin's practice carried with it that critical attitude toward many other forms of Buddhist meditation. But Goenka was criticized by others on various grounds, particularly with respect to how he taught the practice of concentration, or samādhi.

Critics have noted that one aspect of traditional Buddhist meditation is conspicuously absent in most contexts of Goenka's repackaging: the practice of deep states of concentrated absorption (Sanskrit: *dhyāna*; Pali: *jhāna*), usually described as the practice of calm meditation (samatha). In classical Buddhist texts, these states of concentration are the sine qua non of meditation and are foundational for—if not constitutive of—liberating insight. According to tradition, the Buddha himself became enlightened through the practice of concentrated absorption.

U Ba Khin understood this and was quite critical of teachers who taught that such deep states of absorption were not necessary for the attainment of liberating insight. In the only book he ever wrote, he noted:

> In the *Comprehensive Manual of Abhidhamma*, in the chapter on mind, the [supramundane] path and fruition states that accompany the first, second, third, fourth, and fifth absorption meditations (jhāna) are explained. It can thus be deduced that the path and fruition states cannot take place without absorption meditation.[212]

Here U Ba Khin presented a classical Theravada Buddhist understanding of the role of absorption meditation, asserting that it is essential for enlightenment—discussed here using the technical terminology of "path and fruition states," states of mind that constitute enlightenment. In the rest of his small book, U Ba Khin went on to describe the practice of absorption in detail, and he trained a number of students to master these practices. So why did such practices more or less disappear from Goenka's teachings?

The possibility for this development becomes clear when it is understood that, while he took absorption to be necessary for enlightenment, U Ba Khin was unwilling to entirely decouple absorption meditation from states of liberating insight in the context of the Buddha's teachings:

> In this great noble dispensation of the Buddha, wisdom (paññā) is the main thing. Since calming practice (samatha) is not [in itself] reliable [for the purpose of liberation], we might even reply that the Buddha taught calming only because it was necessary.

> The aforementioned answer[s] to modes of practice involving concentration were not obtained merely through the development of calming. It is to be assumed that progress in wisdom by way of insight knowledge had been developed [in such cases].[213]

Since absorption meditation on its own, without the guiding wisdom of insight knowledge, can take one down an unreliable path that may not conform to the path outlined by the Buddha, U Ba Khin developed a novel way of working with his students so they might attain the initial stages of enlightenment by speedier and more reliable mechanisms. What were those mechanisms? As we have seen, U Ba Khin invoked the help of enlightened nonhuman beings that were karmically connected to him and utilized the psychic powers of some of his advanced students to create conditions in which his students could break through to enlightenment even without attaining absorption. In other words, U Ba Khin sought to replicate the psychic force of absorption for a meditator by using forces external to that meditator.

The details of these mechanisms are too complicated to be discussed further here. But we see once again how some of the more esoteric aspects of Goenka's practice background help to explain why his mission took on the character it did as it developed globally. Although they help provide historical and cultural context, such explanations will likely not assuage Goenka's detractors. Quite a few instances of community rupture have taken place because of the apparent absence and devaluation of the practice of absorption meditation in his teachings. A number of his assistant teachers and serious students left the community and sought other teachers when Goenka refused to formally teach absorption meditation, and many of Goenka's assistants and close students speak pejoratively of the practice of absorption. This can appear strange when one compares such attitudes to those voiced in traditional texts attributed to the Buddha.

It is worth pointing out, however, that Goenka's stance on absorption meditation as an integral element of the Buddha's teachings was largely in line with the classical Theravadin take of his teacher. On his longer retreats, Goenka would lay out his perspective on the issue:

> Working with *vipassana*, one reaches the first *phalasamāpatti* [fruition attainment] of *sotāpanna* [the stream-enterer], the second *phalasamāpatti* of *sakadāgāmī* [the once-returner]. Then all importance is given to these four *jhāna*s or eight *jhāna*s. Partly because after becoming *sakadāgāmī*, it doesn't take much time. Mind has become much purer. A purer mind can get concentrated easily. So, these four *jhāna*s and eight *jhāna*s have become easy for one who has become *sakadāgāmī*. And partly because one has practised *vipassanā*, practised *nibbāna*, so there is no danger of this person going mad in any way. It becomes easy. So it is only after *sakadāgāmī* that the *jhāna*s are being practised—four or eight.[214]

Here Goenka made clear that the practice of absorption was part and parcel of his approach to meditation, and on his sixty-day courses he even provided students with a few more practical details on attaining absorption meditation. However, as far as I am aware, he did not publicly clarify in any coherent way why absorption is not necessary for the attainment of the first two stages of early Buddhist enlightenment, the stages of stream-entry and once-returner. We can understand this theory of practice only when we understand how U Ba Khin and Goenka utilized forces external to the meditator to create conditions that attempted to mimic the psychic forces of absorption.

Finally, it should not be forgotten that Goenka's mission, unlike that of his teacher, was to give the "seed of Dharma" to as many people as possible. In the context of that mission, the practice of absorption meditation receded into the background imaginary of the practice, since the idea of anyone attaining even the first stage of enlightenment was largely removed from the equation. So, Goenka's vipaśyanā came to look, on the surface, like a tradition of practice denuded of both its classical and its cultic heritage.

The Global Vipaśyanā Pagoda

On October 26, 1997, a public groundbreaking ritual was performed on a large piece of land on the outskirts of Mumbai. This marked the beginning of a large building project that Goenka had been developing for a number of years, a project that he saw as the culmination of his global mission. The Global Vipaśyanā Pagoda is a replica of the renowned Shwedagon Pagoda in Yangon. The formal ritual of establishment and the enshrinement of the Buddha's bodily relics was conducted in 2006, and the structure was completed in 2008. The Shwedagon Pagoda is a local Burmese version of burial mounds—known variously as stupas, or *caityas*—constructed in early India to house the remains of deceased holy men.

For Goenka, this monument of the Dharma was to serve as a memorial to his teacher as well as a public sign of gratitude to the country of Myanmar for preserving the Dharma taught by the Buddha in its pure form. The massive structure, hollow inside unlike most traditional pagodas, would serve as a gathering place for large groups of vipaśyanā meditators from all around the world as well as a place for those who had not come in contact with vipaśyanā to learn about it. Adjacent to the pagoda is an educational picture gallery with scenes from the life of the Buddha, a library of books on the history of Buddhism, and an educational facility for the study of Pali.

In speaking about the aspiration behind the pagoda project to a gathering of his students on November 1, 2009, Goenka explained the primary meaning and function of the structure:

> We will build a great gateway of *vipaśyanā*. The British built the gateway of India. Now people will remember Myanmar when this gateway of *vipaśyanā* is built.[215]

He also understood the project to be an emblem of the fulfillment of his teacher's most cherished desires about the spread of his teachings:

> From his higher place, my teacher will be feeling very pleased about the work that is being done.

The analogy with the famous British colonial monument, a mark of political and military conquest, reveals a particular aspect of Goenka's perspective on his global mission. As previous chapters have shown, U Ba Khin and Goenka understood the spread of the practice of their meditation to be one involving a conflict of forces, the enactment of a battle between the forces of Dharma and the forces of anti-Dharma. The global spread of vipaśyanā—the sowing of seeds of Dharma within millions of persons around the globe—was the spread of a conquering spiritual force that would revolutionize the world. Goenka envisioned his pagoda in Mumbai as the "gateway" to that global spiritual empire.

But this project also raised questions among Goenka's community of students about the implications of building what appeared to be something like a temple. Would this mark out the organization as a sect? Goenka responded to such concerns on a number of occasions, including in the final pages of his autobiography:[216]

> It is natural for there to arise delusions within ignorant people with respect to this *stupa*. They feel that it has been built as a symbol of some particular sect. But when they see that apart from *vipaśyanā* practice, no sectarian rituals are being performed in this *stupa*—no incense and lamps, no offerings such as ringing of bells and gongs, no trace of the worship of images—then this delusion of theirs will automatically be removed.[217]

These lines present us with Goenka's particular conception of sectarianism. He saw the pagoda as a public site and vipaśyanā as a practice accessible to all. No traditional Indian ritual practices are carried out in the space of the pagoda. But two points are worth emphasizing here. First, only those who have participated in one of Goenka's ten-day vipaśyanā courses are allowed to meditate in the pagoda. Second, the ritual enshrinement of relics of the Buddha was somehow excluded in Goenka's mind from this repertoire of "sectarian" practices. It is also worth noting that while no traditional Hindu ritual practices of the sort to which Goenka referred are carried out at his meditation centers, and no images or icons are on display, Goenka did maintain a private shrine room at his main meditation center, Dhamma Giri. On the altar of that shrine room sat an icon of the historical Gautama Buddha and an image of Sayagyi U Ba Khin, among others.

The Global Vipaśyanā Pagoda, then, was and remains an emblem of the complex overlay of identities Goenka embodied for his various audiences. It is a public nonsectarian symbol dedicated to a powerful guru, a future buddha, to whom Goenka was karmically tied. It is a space for the public dissemination of information about the teachings of the Buddha, the full utilization of which requires an experiential initiation. It is a dome, at the top of which bodily relics have been ritually established and under which a "scientific" technique of meditation is practiced. It is the karmic basis for many healthy and Dharma-filled future lives for Goenka, his family members, and his students, while at the same time it is intended to inspire the aspiration to abandon all karma in this very life and attain nirvana.

The dome of the pagoda is self-standing, without any pillars to support it. It is constructed of large interlocking stones, "one stone gripping and holding the other in ring form."[218] Just as these stones link together to form an architectural marvel, the extensive global network of meditation centers, assistants, administrators, and meditators that Goenka built over forty-four years was and is a miraculous feat of sheer will, powerful charisma, and brilliant ingenuity. When one looks up at the dome, however, the cracks between the interlocking stones are evident. In the monsoon season, water seeps through them, and buckets must be placed here and there to catch the dripping water from the heavy rains. The drip-drop of the rains echoes across the vast space of the dome, and meditating there can feel like meditating in an echo chamber.

Just as there are in-built cracks in the dome of the pagoda, places where water seeps through during the monsoons, there were cracks and fissures in the structure of Goenka's global network in its very constitution. These cracks—at the interstices of where Goenka's various identities and audiences met—became more and more apparent during the last decade of his life. And they became the fault lines of community fragmentation in the wake of his passing.

CHAPTER 7

S. N. Goenka's Dharma

IN JULY 2014, less than a year after S. N. Goenka passed away, two of his American proxies—a couple named Paul and Susan Fleischman, whom Goenka had appointed as ācāryas, or "full teachers," with the specific responsibility of introducing "vipassana to the intellectuals of the West"—circulated an important document to a number of their fellow vipaśyanā teachers and administrators. This document was titled "An Explanation of Some Differences of Opinion among Vipassana Teachers." The Fleischmans wrote in an e-mail that it was "intended to explain recent problems in our tradition to SATs [Senior Assistant Teachers], ATs [Assistant Teachers], or even Ts [Full Teachers] in the West who request further and clearer explanation than they have already gotten."[219]

The "recent problems" the Fleischmans discuss in this document—which often slips into the first-person singular voice and appears to be primarily the work of Paul Fleischman—provide a window into a complex array of conflicts that emerged in the final years of Goenka's life.[220] A number of these involved Goenka expelling some of his closest disciples from the organization and carrying out a series of controversial rearrangements in the authority structure of his global network.

There is no space in this book to fully lay out and properly analyze these somewhat painful developments. However, we may focus here on some of the basic fault lines of community fragmentation that can be discerned in Fleischman's document, fault lines that emerge from the complexities of the history we have partially explored in this story of Goenka's life.

The primary thrust of the document is sadly predictable, but its details reveal the way the missionary strategies of forty years of spreading the seeds of Dharma set up an inevitable breakdown of communication—or what Fleischman terms "complex situations and impaired communication"—within the global network. The breakdown, in its basic form, emerged over issues of how to treat a revered teacher when questions about his decision-making capacities arise. For example, at the end of his life Goenka handed over a number of institutional responsibilities to one of his sons, Sriprakash Goenka, and many of Goenka's students found this troubling. Additionally, questions were raised about how strictly certain guidelines of the ten-day course format should be followed when Goenka laid down instructions that many found too inflexible. As a result of such choices, there were questions about whether Goenka's mental capacities were compromised by old age, and a controversy ensued about where the source of authority within the tradition should lie. Though the organization remains formally intact, there has been a de facto split between the organization of the "Vipassana worldwide tradition" in India and the "Vipassana worldwide tradition" in Europe and America.[221]

Regardless of the particular sources of conflict—which were many—the primary fault line in all of these issues was between traditional South Asian attitudes about the special status of the spiritual teacher and more egalitarian ideals emerging from recent developments such as rights discourse. The latter is a thought framework within which it is difficult to accommodate traditional South Asian notions of spiritual hierarchy such as those that are foundational to early Buddhist tradition.

In his explanatory document, Paul Fleischman framed the issue as follows, after an elaborate discussion of the various ways in which

Goenka was flexible and open to collaboration during most of his teaching career but appeared to have become inflexible and unreasonable toward the end of his life:

> The idea that Goenkaji made all his decisions by himself, and that all his decisions were perfect, and that all his policies should be followed without question, was never true, was never part of the tradition he founded, and is historically inaccurate. Those loving devotees, who understandably revere their brilliant and compassionate Teacher, but who believe that his decision making was perfect, are inaccurately informed about the actual history and evolution of the tradition as we now practice it.

Fleischman then went on to discuss some of the specific actions that led him and many of his codisciples to question Goenka's judgment in the last years of his life, including his dismissal of "many of the Secretary Teachers he had appointed to run the Vipassana worldwide tradition":

> The documents containing these dismissals are part of the public record and can be found on the world-wide web, and their tone of voice is neither the tone of a wise person nor of the Goenkaji who brought our tradition out of Burma to the attention of hundreds of thousands of people around the world. . . . Either his initial decades of judgment, or his final judgment to purge, must constitute a serious error. . . . The decades of service by these dismissed elders was brushed aside with contempt. These dismissals were perpetrated in a manner exactly the opposite to Goenkaji's previous forty years of nurturing, promoting, developing, and when necessary criticizing with a tone of parental affection. The

> dismissals either came from someone other than Goenkaji, or from a Goenkaji under someone else's influence, or from a tragically altered Goenkaji.

I cannot and will not weigh in on the actual conflict that is being adjudicated in these statements; it would be irresponsible for me to do so. However, from the perspective of the historian interested in the way that Goenka and his missionary institution developed, I would suggest that the perspective presented here—and the "impaired communication" within the organization that it exemplifies—is illustrative. It reveals what appears in hindsight to be the inevitable outcome of a series of choices made in the process of developing the Vipassana worldwide tradition. Perhaps the most consequential of these choices was the split from Mother Sayama and U Chit Tin.

Fleischman's main priority in this document was to prove, by way of strident argument and historical example, that Goenka was a flawed human—someone who made choices that were, in many cases, objectively incorrect. This comes out most powerfully in his claim that Goenka's concerns for his sons and their family business led him to lapses in ethical judgment:

> There has been widespread confession by the participants in one set of events that Goenkaji solicited loans from some of his close, long term students and appointees to run his family business. Not all of these loans were returned as due. We cannot accept this as proper conduct for any kind of teacher at all, even the most mundane, to use the trust his position garnered for material solicitation. Once again, with forgiveness and affection, we can see that our Teacher's magnificent strengths were not accompanied by perfection in every domain. The people who currently believe that every deci-

> sion Goenkaji took was unquestionable, and that his late life decisions should not be subject to courteous and courageous review, are self-deluding followers of an already disproven daydream. The public information that Goenkaji solicited loans from his students, even if it was benevolently intended, establishes the fact that even before he became ill in his final years, his decision-making could be inappropriate.

We find echoes here of Goenka's "Notice of Change," in which he questioned the ethics of his colleagues at the International Meditation Centre on the grounds that they were taking money from students for meals and course maintenance. We saw in that instance, however, that the suggestion of ethical impropriety—which became the primary narrative leverage point for explaining why Goenka turned his back on his own teacher—served primarily to solve other kinds of problems that emerged from Mother Sayama's identity and her cultural and religious commitments.

History repeats itself, it seems—or perhaps Goenka's karma caught up with him. By showing that Goenka's ethical decision making was objectively faulty even before some of his more radical late-life rearrangements of the organization, Fleischman made a similar move, since his primary target was indeed a larger issue of cultural and religious identity.[222] This basic fault line in the Vipassana worldwide tradition appeared most powerfully toward the end of the document, when Fleischman spoke in strident critical terms about loyalty as it is understood in Asian guru traditions:

> We affirm our full loyalty to Goenkaji as a person, and to the noble Vipassana tradition that he spread around the world. Our loyalty consists of unwavering reproduction of every course in the traditional manner that we ourselves took that course. Our loyalty also consists of discussing policy, even

> to the point of challenging Goenkaji as he wanted and often asked us to do. Our loyalty consists in seeing him analogously to the way that the Pali Canon encouraged us to see the Buddha, as a human being who grew old, sick, and died. Our deepest gratitude and hard work as Vipassana Teachers is now directed toward making sure that this beautiful living tradition of Dhamma does not deteriorate into religious deification or guru worship. . . .
>
> My personal agenda is based upon the belief that neither my son, nor his generation in the West, nor his generation in the New India, will become guru worshippers, nor imagine that any human being is perfect and a flawless decision-maker. I believe that the upcoming generation in both India and the West consists of well-rounded, intelligent, autonomous adults, who will not participate in a personality cult. Therefore, I believe that the deification of a great human being into a perfect guru will destroy the future of Dhamma. . . .
>
> I myself have never joined any sect or cult and I do not belong to one now.

We have seen in the course of this book that while Goenka publicly played down his role as a Guru with a capital G, he was fully immersed in a world of experience in which his own teacher was much more than just a simple teacher. By extension, he certainly considered himself to be much more than just an ordinary human. Like U Ba Khin—currently abiding in his "higher place"—Goenka was karmically destined for greatness, and his development into a global teacher, a viśvaguru, was a development into a guru worthy of worship, worthy of emulation.

We have also seen that the structure of Goenka's courses and the assistant teacher model he developed to disseminate his teachings to a mass audience were predicated on the notion of a tiered channel that allowed him to serve as a medium for the psychic power of U Ba Khin and to support his assistants by means of distant control. Goenka and his students served and continue to serve as channels for U Ba Khin's Dharma. At the same time, when he disavowed Mother Sayama, Goenka made a strategic public criticism in which he encouraged students "to take refuge in Dhamma, and not in any personality." This early discrepancy between what Goenka was actually doing in practice and his rhetorical strategies to justify his break from Mother Sayama and draw in a global audience set the stage for the conflicts that emerged at the end of his life. These conflicts come forcefully to the surface in the 2014 document.

Some of the divides delineated by Fleischman are telling. He wrote of "the West" as if it were a real place and not a social imaginary. He also wrote of the "New India," a place where I have never been, though I have spent nearly a decade living and carrying out research on the Indian subcontinent over the past twenty years.[223] He invoked a Pali Canon that "encouraged us to see the Buddha, as a human being," even though any Pali scholar can tell you that in these texts, the Buddha is categorically no longer a human being once he becomes the Buddha but is certainly a powerful deity in his penultimate birth.[224]

The global Goenka who came fully into being in the course of the 1980s was the only Goenka with whom Fleischman and many others were comfortable. When confronted with a Goenka who appeared different from the global one who had been formed in their own image, these "intelligent, autonomous adults" often found what he actually practiced and believed to be backward and ignorant. While I can't comment on this at the level of ultimate truth, it appears obvious from a historical perspective that Fleischman's "tragically altered Goenka" may simply be a Goenka that many with certain commitments—from all sides of the ideological spectrum—had chosen to willfully ignore. This is not simply the story of Goenka and his movement, but a story that is playing out today in a variety of contexts when ancient wisdom traditions with long, complicated histories get appropriated, repackaged, or repurposed.

Fleischman's final statement is particularly revealing. It discloses how many people who find the experiences encountered within traditional contemplative contexts compelling choose to overlook aspects of the tradition that do not appeal to them. Goenka himself encouraged such an approach to his teachings and insisted that anyone and everyone might practice and benefit from it, regardless of their broader commitments. Many of Goenka's students took this approach quite seriously, but it meant they had to ignore or tolerate the apparent contradictions and multiple layers of identity that Goenka embodied.

In doing so, many of these people had to overlook or chose to overlook the historical Goenka himself, because a true examination of his very complex identity would have forced them to reassess their own identities in uncomfortable ways. This can be said of quite a few people, from all walks of life, who participated in and committed themselves to Goenka's mission during the four decades when he was alive and into the present. This is also the reason that even in being "overlooked no more" in David Gelles's obituary, Goenka was, for the most part, overlooked again.

The preceding chapters have shown Goenka to be a complicated person whose life spanned some of the most transformative developments in modern global history. He lived and migrated through the Second World War, independence from colonial rule in multiple national contexts, and a military coup. He grew up in a cultural context in which child marriage was the norm and girls were not educated, and he came to be an unwitting participant in the counterculture movement of the 1960s when a wide range of traditional, conservative social norms crumbled under the weight of radical social forces.

Although Goenka insisted that the Dharma taught by the Buddha is *sanantano*, an ancient transmission not bounded by limitations of time and context, I suggest that Goenka's Dharma—as he experienced it in his encounters with his teachers in colonial Burma and as he came to present it to his multiple audiences in India and elsewhere—can best be understood in light of these various historical and cultural contexts. It is imperative that we situate Goenka's actions in those contexts. It is imperative that we allow the narrative of Goenka's Dharma to be a layered narrative and that we allow the many identities Goenka embodied and the many communities he reached to be represented in his story. Like a multifaceted gem, Goenka's Dharma has many aspects. It glitters, reflects, and cast shadows, depending on where you stand.

Goenka was undoubtedly one of the most important and influential meditation masters of the twentieth century, and he was a master par excellence. This story reveals that he was, like all great bodhisattvas must be, inscrutable. That was his magic. That magic continues to work into the present, touching thousands upon thousands at meditation centers around the world.

The Writings and Teachings

CHAPTER 8

Selected Poems of S. N. Goenka

from *My Poetry, Written in Burma*

My Poetry, Written in Burma *is a collection of fifty-one of S. N. Goenka's poems. It was published not long before his death in 2013. The collection is divided into eight sections: literary poems, poems about love of country, poems dedicated to political leaders, poems about Burma, poems about social issues, poems about the Hindu Festival of Lights, translations of famous Rajasthani poems, and poems about family. These poems were mostly written in Goenka's early adulthood, when he was immersed in the study of Hindi literature and the culture of Indian nationalism and Hindu devotionalism. Some of the poems were written in his youth, and others, like the last poem presented here, reflect later influences, after he took to practicing vipaśyanā meditation.*[225]

1. The Power of Faith

It's midnight, and in the deep darkness
The whole world sleeps, under the rule of silence.
By the shore of the ocean, on the floating rocks,
Is the *chap chap* sound of the lapping waves.

Weary from a day of hard work, the bears and monkeys
Sleep restlessly, here and there on the ground.

Similarly, Rama, lord of the Raghu lineage, is sunk in thought.
What is the conundrum? What is the secret?

He reflects on what an improbable thing it is,
This miracle of Nila and Nala.[226]
"What miraculous force is there in my name,
Such that stones might float on water without support?

"How is it that today the law of nature is broken?
What sort of sorcery, what illusive work is this?
Why don't I go myself and verify it?
Surely there is something concealed, some secret."

Suddenly, Rama moves in the stillness of the night.
Behind him, hidden, follows Hanuman.
Standing like a portrait, on the shore of the ocean,
He surveys the floating pieces of rock.

Marked with Rama's name, the rocks had become like wood.
They floated, and this he could not believe.
Suddenly he picked up a stone from the shore,
And hurled it into the dancing waves.

"Hey, what's this? Why does it not float?"
It sunk, plunging to the depths of the ocean.
Annoyed, Rama spoke: "It's a lie, a fraud,
The monkeys' trick, sheer deception.

"If a stone from my hand can't float,
How is it that these pieces of rock float in my name?"
Quickly stepping forward, Hanuman spoke with joined hands:
"Lord, today you have broken beyond your limits.

"When Rama takes something up,
Does he ever let it go, as you did just now?
Enough, king of the Raghu lineage, may no one else come to know
Of tonight's mysterious episode."

Hearing that Rama took hold of something and then let go,
People will withdraw their trust in him.
Who else is possibly going to support
Someone whom Rama took hold of and then let go?

Whether it is a stone or a rock, a man or a woman,
It will surely sink if thrown by Rama.
When Rama, dumbfounded, returned to his camp,
The mystery of the riddle of the monkeys became clear.

Great is the majesty of devotion, of faith.
Puny is God in [light of] the majesty of the devotee.

In the deep darkness of midnight,
Once again the shore becomes deserted.
Pieces of rock drift in the lapping waves
While a helpless stone curses its destiny on the ocean floor.

And the entire world, the whole army of monkeys and bears,
Was sleeping, as before, in the stillness of the night.
It was midnight, and in the deep darkness
The whole world slept, under the rule of silence.

2. Hindustani (1955)

I have seen Indians
Who are ashamed to call themselves Indians,

Yet are quite proud to be called Hindu,
Very gratified upon being called Muslim,
Take it as a point of pride to be called Sikh,
Delight in being called Farsi, Jain, or Buddhist.

When I look at this clan of Indians,
I know not whether to cry or sing!

How self-absorbed all of these people have become,
Taking pleasure each in their individual instruments.

Someone says, "No one is better than me,
I am in the lineage of Rama and Krishna, of Rana Pratap.[227]
My ancestors were world teachers, sovereigns,
Known throughout the land.

"When the whole world was uncivilized and illiterate,
We were civilized and cultured.

"Because of this, how could anyone be like us!
Because of this, our Mathura is the most unique.
Precisely because of this, it is the right of those of this land
To simply speak of themselves as Hindus."

Now listen further!
Whoever forsook their religion (*dharm*) due to fear of punishment
To adopt Islam at some point many centuries ago,
Is said to be in this way a Muslim of the South.
"My great grandfather came from an Arab country."

These heathen uncivilized Kafirs
Were at some point taught true faith.

They are my Mughal, Turkish, and Afghani ancestors,
Who organized into Islamic sultanates.

The Taj Mahal, the Jama Masjid, the Moti Masjid,
The Red Fort, these are symbols of their accomplishments.
Whether these remnants of Mughal rule
Belong to the Muslims is meaningless.

Why is it so? Listen further—
These are the disciples of that Guru, who was saved from Hindu Dharma.
Those who are the faithful of Nanak, of Guru Gobind, are called Sikh.

Listen, then, to what they say:
"Wherever the Guru's congregation is held,
There, at least, the Khalsa must seek self-determination.[228]
What social intercourse do we have with these Hindus?
We need our own Sikhistan."

Why is it so? Listen to something more, factionalist!
Some speak like this: "The south of the country is ours.
If North India is lost, then what of us?
We love our Dravidian country dearly."

Some say, "Keep your state,
Let us establish our Maharashtra.
If our heart's desire is not fulfilled,
We will fill the streets and lanes with the blood of our brothers."

Another says, "Break up Maharashtra,
Make a state, Vidarbha, from one part of it.

Otherwise, we are worse than sham heroes.
Show us both of your hands."

And next, listen to what is said there in Bihar:
"Why has my land been given to the Bengalis?
This is the earth of my grandfather and great-grandfather.
Tell me what right to it have the people of Gaur?"

The Assamese is saying, "This country of Assam is mine,
But now the Bengalis are circling the bed of this house."
"Just this Odisha is ours," [say] the Odishans.
"Why then can't the Bengalis simply have Bengal?"

When everyone remains embroiled in quarrels of this sort,
How might the country not remain impoverished?

"If the language of the government becomes Hindi,
We will sprinkle the oil of our lives on the oblation fire.
It is well and good that our regional language continues to die out,
But the foreigner's English should always remain intact."

Seeing this state of affairs, I sink into confusion.
I find myself at a loss; should I laugh, or should I cry?

You say I should become one among them!
I should choose one of these various approaches.
But I discern no difference between them.
Should I listen to my own heart or to the concerns of others?

It is possible that my heart advises falsely,
That it might take me in the wrong direction.

It is possible that it is a complete fool, a lunatic,
But this madness is what appeals.

In the midst of this madness, I dreamt
Of how great my undivided India will be,
Where all will live equally,
Without distinctions between high and low.

These foolish wise men, learned in their various traditions,
Will not be hindered on their paths.
These mullahs, these leaders of sectarian groups,
Will not be impeded in their progress.

But in the end, dreams are just dreams.
They disappear after they have been seen.
Unsolicited, the country has become two,
And who knows now, how much further things may go?

Reflecting on this, I find myself tormented,
Perpetually crushed by anguish.
Who might I tell about my inner troubles?
I have no choice but to remain silent and helpless.

When an Indian says,
"I am ashamed to be called an Indian,"
I tell him straight,
"I cannot fathom your innermost torment."

3. The Magnificent Sun of India (Mahatma Gandhi)

Spread your golden rays, to break through the canopy of darkness.
In the midst of the darkest moment of crisis, a soft beam of hope shines through.
You have descended, divine messenger, bringing a providential message to humanity.

The India that has been forgotten was by nature glorious. It had the breath of happiness and peace taken out of it.
In a noose controlled by others, it became the bonded servant of a foreign country.

Trapped in a cage, the lion becomes sluggish, with sleepy eyes.
Bestowing consciousness to dead matter, you broke through this restless sleep.

You aroused a long dormant vitality and sounded the ferocious cry of awakening.
Breaking through the dreamy illusion, you removed the intoxication of listless weariness.

You blew new life into the people, with new lifeblood they were transfused.
The country, [now] alert, is with great energy infused.

4. Mother Durga

Dark, skeletal, dreadful.
Torso, head, and skull cup.
How should I worship you, who bears the marks of ferocity and horror?

Dasahara[229] has come once again today,
And this doubt is deep in my mind:
How should I pay respect to you, you who drink the blood of the dead?

That mute tongue, that meek heart,
It wails, it weeps, the fearful creature.
When the offering is made, you are satisfied. How hard-hearted can you be?

She creates the dance of destruction.
She arranges the spectacle of death.
Still she is called "mother," though she devours living beings.

This terrifying atom bomb,
This bomb of destructive creation,
The red of your eyes, flaming, brings about annihilation.

You have erred, lost the path.
What were you yesterday? What have you become today?
You were gentle, peaceful, soft as moonlight, but have become a ferocious demoness.

When you see troubled humanity,
You are moved to remove the demonic.
But you yourself remain a demon, a poisonous snake—bitter, crooked, twisted.

You should understand the thing
That is your great defeat.
The weak take life, while the strong forgive.

You have eight arms, one hundred, one thousand,
A tall victory flag from the battlefield.
But as long as you have not conquered the self, all [other] victories are empty.

Once you have won such a victory,
Then no defeat is possible.
The victory that can change into defeat is an entirely illusory victory.

When is the victor fearless?
When does he sleep the peaceful sleep of conquest?
He indeed is mighty who is established in wisdom (*sthitaprajña*), victorious in defeat or victory.

When has anger quelled anger?
When has hatred tamed hatred?
Mother of violence and aggression, you are deliberately intoxicated by conflict.

Arise now, you senses.
Wisdom is awakened, a great blessing.
Not to become again either human or demon, make yourself a protector of the True Dharma.

The dark luster of your divine body has become weary,
Its brilliance obscured.
Stop now the dance of destruction and become the verdure of the fields.

Relinquish your fire, your storm,
The ferocious wail of death.

Put down the skull cup, sword, and scimitar, and take in hand the
cup of deathless nectar.[230]

Enough, there has been much of the dance of destruction,
[Much] horrific howling and ferocious threats.
Now drop the cursing and vehemence, and bring auspiciousness,
delighting in what is pure.

Become one who provides sustenance and removes suffering,
Become the autumnal Lakshmi, who brings happiness.
Fill the mind with unparalleled compassion, and, since you are a
mother, offer your motherly love.

Calm the mind, bestill the heart.
Become sympathetic, merciful, protective.
Then every particle of the universe will vibrate with repeated
tribute: "Glory to the Beautiful Mother!"

You must become the Perfection of Wisdom,
Loving-kindness, compassion, sympathetic joy.
You must put down the pot of poison and take up the cup of
deathless nectar.

5. The Highest Good[231]

Those who seek spiritual benefit,
Deities or humans, are concerned:
"May the Blessed One himself tell us
What is the highest good."

To avoid the company of fools
To make contact with the wise

To worship those who are worthy of worship
These are the highest good.

To live in a favorable country
To heap up karmic merit
To keep one's mind concentrated
These are the highest good.

To train in a skill and to be very knowledgeable
To follow the rule of law
To perform proper conduct of speech
These are the highest good.

Service to mother and father
Care of family members
Avoidance of bad karmas
These are the highest good.

Giving away wealth and living a life of Dharma
Supporting friends and associates
Avoiding blameworthy karmas
These are the highest good.

Not delighting in evil
Forever abstaining from liquor
Being vigilant in the observance of Dharma
These are the highest good.

Honoring others and always greeting people with respect
Remaining grateful and contented
Listening to the Dharma at an appropriate time
These are the highest good.

Becoming tolerant and obedient
Visiting saintly ascetics
Participating in discussions about Dharma at an appropriate time
These are the highest good.

Observing vows of self-discipline and celibacy
Seeing the four noble truths
The realization of nirvana
These are the highest good.

Remaining unmoved when touched by conflicts
In the form of pleasure and pain
Free from sorrow, pure and fearless
These are the highest good.

Following these dharmas
Win victory in every sphere.
These are the highest goods
Of those who are always happy.

CHAPTER 9

The Buddha Made India Weak

from the *Autobiography, Part 1*

S.N. Goenka wrote a variety of autobiographical material over many years, particularly in the pages of the Vipaśyanā *newsletter. In 2003, the first volume of a formal autobiography appeared. In this volume of the autobiography, or* Ātmakathan, *Goenka frames his mission to spread the teachings of the Buddha in India as a project to overturn the classical Hindutva narrative that Buddhism weakened India politically. The opening pages of the book are presented here.*[232]

QUESTION: Did the Buddha truly make India weak? Did his teaching reduce the country to a state of slavery?

ANSWER: Yes, this is absolutely the truth. It is true that the Buddha was great, and that because he is globally respected due to his great compassion, India came to be admired throughout the world. But it is equally true that his teaching, "nonviolence is the supreme Dharma" (*ahiṃsā paramo dharmaḥ*), was harmful to the country and weakened its military power. More value was given in the country to the extensive community of monks who forsook the valor of the warrior, abandoned household life, and promulgated [the] peace [of renunciation]. His teachings against [taking up] weapons sowed confusion when, [under their influence], India's powerful emperor

Aśoka, after conquering Kaliṅga, understood the victory to be a loss, broke his sword, and vowed not to wage war [again]. The negative influence of this [teaching] affected the nation for centuries. It weakened its capacity to confront foreign invaders. As a result, it became prey to foreign attacks, and remained bound in the shackles of slavery. Because such harm to the country developed from this, how could it have been good?

Since my adolescence and into early adulthood, I was totally convinced by these [statements] or ideas of this sort. Living in prewar Burma (now Myanmar), as much as I was filled with faith toward the personality of the greatly compassionate Blessed Buddha, I found fault with his teachings. In those days, of the many flaws I looked for in his teaching, this deficiency seemed the most important and also the most harmful.

Life in Prewar Burma

Living in prewar Burma, my respected grandfather Basesarlalji used to have me read out loud to him the Hindi-language periodical, *Burma News*, published in Rangoon (now Yangon). Because of his old age, his eyesight had become weak, so he could not read by himself. Reading the newspaper was quite a hobby of his, since he had great interest in Indian politics. It was the early 1930s, and the activities of Congress and Gandhi[233] were reported daily in the newspaper headlines. Grandfather was a devout [Indian] nationalist. Even at his age, he remained anxious about the country's independence. For this reason, even at that young age, my mind was strongly influenced by his ideas about the nation.

When I was a bit older, I came in contact with the local Arya Samaj organization. And fortunately, I had good teachers in school.

So my interest in the political activities of India increased. In those days, one mode of thought continually arose in my mind: Gandhi is to be respected and lauded, since he alone brought about a powerful aspiration for self-reliance in the country, which is truly remarkable. Yet independence would not be attained by mere reliance on his "love and nonviolence." The power of the colonists relied on arms. It was also necessary for us to use weapons. In those days I also came to think that Gandhi was deeply influenced by the love and nonviolence of the Buddha, which was responsible for the fact that there would never be an armed revolution in the country. While I was compelled by reverence and respect for the Buddha's personality, there was a struggle in my mind, which was due to a deep distrust of his extreme advocacy of nonviolence.

For this [same] reason, while I retained faith in and respect for Gandhi, my mind was more inclined toward the side of armed revolution. Through a bookseller I knew in Burma, I would secretly request books like Manmath Nath Gupta's *History of Armed Revolution in India*, which were banned by the government, and read them with great interest. Revolutionaries such as Bhagat Singh, Sukhdev, Rajguru, and Chandra Shekhar Azad were great men in my eyes. I was greatly delighted when Subhas Chandra Bose succeeded in evading the British and escaping the country.[234]

CHAPTER 10

Vipaśyanā as Practical Knowledge for Affirmation against Denial

from *Was the Buddha a Denier?*

S.N. Goenka wrote Was the Buddha a Denier? *in 2008 as the culmination of a long-term project to argue against what he considered to be false characterizations of the Buddha prevalent among Indians. These characterizations strongly influenced Goenka himself during his upbringing. This book is a complement to his* Was the Buddha a Pessimist? *published in 2001.*[235] *This chapter presents four short sections of the book, which aim to render the Buddha's teachings compatible with the teachings of the Bhagavad Gita, argue for why the Buddha must be understood as one who positively affirmed traditional moral codes, explain how he worked to confront those who advocated the denial of such codes, and delineate how his practical teachings make experientially manifest such affirmation through the practice of vipaśyanā.*[236]

The Practice of Vipaśyanā and the Theory of the Gita

When I joined a vipaśyanā course, the aforementioned incident [when Bhadant Anand Kausalyayan informed Goenka that the Bhagavad Gita had been influenced by the teachings of the Buddha] had no special significance in my mind.[237] At that time I had to see for myself, through my own effort, the wisdom of vipaśyanā that the Blessed Buddha had taught. Whether the Gita was composed before or after the Buddha, my confidence in it was unyielding. Since my adolescence and into early adulthood, I had boundless faith in the Gita and the teachings of the Gita, particularly those on [the concept of] establishment in wisdom (sthitaprajñatā).[238] In the meditation practice of those ten days of vipaśyanā, I saw that I had been taught the applied aspect of the great theoretical ideal of the Gita's teachings. I had been taught to observe good conduct, which is the foundation and cornerstone of Dharma. I had been taught to perform wholesome action while avoiding unwholesome action. In order to strengthen it, I was made to actively practice making the mind one-pointed. Then I was taught to actively get established in wisdom, such that a meditator might gradually

> be able to "have a mind free from aversion towards sufferings, be free of desire for pleasures," and "be devoid of passion, fear, and anger." (Gita 2.56)

> "He neither delights nor detests," (Gita 2.57) and so, "he is free of identification, free of self-making, a stoic for whom pain and pleasure are the same." (Gita 12.13)

I had been made to actively practice the theory in line with such statements. I had been taught to develop my equanimity (*samatā*) toward the experiences of pain and pleasure.

The main teaching of the Gita is to remain established in equanimity (*samatva*) through detachment:

> ". . . Equanimity is called *yoga*." (Gita 2.48)

In vipaśyanā, I had seen revealed the entire path of meditation through the training of equanimity: equanimity in every state, equanimity from moment to moment. Vipaśyanā and equanimity became synonyms.

I learned how the mind gets purified of its own accord due to the active practice of equanimity and how one becomes suffused with the wholesome qualities of goodwill.

Felicity arose in me when I learned to cultivate auspicious loving-kindness, which allowed for the arousal of sublime states: "Without enmity, one is friendly and compassionate toward all beings" (Gita 12.13).

Here a scientific method had been taught that made available those states that I had always believed to constitute the ideal of my own spiritual life. The teachings of the Gita, which have continued to fascinate me up until now, no longer remained just teachings. I was filled with delight, thrilled to have found an accessible method that allowed me to bring them into daily life.

Since childhood, in my mind, there remained a firm intention to attain one ideal state:

> *ke tohi lāgahi Rām priya, ke tū Rām-priya hoya*[239]
> "Either make Ram dear, or become dear to Ram . . ."

At that time this statement appealed to my adolescent mind. But I adjusted it slightly.

Saints have said that we should choose one of these two options for our benefit.[240] But I found fault with this. Why should I choose only one? Since he is my Lord, he is indeed dear to me. If he weren't dear [to me], then how would so much devotion, so much faith, arise? A text states: "You are the merciful, and I am wretched. You are the donor, and I am the beggar."[241] A wretched person and a beggar will naturally have a respectful feeling of affection toward a merciful person and a donor, respectively. There is no need to make any particular effort or choice.

So, in those days, I thought that I did not have to choose between the two options. If one were to be chosen, I would also have to choose the other. Since he was my Lord, he was indeed dear to me. In this way, I also made myself dear to the Lord. But how should I do so? Every morning, with the picture of the Lord before me, feigning tears, I was unable to make myself dear to him by merely praying that I might be free of defects. I also could not become dear to the Lord merely by repeatedly reciting thousands of verses of praise. How might I become dear to the Lord? Only one solution to this problem seemed clear.

As an adolescent, when I read the Gita, [the teaching on] getting established in wisdom in its second chapter became my life's ideal. I should become established in wisdom, then I would be able to become dear to the Lord. Otherwise, how [to become] dear to the Lord? Further, in the twelfth chapter it is stated that if the qualities of a devotee become evident in life, then one can become dear to the Lord. This was the clear pronouncement of my Lord:

> *anapekṣaḥ śucirdakṣa udāsino gatavyathaḥ* |
> *sarvārambhaparityāgī yo madbhaktaḥ sa me priyaḥ* || (Gita 12.16)
> That devotee of mine who is impartial, clear, skillful,
> indifferent, unphased,
> who fully abandons all undertakings, is dear to me.

If these excellent qualities are present, then, as the Lord himself states, *yo madbhaktaḥ sa me priyaḥ* —"Such a devotee is dear to me." How might I become such a devotee, so as to become dear to the Lord?

I can become impartial by keeping all expectations, cravings, longings, and desires at a distance. [To be] clear means that I should be pure of heart. Actions of mind, speech, and body should be pure. "Skillful": whenever any pollutant is active in the mind, at that time I should skillfully remove it. "Indifferent": the mind should remain indifferent in the face of the vicissitudes of life. That is, it should remain established in equanimity. When one remains established in equanimity, then one is unphased—all distress is at a distance. When that is the case, one naturally "fully abandons all undertakings." That is, one does not allow for the undertaking of bad action. I understood well that I would become dear to my Lord when these excellent qualities would be incorporated into life; otherwise, not.

In my very first vipaśyanā course, I saw that here I was made to carry out the active practice of all these [qualities].

After the course, in order to understand the words and teachings of the Blessed Buddha more fully, I read his words for the first time in the well-known book, the *Dhammapada*. As I continued to read it—once, twice, three times—I was thrilled. I saw that in the words of the Blessed One there remained a highly elevated spiritual philosophy, a pure spirituality replete with spiritual concerns.[242] The entire training was precisely for the purpose of the absolutely faultless, unpolluted Noble Dharma.[243]

As I continued to read the *Dhammapada*, I saw that in it were explanations of those excellent qualities that I had aimed to take on in life ever since I had been living it. Here was the glorious ancient and eternal spirituality of India—how one might strengthen these excellent qualities and keep bad qualities at a distance. The *Dhammapada* contained clear explanations of how to remain fully endowed with excellent qualities, and it was replete with wholesome guidance on how to keep harmful, negative qualities at a distance. On one side, I had actively practiced vipaśyanā. On the other side, the brilliant nature of the Dharma was illuminated in my mind as I read this immortal language of the *Dhammapada*.

During the first course, my mind was convinced that the wisdom of vipaśyanā clearly gave fruit, brought benefit, and destroyed negativity. Not a trace of fault did I see in it.

After the course, two questions necessarily emerged in my mind.

One was for Blessed Krishna: Why did he not teach practical wisdom such as vipaśyanā so that one might become developed in the unparalleled dharmic teaching such as getting established in wisdom? In the absence of such [practical wisdom], nearly all the characters of the *Mahābhārata* remain enmeshed in a proliferation of lies, deceit, duplicity, pretext, and trickery. No one is able to avail themselves of the true effects of the teaching of getting established in wisdom.

The second was for the Blessed Buddha: Why did he not accept the existence of the self and the ultimate self along with a wisdom that so clearly gives good fruit? [If he had done so,] the brilliance of this entirely faultless wisdom [would] not have been marked by the dark stigma of nihilism.

Both questions were indicative of how incomplete my knowledge was at the time.

The Blessed Buddha's Establishment of the True Dharma of the Affirmers

The Blessed Buddha brought immense benefit to humanity by establishing the virtuous, true Dharma, which went against teachings replete with denial, such as [of those advocating hedonism and the disbelief in karma and rebirth]. The Blessed One taught the affirmative Dharma of truth to save people from the teachings of denialist teachers. [Such teachers] allowed people to neglect good actions and encouraged bad actions, [while the Buddha] encouraged them to engage in wholesome actions. In this respect [he gave] primacy to morality, good conduct. Then there was the practice of concentration, control of the mind (*man*), in order to strengthen such [good conduct]. Likewise he taught the method of fully purifying the mind (citta) by getting established in wisdom. He offered a teaching [that allowed people] to get established in the True Dharma on the basis of loving-kindness, compassion, and goodwill through the destruction of habit patterns that incline toward bad karma. In this way, he taught the pure Dharma of the absolutely affirmative Eightfold Noble Path.

The doctrine of enjoyment—[the encouragement to] "eat, drink, and enjoy life" of denialist left-handed practitioners—remained in vogue. They continued to emphasize indulging in bad conduct associated with drinking alcohol and sensual indulgence. To counter these [teachings], these two important parts of the five precepts were taught: (1) *kāmesu micchācārā veramaṇī* (to abstain from wrong actions associated with sensual indulgence, specifically adultery); and (2) *surā-meraya-majja . . . veramaṇī* (to abstain from alcohol and any kind of intoxicating drink). These two [precepts] were given great importance so as to rescue people from the wanton freedoms of the left-hand path of the denialists. For this reason, the teaching of abstaining from adultery was prescribed for householders, and the strict rule of observing absolute celibacy was instituted for monks.

It is not possible to say with certainty whether there were organizations of people practicing sensuality, advocating the left-hand path, during the time before the Buddha. But in the society of the Buddha's time, these teachers advocating denial organized such people in the form of sects.

By fully establishing and spreading in an organized form the Noble Dharma— perfected through concentration and wisdom based on morality and good conduct—the Buddha weakened the denialists' grip on the society. He reestablished the ancient affirmative lineage in the form of morality, concentration, and wisdom. Pure Dharma was once again established in society. Because of this, we have seen that the denialist teachers of the time in the northern region of India were unable to counter this Noble Path of the affirmers. Due to fear of public condemnation and public humiliation, they were unable to counter it. This was because of the diffusion of the pure Dharma.

It is clear from the words of the Buddha that in those days some people accepted the importance of affirmative good conduct but were hesitant to accept the idea of the existence of a resulting pleasant afterlife beyond death. The Blessed One made such people understand that even if they were only to accept the reality of this life and not the next, still, by living a dharmic life of morality and good conduct here and now, they would remain happy and respected by the wise people of society. Since you get such immediate results in this very life, if there is actually an afterlife, then you will also attain happiness there after death. You lose nothing by living a life of good conduct in this world; rather, you continue to benefit from it. So a life of good conduct is both faultless in every way and advantageous. This teaching of good conduct by the Blessed Buddha weakened the grip that denialists had on the society of his time.

Countering the Teaching of the Deniers

Giving, Morality, and the Afterlife

The denialist teachers believed that it was useless to give donations and observe morality. The Blessed Buddha gave importance to giving and observing morality. In the same manner that all buddhas properly establish the True Dharma, the Blessed One, Gautama Buddha, gave this teaching:

> This is the law (sāsana) of the buddhas: Give donations with faith, protect morality at all times, and delight in meditative cultivation. (*Dhammavandanā, Pubbaṇhasutta* 6)[244]

The teaching of all the buddhas is that one should give donations with faith. Faith means the belief that one will necessarily obtain good consequences from generosity. It was also their teaching that one should always observe morality and good conduct. To get fully developed in this, one should cultivate meditation, which comes about through the direct experience of concentration and wisdom. That is, one should remain immersed in the experience of practicing concentration and wisdom so that one might be *bhāvito bahulīkato*, or fully accomplished in the experiences in great measure. One should develop through repeatedly entering into the experiences many times. Once these practices are developed, morality and good conduct will naturally develop.

The deniers did not accept the existence of this world and the next; and since those were not accepted, they likewise did not accept the existence of karma and the fruit of karma. The Blessed Buddha accepted both, and taught [others to accept them]:

> *Idha nandati pecca nandati, katapuñño ubhayattha nandati.* (*Dhammapada* 1.18)
> Whoever performs good deeds is joyous in this world, and after death he is also joyous. He is joyous in both places.

> *Idha tappati pecca tappati, pāpakārī ubayattha tappati.* (*Dhammapada* 1.17)
> Whoever performs evil deeds burns in this world and also burns after death. He burns in both places.

It is clear that the Blessed One gave full importance to giving, morality, and good conduct and to the fruits of karma in this world and the next. Denialist teachers neglected these, and therefore they were deniers. The Blessed One accepted them, and therefore he was an affirmer. Those teachers like the Buddha who were affirmers were ridiculed by the denialists. We have seen that the denialist Ajita Kesakambala mocked the affirmers, believing their statements about the fruits of giving donations and observing morality to be empty and false.

Against Wanton Sexuality

These [teachings of] wanton freedom associated with the enjoyment of sensual pleasure had become formally established by teachers of left-hand practices during the time of Gautama Buddha. Wherever people did not agree with the observation of good conduct and did not oppose the madness of sensual enjoyments, there communities of denialist teachers naturally grew. Common people always continue to be drawn, like animals, to the path of enjoyment. It would also not be wrong to assume that these teachers who gave people the liberty to abandon morality and good conduct and sexual relations would themselves increasingly take such liberties, even while being renunciants. Because of the spread of this denialist teaching—which was devoid of good conduct—the True Dharma was deteriorating and disappearing. True Dharma continued to diminish, True Dharma continued to weaken. The influence of the anti-Dharma was increasing. The Blessed One made immense effort to dispel this corrupt influence.

The Noble Middle Path of the Aryans That Avoids Two Extremes

After attaining full enlightenment, the Blessed Buddha gave the first Dharma teaching, correctly and meaningfully called the *Dharmacakrapravartan* [Turning of the Wheel of Dharma]. At the beginning of this teaching, the Blessed One states clearly the two sorts of extreme paths that the renunciant teachers of those days might traverse.

The first is that which is *attakilamathānuyogo dukkho anariyo anatthasaṃhito*. It is a path of bodily torture and self-oppression that brings suffering, is practiced by ignoble people, and is ineffective.

The second is *kāmesu kāmasukhallikānuyogo hīno gammo pothujjaniko anariyo anatthasaṃhito*. It is that which remains immersed in the pleasures of sensual enjoyment and is base, crude, barbarous, practiced by commoners and ignoble people, and ineffective.

The Blessed One gave a teaching on walking the Noble Path of moderation by avoiding these two extremes of ignoble practice. The Blessed Buddha reestablished the true Noble Dharma of the ideal affirmers by illuminating this Noble Path. We speak of reestablishing in the sense that before the Blessed One, Gautama, there had been many other buddhas. Three fully enlightened buddhas, Kakusaṃdha, Koṇāgamana, and Kāśyapa had come before him in this aeon. The first two were born near Kapilavastu. All fully enlightened buddhas establish the ancient and eternal Noble Dharma. Upon their disappearance, there comes a time when the force of the pure true Dharma begins to wane. The liberating wisdom of vipaśyanā disappears entirely from the human societies of the world. The doctrine of karma, which is the original foundation of the true Dharma, begins to decline. Those who are against morality and good conduct, and the denialism that neglects the truth of how the fruit of karma is attained in accordance with karma, become prevalent. Because the fruits of all karmas do not manifest in just one life, and because of the resulting neglect of the truth of rebirth, a strong trend emerges toward this denialism, which encourages the proliferation of bad conduct. In this way, the Dharma begins to decline. It starts to become decrepit. In such a situation, a bodhisattva fulfills all of the perfections of good deeds and takes his final birth. He discovers the lost practice of vipaśyanā, attains for himself the state of full enlightenment, and upon becoming a fully enlightened buddha, reestablishes the pure Dharma by giving the following teaching:

> *sabbapāpassa akaraṇaṃ*—to abstain from all evil karma.
> Evil karma is whatever defiles the mind and makes a person into an ignoble person.
>
> *kusalassa upasampadā*—to become endowed with wholesome karma constituted by good deeds.
> Good karma is whatever makes the mind pious and makes a person happy.
>
> *sacittapariyodapanaṃ*—one should purify one's own mind entirely, not just partially.
>
> *etaṃ buddhāna sāsanaṃ*—this is the teaching of the buddhas.

This true, eternal Noble Dharma is not the teaching of just one buddha. It is taught and laid down as law by all buddhas for the infinite benefit of the world.

The harmful and negative teachings of the denialists get struck down by this teaching, and the teaching of the affirmers—which brings benefit to all people—is established. People attain the path of liberation to remove themselves from the grip of denial.

The Practical Wisdom of Vipaśyanā

The Buddha did not get wrongly embroiled in intellectual debates with the ineffective teachings of denialist teachers. Rather, he strongly refuted them by teaching the practical wisdom of vipaśyanā.

Denialists stated that one does not obtain any painful or pleasant fruit of evil or good deeds. The Blessed One taught the wisdom of vipaśyanā, and people understood through experience that all actions of body and speech arise first in the mind. When the mind has reacted to an experience of pleasure or pain, which is the result of a sensation on the body, it produces evil and good deeds. A meditation practitioner understands well through the experience of vipaśyanā this truth taught by the Blessed One: *vedanāsamosaraṇā sabbe dhammā* (*The Numerical Discourses* 3.8.83, *The Section on Mindfulness*).[245] That is, whatever emerges in the mind begins flowing in the form of sensations on the body.

It is truly miraculous how that great scientist of the spiritual world—simply through the power of meditative attention and without any scientific contraptions—made such an important discovery.

He revealed two aspects of the truth. One is the conventional truth, or truth as it appears. This is the truth that remains clearly evident.

The second is ultimate truth, or the actual truth.

On the basis of these two truths, he discovered that not just our physical bodies, but all the physical realities of the universe are in fact not solid, though they appear solid. They are made of the tiniest subatomic particles, wherein one finds no trace of solidity. Throughout the entire universe, at every moment, there is ongoing combustion and oscillation.[246]

Our minds also, when they are affected by the impurities of anger, hatred, ill will, and so on, feel gross and solidified. In actuality, in this case as well, there is ongoing combustion and oscillation. Whether animate or inanimate, everything is vibrations, perpetually arising and perishing.[247] Nothing remains stable for more than a moment.

Due to this constant oscillation of body and mind, living beings feel various types of sensations, which are either pleasant, painful, or neither pleasant nor painful.

When these sensations feel pleasant, a living being begins to crave them. When they are painful, one feels aversion toward them. One wants the pleasant to remain, to increase, and never to be destroyed. In this sense, one gives rise to the thirst of craving it. One wants what is painful to be removed, to diminish. In this sense one gives rise to the thirst of aversion to it.

Whether it's the thirst of craving or the thirst of aversion, thirst is thirst. It makes a living being suffer.

It is obvious that a painful sensation is painful, but a pleasant sensation also does not remain permanent, perpetual, or fixed forever. It transforms into pain and makes us suffer. It is the habit pattern of these sensations to keep changing. They are born from the conjunction of the physical body and the mind, and these both go on changing every moment. Like the body and the mind, these sensations are also impermanent, destructible, ephemeral, and liable to transformation.

This great scientist [the Buddha] also made one more important discovery.

Conventional, or manifest, truth tricks us into giving rise to craving when we feel good and aversion when we feel bad, in the context of the interaction of sense faculties and sense objects: the eye and forms, colors, lights, images and so on; the ear and sounds; the nose and scents; the tongue and tastes; the body and the touch of any physical thing. This great scientist discovered that this is not actually the case. It was a truth of the sort he had not heard previously: that it was a great error to think that because of the contact of the sense faculties, one gives rise to craving for objects that are pleasant and aversion toward objects that are unpleasant. The truth was this: when the mind makes contact with any sense object, some sensation inevitably arises in the body. There is pleasure when one takes that sensation to be good and pain when one takes it to be bad, and at the same time, craving arises toward the pleasure and aversion toward the pain. In the process, a living being comes to suffer.

The great scientist also discovered one more thing: in addition to these five sense faculties, the mind is also an important sense faculty. In this respect, when one conceptualizes and considers something to be pleasant, craving arises. When one considers something to be painful, aversion arises. This also is the simple, apparent truth. The [deeper] truth is that at the very same time that anything arises in the mind, some sensation arises on the body. This is the irrefutable law of nature. It is not possible that a thought will arise in the mind without some sensation arising in the body. That is, the reactions of craving and aversion are not caused by what arises in the mind. Rather, craving and aversion arise from whatever sensation arises on the body.

This great scientist understood the disease, and he understood the actual cause of the disease. Yet he also understood that it is not enough for a doctor to simply understand suffering and its cause. He knew well that humans become diseased and disturbed because they give rise to the thirst of craving or aversion toward sensations that arise on the body. But it was even more important to discover a method to prevent this [disease]. The sensations continue to manifest throughout the body at every moment. It was important to figure out how not to give rise to thirst toward them. For this purpose, he discovered the ancient meditation practice method of vipaśyanā that had been lost to India of those days.

It is easy to be aware of the gross sensations in the body, such as heat, perspiration, heaviness, pressure, pain, tension, and so on. It is not easy, however, to understand all of the sensations in the body without treating the disease. When we are not aware of all types of sensations that are going on in the body, we give rise to craving and aversion toward them, since we are ignorant of them. To remedy this, it is necessary to make the mind one-pointed, to the extent that it becomes subtle and sharp, so that it can fully experience all the sensations on the body.

Some sensation exists on the body, and the mind reacts and gives rise to evil and good karma. Because of these, another sensation on the body becomes solidified. In this way, meditators begin to be aware, through their own experience, that when they react to any sensation on the body resulting from an external event and give rise to evil, they themselves suffer. One begins to understand well that when one performs bad karma of body and speech in order to bring suffering to another person, one first gives rise to karmic impressions of anger, aversion, ill will, and so on in one's own mind and makes oneself suffer. Before striking down anyone with a weapon, one must first give rise to harmful defilements in the mind and strike down peace and happiness within oneself. Meditators come to understand through their own experience these words of the Blessed One:

> *pubbe hanati attānaṃ, pacchā hanati so pare.* (*Verses of the Elders* 139, *Verses of the Elder Vasabha*)
> First one strikes oneself, afterward one strikes another.

The painful fruit of striking someone is *akāliko*. That is, one encounters it immediately. The bitter seed of bad karma makes us begin to suffer immediately, and when it ripens into a bitter fruit in the future, it will make us suffer further. This truth is not accepted merely at the level of doctrine. Rather, it is *sandiṭṭhiko*. That is, one enters into the experience at that very moment. For this reason, a meditator accepts it. Before one performs any bad action of body and speech, that person first gives rise to defilement in the mind and experiences suffering for themselves. The encounter with the fruit of evil is initiated at the very moment of the karma. As it is with bad karma, so it is with good karma. If one should perform good karma with the body, first a wholesome feeling arises in the mind. When one gives a donation, first loving-kindness, compassion, and goodwill arise in the mind. At that very moment there is a pleasant experience in the form of the fruit of that karma. The encounter with the fruit of good deeds is initiated at the very moment of the karma.

This is not simply a matter of doctrine. It is a truth to be entered into through the experience of a meditation practitioner. Becoming aware at the depths of vipaśyanā, a meditation practitioner sees for himself that:

> *manopubbaṅgamā dhammā, manoseṭṭhā manomaya.*
> The entire world [of concepts] is [a world] of the mind. Karma is initiated by the mind itself. One begins to experience the directly evident fruit [of karma] through the mind itself.

The initial fruit of good and evil deeds does not, itself, persist. A meditation practitioner sees that:

> *manasā ce paduṭṭhena, bhāsati vā karoti vā.*
> When karma of body or speech is performed on the basis of a defiled mind,
>
> *tato naṃ dukkham anveti, cakkaṃ va vahato padaṃ.* (*Dhammapada* 1.1)
> Then suffering of that sort follows behind, just as the wheel of the oxcart follows behind the ox yoked to it.

A meditation practitioner also sees clearly how the experience of dislike continues to emerge again and again from defilement produced in the mind one time, based on the experience of dislike. Because of this, one goes on giving rise to that kind of defilement in the mind. Then the habit pattern of giving rise to defilement in the mind is strengthened, and along with that, suffering is strengthened. So indeed:

> *manasā ce pasannena, bhāsati vā karoti vā.*
> Anyone who does action of body or speech with an undefiled mind,
>
> *tato naṃ sukham anveti, chāyā va anapāyinī.* (*Dhammapada* 1.2)
> Happiness follows behind him like a shadow that accompanies him and never leaves.

As the habit pattern of performing karma with an undefiled mind gets stronger, so the accompanying pleasant fruit of the experience of that karma becomes cemented and strengthened.

The Blessed One revealed this scientific truth of the cosmic order, the truth of the cosmos:

> *cetanāhaṃ, bhikkhave, kammaṃ vadāmi.* (*The Numerical Discourses* 2.6.63, *Discourse on the Penetrative*)
> Oh, Monks! I teach that the intention of the mind is indeed karma.

Vocal and bodily action are the mere offspring of the intention of the mind. A good vipaśyanā meditation practitioner begins to understand and accept this truth based on his own experience. Consequently, one avoids the wrong belief of the denialists—that there is no fruit of good and bad deeds—and makes oneself a strong affirmer.

CHAPTER 11

Discourse on Matter

from the *Vipaśyanā* Newsletter (June 1973)

This short article is the first in a series of three pieces—published consecutively in the June, July, and August 1973 editions of the Vipaśyanā *newsletter—on the topic of matter, the material or physical world. It presents S.N. Goenka's particular approach to traditional Theravada Buddhist doctrine. This approach was a key aspect of Goenka's early attempts—following the lead of his teacher, U Ba Khin, and his guru-brother Robert Hover—to show that the experience of vipaśyanā brings direct access to the ultimate truths of matter discovered by modern science.*[248]

The Buddha's Words

kiñ ca, bhikkhave, rūpa[249] *vadetha? rūppatī ti kho, bhikkhave, tasmā 'rūpa' ti vuccati. kena ruppati? Sītena pi ruppati, uṇhena pi ruppati, jigacchāya pi ruppati, pipāsāya pi ruppati, ḍaṃsamakasavātātapasirisaṃpa-samphassena pi ruppati; rūppatī ti kho, bhikkhave, tasmā 'rūpa' ti vuccati.*[250]

Monks, why is matter called "matter"? Because it gets transformed, therefore it is called "matter." What transforms

> it? It is transformed by cold, it is transformed by heat, it is transformed by hunger, it is transformed by thirst, it is transformed by contact with gnats, mosquitoes, wind, sun, and creeping animals. Monks, because it gets transformed, therefore it is called "matter."

We have seen that the cause of all sufferings is craving, attachment. But to be able to understand this more clearly, we need to go more deeply into this truth. We have to make a more detailed analysis of the many other facets of reality connected with this [truth].

First we must ask ourselves, "What is this craving, after all? Who is it that becomes miserable by dint of this craving? Who is [this person]? What is it that one continues to conceptualize as 'I, I,' that one continues to conceptualize as 'mine, mine'? That is used to prop up the ego and thereby arouse this craving? That is used to prop up a sense of ownership, thereby increasing this clinging?" To understand this truth, we have to look at ourselves. Through self-examination and self-inspection, we come to understand, what is this "I"? Who am I? How am I?

We take the very first step in the direction of this search for the self [when we look] right in front of ourselves at this gross physical body to which we very clearly [ascribe] a sense of self. From reading many scientific books, from hearing many discourses on Dharma theories, we know very well at the level of the intellect that this body is not "I," that this body is not "mine," that the identification with the body is false and problematic. But this is all an intellectual coating that we have applied to the surface of the mind again and again through intellectual musings. These coats have no impact on real life. We go on identifying this body as "I," identifying it as "mine." We go on identifying the pains and pleasures of this body as "my" pains and pleasures. How deep is the state of identification with this body of ours! For our common worldly conventions, the use of the words

"I" and "you" is another matter. But how much deep attachment has come about toward this body because of self-identification?

And so [I say], come, first we should look at our bodies and understand, What is this? How is it? What natural qualities does it have? In order to make a proper investigation of its true form, we will have to divide it up and look so that we can remove the illusion of its conventional form and be able to see and understand it in its ultimate form. Whatever we see in the material world that is gross or compact, that is what we call conventional truth. Conventional truth means that truth which is made manifest directly to our gross eyes and our gross intellect. Such a gross truth is that which a common person does not find difficult to see and understand. But taking apart this manifest truth, when we reach a stage where we can no longer take things apart further, we come to a deep and most subtle [aspect] of that gross truth. We will call that the ultimate truth.

In every manifest truth there is the ultimate truth combined with illusion, just as in sesame seeds there is oil or in sugar cane there is juice. When one looks further, one does not see sesame oil in sesame seeds, and one does not see juice in sugar cane. But one who possesses the skill of pressing oil or juice simply does so. In the same way, the person who knows the method of realizing the less evident ultimate truth within the illusory manifest truth can do so easily. Through vipaśyanā meditation, we can use this method to go from the manifest in the direction of the ultimate, from the evident to the less evident, from the gross to the subtle, from the seen to the unseen, from the known to the unknown, from this side of the coin to that side of the coin, reaching finally the realization of ultimate truth.

As we progress from gross truth toward subtle truth, it becomes clearer and clearer that the illusion of the solidity of things that is produced is a great barrier for seeing and understanding their real form and their real nature. In truth, solidity is an illusion, a mirage, a deception, a falsehood, a delusion, an error. Precisely when the perception of the solid is destroyed, so also the curtain of illusion is removed, and the ultimate truth begins to emerge. When we break through the illusory gross solidity, and the unobstructed subtle truth in its actual form appears, then naturally attachment is broken apart. Dwelling in darkness, we clutch in our fist what we take to be a precious diamond. Coming into the light and seeing that it is but mere gravel, we come to realize that our clinging was in ignorance. Therefore, this journey from the conventional to the ultimate is a journey from darkness into light. It is a journey from the delusion of ignorance to pure awakening. It is a journey from the bonds of attachment to liberation.

Until we look at the dense, integrated form of our own solid bodies, we continue to generate attachments of "I" and "mine," though fully determined not to do so. In the same way, we also continue to generate a strong sense of "you" and "your," "he" and "his," toward the solid, integrated bodies of others. In order to counter this [tendency], there is the practice taught by those advocating the discrimination of observing the body in the body. The research scientist is ever an advocate of discrimination. Having removed the illusion of integration, he discriminates and arrives at the essence of the truth. The proper discovery of the truth—seeing that what is joined together can be taken apart, that what comes together can be separated, that [elements of] a conglomerate mass [can be made] distinct—occurs precisely by seeing by way of distinguishing.

When we look at any being, we see the gross, conventional bodily form, and we refer to it as a man or a woman or a horse or a cow and so on. If it is a woman or a man, [we call her or him] Ramu or Sita, Shyamu or Gita, and so forth; fat or thin, dark or fair, heavy or light, crooked or straight. By the force of these identifications of conventional bodies, we come to believe that this is what "I" am, that this body is "mine." We come to believe that this is "you," and this is "your" body. We come to believe that this is Shyamu, and this is Shyamu's body. I-mine, you-your, he-his—so begins this facade of gross truth, and it seeps into the depths of the subconscious mind, transforming into deep attachment. As long as we are trapped in the sphere of this gross conventional truth, we are not able to see the actual form of the truth and are not capable of freeing ourselves from the illusion—produced by attachment—of "I," "mine," "you," and "your."

Then [I say,] come, look part by part at this apparent, gross, integrated mass of a body and understand, What is it? What is in it? What parts is it made up of? What things constitute it?

As we progress, we see that this body has two hands, two feet, two eyes, two ears, a nose, two lips, a chest, a stomach, a back, a waist, and so on. This is a very gross discrimination of this body. Discriminating to this extent, we remain in a very gross, conventional field. Despite this discrimination, my hand is still my hand. Ramu's hand is still Ramu's hand. Finally, who made this hand, foot, torso, and so on? Is there, even at that subtler level, any common distinction in Ramu's body and my body? In order to see about this, we have to further dismantle the body. It would be good to be present in a hospital morgue when a doctor carries out an autopsy and is inspecting a corpse. Then we would see that for the various forms we see from the outside—hand or foot, head or torso—there is, from the inside, simply one state of being matter. Slicing open and looking at the body, the clear, distinct, and subtler true form of its outsides and insides becomes manifest. What is it that we refer to as the body? Head hair, body hair, nails, teeth, skin, flesh, tendons, bone, bone marrow, kidney, heart, liver, spleen, lungs, the large and small intestines, food and drink in the stomach, the medulla of the brain, bile, phlegm, pus, blood, sweat, tears, fat, spit, moisture, saliva, feces, and urine.[251] By looking into this body, we will come to feel that just as my body is, so also is Ramu's body. So also is Shyamu's body. So also is the body of every person. Flesh is just flesh, blood is just blood, and feces is just feces. We would certainly not like to identify with it.

Even progressing this far, however, we have not arrived at ultimate truth. We are still wandering in the field of conventional truth. Flesh is just solidified flesh, and bone is just solidified bone. A biologist will inform us that this flesh and bone are made up of innumerable tiny cells. But there is a reality even more subtle than these tiny cells. Until one has realized for oneself this reality, one has not yet witnessed the most subtle realization of the truth. To reach this subtlest stage is the distinctive quality of the practice of vipaśyanā meditation. By observing the body in the body and sensations in sensations,[252] one can arrive at the subtlest subatomic unit of the body and can experience for oneself the condition of the truth by virtue of sensations at that subtlest level. It is in this direct experience that the entire delusion of conventional truth is rent asunder, not before it. Upon the destruction of solidified perception, the gross delusion of solidity is removed. Whether flesh or bone, skin or blood, every bodily organ, all aspects of the body are made up of the very same extremely subtle physical particles. When one can directly experience such a collection of particles within oneself by virtue of the wisdom of vipaśyanā, one has reached the stage of ultimate truth. There no longer remains awareness of any consolidated gross thing. There no longer remains the difference between a gross foot or a gross hand. There no longer remains a distinction of gross flesh and gross bone. The entire body is dissolved. The "I" does not remain, and "mine," "you," "your," "he," "his" do not remain. Attachment certainly cannot function in that state of realization of no-self where the whole bodily mass comes to appear simply as a collection of innumerable *aṭṭhakalāpa*s.

What is this aṭṭhakalāpa? *Kalāpa* means "a conglomeration." *Aṭṭhakalāpa* means "a conglomeration of eight." Of which eight?

Earth, water, fire, wind—[a conglomeration] of these four great elements and of their various respective qualities–natures–habit patterns. This kalāpa is extremely subtle. It is more subtle even than an atom. It is more subtle even than a subatomic particle. It is the subtlest unit of the physical world. And still eight [aspects] are coming together. In every kalāpa these eight are consolidated, not disintegrated. They are together, not apart. They are connected, not disconnected. This aṭṭhakalāpa cannot be divided, penetrated, or broken apart. This does not mean that in this [physical] unit there is any solid core or essence that does not decay or die, that is permanent, perpetual, or fixed. On the contrary, because of the habit pattern of this kalāpa, it is impermanent, decaying, breaking up, liable to transform. For this reason, we also call it a *rūpakalāpa,* or "a conglomeration of matter." Today the common meaning of *rūp* is "apparent form."[253] Various physical forms are indeed made from the coming together of these kalāpas. In this sense these physical forms can be called *rūpa*. However, the original meaning, based on which these are called rūpa, is entirely different. In the language of the people of India twenty-five hundred years ago, they used *ruppana* to mean "break up, get destroyed, get altered." And so, *ruppa atyena rūpaṃ.*[254] The word *rūpa* was used in the sense of being altered. Because it has the characteristic of being altered, matter is called rūpa. *Sītuṇhādi virodhi paccayehi ruppatīti rūpaṃ:*[255] "Because it gets transformed by the opposing conditions of heat and cold and so on, it is rūpa."

Every single rūpakalāpa arises, exists, and is destroyed, [and this happens] innumerable times every moment. This is its natural habit pattern. In this way, a mass of many rūpakalāpas arises in a conglomeration, decays, and is destroyed. This is likewise the natural habit pattern. All embodied living beings in the world have bodies made up of these rūpakalāpas, with the element of space as the emptiness between them. So bodies made up of matter, for this or that reason, sooner or later are transformed and reach destruction. Transformed by cold or heat, they are destroyed. Transformed by hunger or thirst, they are destroyed. Transformed by the bites of various creatures, they are destroyed. For some reason or another, they are transformed and destroyed. Now there is no living being whose body is not transformed and then destroyed in this way. And not just the bodies of animate beings, but the entirety of inanimate physical reality is also made up of these rūpakalāpas, and for this reason there is no physical thing that does not decay and get destroyed. This is indeed the nature of this rūpakalāpa and of these conglomerations of kalāpas.

Because they are the ultimate units of the physical world, they are referred to as ultimate truth. The object of ultimate truth is never permanent or fixed. They can't be further divided, and so it is said that the elements of fire, water, earth, and wind in an aṭṭhakalāpa, along with their various respective qualities-natures, can't be separated. It is not that a fire element particle is separate, a water element particle is separate, and so forth, and these are joined together to make an aṭṭhakalāpa. The four great elements arise together, they remain together, and they are destroyed together. They are, therefore, conascent, coexistent, and "co-dying." It is not possible for any one great element to abide separately from the other three. Yes, in any conglomeration of kalāpas, any of the particular great elements may at times flare up as more active and predominant. Whenever the activity of the fire element manifests, feelings of burning predominate. Whenever the activity of the earth element manifests, feelings of heaviness and lightness become predominant, and so on. Ultimately, this subatomic particle, or aṭṭhakalāpa, is not always uniform like material building blocks are when they are cast in a mold; all the eight fundamental substances are not mixed together in a single fixed quantity and size. If this were the case, the physical world would be ready-made from these building blocks and remain forever a single substance. But this is not the case. The reality is that the entire physical world—this earth, this moon, this sun, the planets and asteroids, the stars and constellations, the infinite space of this unfathomable solar system—is transformed every single moment. This is because every physical thing, big or small, is made up of these subtlest rūpakalāpas, which are themselves liable to transform every single moment. The proper practice of vipaśyanā, proper insight, is to realize directly through one's own experience how rūpakalāpas have the basic characteristic of being liable to change. This is the subtlest vision of the truth of the physical world. It is the actual vision of ultimate truth that is devoid of illusion and devoid of delusion!

AUSPICIOUS FRIEND,
Satyanārāyaṇ Goenka

CHAPTER 12

On the Foundations of Mindfulness

from a Dharma Talk during a Ten-Day Meditation Course in Varanasi (December 1974)

In the autumn of 1974, one of S.N. Goenka's young American students, Joseph Goldstein, taught his first meditation course in America. It was a course on "the foundations of mindfulness" (satipaṭṭhāna). A month later, Goenka took the time on one of his meditation courses in Varanasi to explain in a Dharma talk the meaning of satipaṭṭhāna in light of his meditation teachings and in connection with a "big confusion in the minds of Western students with these words of satipaṭṭhāna *and* vipaśyanā." *What follows is an excerpt from the beginning of that Dharma talk.*

TRY TO DEVELOP self-confidence, understanding—the basic rules of the game, what we are doing here, what is our aim. What is this technique? When the basic principles are fully understood, then these basic principles will be your guide.

Only when there is a real complicated situation, a big confusion, then of course a guide might help you. Or, taking mettā [loving-kindness] vibration from the guide is also understandable. But taking guidance for every small little thing that you come across will be developing the habit of weakness, developing the habit of relying on others. And the more we keep relying on others, the less is the possibility of our getting liberated, because the liberation comes with self-reliance. You have to be self-dependent.

So let us, today, understand, [let us] review, the basic principles of what our practice is. Understand [there are] two major divisions of this practice. One is called samatha [calm], the other is called vipaśyanā [insight]. *Samatha-bhāvanā* [cultivation of calm], *vipaśyanā-bhāvanā* [cultivation of insight]. Samatha is the field of samādhi [meditative concentration], where we have these three: *sammā-vāyāma*, efforts, the right effort to remain concentrated; *sammā-sati*, awareness, awareness, awareness; [and] *sammā-samādhi*, continuity of awareness, continuity of awareness.

For this practice, we have chosen respiration as our object. The Buddha gave forty different objects on which we could have practiced, anybody could have practiced. We have chosen this, *ānāpāna* [respiration]. And because it has suited you all right, you have worked on this. Better stick to it. To develop your awareness, we have asked you to keep attention on a smaller area. And we have chosen the area below the nostrils, [the] entrance of the nostrils.

There are some schools where students are asked to be aware of their respiration [but] not limited to this small area. They gave bigger areas. In some schools, they are asked to follow the breath deep inside their lungs. And even when the breath goes out, [they] make their imagination a bit . . . how far it goes in the air. And things like that, a big area. The mind is to be kept in a big area—of course, related to the breath. In some schools, students are asked to keep their hand on their abdomen, on their belly, and be aware of that big area of the belly as it rises, falls, along with the movement of the breath coming in, going out.

We have straightaway taken a small area and seen that it works.

Not necessary for us to go to bigger areas. On the other hand, we try to narrow it, narrow it, narrow it. Higher states of concentration cannot be achieved by keeping an object of big area. The smaller the area, the longer the periods of awareness, the deeper the samādhi, the stronger the samādhi. So we straightaway started with the big triangular area, including the nostrils—inside [and] outside—and the base of the upper lip. And we restricted our attention—didn't allow it to follow the breath inside the body—and of course, no question of following imaginary breath going out in the air. We limited the awareness of the entire length of the breath within this small area because we wanted to narrow down the area where we have to develop our concentration. And we kept narrowing down, narrowing down, until we came to the smallest area possible.

As I was now explaining to other students—old students—although you are in vipaśyanā now, many times you will find your mind has entered a big storm. [This may be] due to some external reasons, but most of the time not external reasons—reasons within yourself. Some deeply rooted impurity has been shaken. Some complex in the subconscious or unconscious has been shaken, and then it comes on the surface, [the] surface of the flow of consciousness. And naturally, the mind gets very agitated, and there's a big storm. Then it becomes difficult for you to continue your vipaśyanā. You take shelter, you take refuge, again in samatha, again in ānāpāna. Again you come to the breath—sometimes conscious breath, hard breath, intentional breath, and from that coming back to unintentional, natural, normal, soft breath. And then, narrowing down the area to the sensation on the small area, start your vipaśyanā.

When should you take [the] help of ānāpāna? Nobody else can tell you. So come out of this habit of asking a guide, "What I should do now? My mind is very agitated. What I should do now? My mind is very turmoiled, very drowsy."

Understand, this is what you have to do: Again, come back to ānāpāna. Again, come back to the samatha, because vipaśyanā is too hard for you now. Again come back to samatha, come back to ānāpāna, strengthen your mind—and then switch over to vipaśyanā as quickly as possible.

The field of vipaśyanā we have chosen: the awareness of breath. There are some schools—of course, as for the teachings of Buddha, all right—some schools where a student is asked to take [as] the object of his concentration, the object of his awareness, the grosser activities of the body. [This is] what we were discussing a few minutes back and what I advised: during the recess periods, be aware of the gross activities of your body—walking, walking, walking; eating, eating, eating. And whatever else you do. There are schools where the whole practice starts with that. Nothing wrong. The aim of those schools is also the same: you start with the gross activities of the body and come to the subtler activities of the body. All subtler activities are going on in the body.

[There is] a big confusion in the minds of Western students with these words of satipaṭṭhāna and vipaśyanā. Awareness of walking, walking, walking, awareness of eating, eating, eating is taken up by many students as satipaṭṭhāna. And awareness of sensation, subtle sensations in the body, is taken up as vipaśyanā, which has created a lot of confusion.

The word *sati* means "awareness." *Patthāna* means "getting strongly established." And sati is, the awareness is, really strongly established when there is paññā with it, wisdom with it. Otherwise, it remains in the field of samādhi only, samatha only. You can be just aware, but without wisdom, without paññā, you cannot get established in Dhamma. So the whole discourse of Buddha, called *Satipaṭṭhāna-sutta,* or *Mahāsatipaṭṭhāna-sutta*, is for training the mind for both: awareness and wisdom.[256] Awareness and wisdom. *Sati-sampajāna, sati sapaññā*: wisdom, awareness; wisdom-awareness.

Because of not understanding the real purpose, those students who have started developing wisdom by experiencing subtler realities, many times just out of their inquisitiveness, they start practicing some new practice—that means something new that's going on in other schools—with these grosser objects of the grosser activities of the body. Nothing wrong. But what's wrong is, by forgetting all about the subtler realities, they get themselves so much engrossed in these gross activities of the body that they start losing all the subtle sensations. The entire body gets once again blocked up. Although the poor teacher—the guide who gives this so-called satipaṭṭhāna—says very clearly that you have to go [to] the subtler stages, but because of this not understanding the whole basic theory behind Buddha's teaching of practice, they again make themselves, their minds, so blunt—though aware of the grosser things—that for them it becomes a big thing to go to the subtler stages of the body and mind. In this tradition, we start with ānāpāna because out of all the gross activities of the body—like walking, eating, or anything—among them, the subtlest is breathing.

We stop all other activities of the body, because we sit down quietly. And when there's no other intentional activity of the body, what is left now? For someone who can't experience still subtler things going on in the body, what is left now is only the breath, which unintentionally keeps coming in, going out, coming in, going out. We start from that station and go deeper, deeper, deeper. And with that, you have started experiencing what is going on throughout the body at a subtler level.

Having reached that, you have to maintain that. Maintaining that, then the second paragraph of *Satipaṭṭhāna-sutta* can be used, nothing wrong. The first paragraph starts with ānāpāna and takes you to the final goal. The second paragraph starts with these gross activities of the body, and taking you subtler, subtler, takes you to the final goal. And like that, every paragraph.

Now you want to try the second paragraph, nothing wrong. One should try, and in this path also, in this practice also, training is given for that—not for the beginners, because you already began with something subtle and have gone to still subtler layers. Now we will add this, this subtlety, awareness of our subtlety, to all of our gross activities. We will walk with the awareness of the subtle, with the awareness of the subtle sensations. We will eat with the awareness of subtle sensations. The subtler the awareness, the bigger the progress.

If you understand what vipaśyanā is, how it is defined, the whole *Satipaṭṭhāna-sutta* is nothing but vipaśyanā, vipaśyanā, vipaśyanā. *Kāyānupaśyanā*—observing the body; *vedanānupaśyanā*—observing the sensations on the body, related to the body; *cittānupaśyanā*—observing the mind; and *dhammānupaśyanā*. It is a very wide term, Dhamma, and it includes everything, practically everything, all the waves that arise in the mind. And the law, in full detail—not only at the intellectual level but at the actual level, by experience—you understand the entire law, the entire Dhamma, that is dhammānupaśyanā. And observing the entire law of the sensual field, of the field of relativity from the grossest to the subtlest, you transcend that and experience the law of nibbāṇa, which also comes under dhamma.

So the entire *Satipaṭṭhāna-sutta* is nothing but vipaśyanā: *kāyānupaśyanā vedanānupaśyanā cittānupaśyanā dhammānupaśyanā*. And what is vipaśyanā? "*Paññatti ṭhapetvā, visesena paśyatīti vipaśyanā.*" Breaking the entire field of apparent truth, conventional truth, and reaching the stage of ultimate truth—that is vipaśyanā. If we are just observing the conventional truth all the time and keep ourselves limited to the gross, apparent, conventional truth only, then it can be a very good sati, awareness, but it has nothing to do with vipaśyanā and nothing to do with satipaṭṭhāna.

CHAPTER 13

Worshipping the Buddha, the Body of the Buddha, and the Qualities of the Buddha

from *The Perfectly Enlightened Buddha in the Tipiṭaka*

The Perfectly Enlightened Buddha in the Tipiṭaka *is S.N. Goenka's magnum opus on the doctrines of the Buddha. First published in two volumes in 1995, it is the result of an extensive excavation of the Pali scriptural corpus of the Theravada Buddhist tradition. It is the culmination of many years of scriptural study, Goenka's attempt to present his understanding of the Buddha's teachings comprehensively in one place. An excerpt from the fourth section of the first volume of the book, on the topic of the Buddha's Dharma-body (*dharmakāya*) appears here.*[257]

The Correct Way to Worship the Buddha

The time of the great final enlightenment of the Buddha was approaching. It was raining sandalwood powder and sweet-smelling flowers in honor, in worship, of the Blessed One. Seeing this, the Blessed One spoke:

> *na kho, Ānanda, etāvatā tathāgato sakkato vā hoti, garukato vā mānito vā, pūjito vā, apacito vā.*
> Ānanda, this is not the actual way that the Tathāgata is felicitated, revered, honored, worshipped, and respected.

What, then, is the correct way to worship the Tathāgata? He explained:

> *yo kho, Ānanda, bhikkhu vā bhikkhunī vā upāsako vā upāsikā vā dhammānudhammapaṭipanno viharati sāmīcippaṭipanno anudhammacārī, so tathāgataṃ sakkaroti garuṃ karoti māneti pūjeti apaciyati paramāya pūjāya. . . . evañ hi vo, Ānanda, sikkhitabbaṃ.*
> Ānanda, when a monk or nun, layman or laywoman, enters upon the path of Dharma and lives it, enters upon the right path and lives it, acts in accordance with Dharma, that is genuine worship. Through this supreme form of worship, the Tathāgata is felicitated, revered, honored, worshipped, and respected. . . . Ānanda, train yourself in this way.

For this reason, this lineage of practice carried on:

> *imāya dhammānudhammapaṭipattiyā buddhaṃ pūjemi.*
> I worship the Buddha by following the tradition of Dharma.

How is someone one who follows the tradition of Dharma?

> *rūpassa ce, . . . vedanāya ce, . . . saññāya ce, . . . saṅkhārānaṃ ce, . . . viññāṇassa ce, bhikkhu, nibbidāya nirodhāya paṭipanno hoti,*

> Monks, whoever has practiced to bring about disgust and dispassion for and cessation of these five aggregates—matter, feeling, perception, karmic reactions, and consciousness,
>
> *dhammānudhammapaṭippanno bhikkhū ti alaṃ vacanāya.*
> is one worthy of being called a monk who is practiced in the tradition of Dharma, in the correct sense. (*The Connected Discourses* 2.3.115, *Discourse on the Dharma Speaker*)[258]

One who has arrived at the final stage of liberation by progressing step by step from gross states to subtler ones is one who is practiced in the tradition of Dharma.

This is the correct worship of the Dharma-body of the Buddha, the correct salutation. For this reason, those genuine meditation practitioners who take refuge in the Buddha, in accordance with the teachings of the Buddha, do not take refuge in anyone else. One takes refuge in oneself, takes refuge in the Dharma. For true refuge one makes oneself an island, one makes an island of Dharma:

> *tasmātih' Ānanda, attadīpā viharatha attasaraṇā anaññasaraṇā.*
> Ānanda, it is indeed because of this that you should dwell as an island unto yourself, as a refuge unto yourself, not taking anyone else as a refuge. (*The Long Discourses* 2.165, *The Discourse on the Great Passing*)[259]

Battered in a storm, a boat seeks an island in order to save itself. Battered on the ocean of existence, for the boat that is an individual life, there is an island within that gives security. It is not to be found outside oneself. One should make that a refuge.

> *dhammadīpā dhammasaraṇā anaññasaraṇā.*
> Dwell with Dharma as your island, with Dharma as your

> refuge, not taking anyone else as a refuge. (*The Long Discourses* 2.165, *The Discourse on the Great Passing*)[260]

The actual refuge, then, is the refuge of Dharma. Dharma is also what arises within oneself. Aroused within oneself, Dharma gives us refuge in its true sense. It gives us protection. When one sees the Dharma within oneself—in other words, *dharmānupaśyanā*—it produces a vision of the Buddha. It produces a vision of the Buddha's Dharma-body. These words of the Blessed One make this clear:

> *yo kho, Vakkali, dhammaṃ passati, so maṃ passati.*
> Vakkali, whoever sees the Dharma sees me. (*The Connected Discourses* 2.3.87, *Discourse to Vakkali*)[261]

Seeing the Dharma within oneself, a meditation practitioner sees the habit pattern of the five aggregates, the Dharma of arising and passing away. That is, they experience it. These vibrations of Dharma that awaken one to the reality of impermanence at a high level of vipaśyanā are identical to the Dharma vibrations of the Blessed One. Alternatively, when a meditation practitioner realizes the deathless *nirvāṇa* that transcends the five aggregates and is beyond the senses, [the vibrations] automatically become identical to the *nirvāṇa*-element of the Blessed One. Whoever sees the Dharma sees the Buddha. They see the Dharma-body of the Buddha.

In this context, it is good to give attention to an incident from a past life of the Blessed One.

At that time, working for the welfare of the world as a bodhisattva and fulfilling his karmic perfections, he was living the life of a bodhisattva by the name of Śarabhaṃga. Once he was giving a Dharma talk to the kings Aṭṭhak, Ugratej of Kaliṃga, and Bhīmarath. While they were listening to this talk, there arose in the minds of the three kings a strong urge to practice the Dharma, and at that very moment all clinging to the enjoyments of sexual pleasure was eradicated from their minds. Having seen this with his power of reading the minds of others, the bodhisattva Śarabhaṃga was delighted and said:

> *mahattiyaṃ āgamanaṃ ahosi, tavam Aṭṭhakā*
> *Bhīmarathassa cāpi.*
> *Kāliṅgarājassa ca Uggatassa, sabbesa vo kāmarāgo pahīno.*

> It was a great thing that all of your attachment to the enjoyments of sexual pleasure, and that of Bhīmaratha and Ugratej the King of Kaliṃga, was eradicated. (*The Past Lives of the Buddha* 2.17.86, *The Story of Sarabhaṅga*)[262]

When they heard this, the three kings were astonished. How could the bodhisattva know their present state of mind? They requested that they might be given an opportunity to attain such an ability. Then the bodhisattva said:

> *karomi okāsam anuggahāya, tathā hi vo kāmarāgo pahīno.*
> *pharātha kāyaṃ vipulāya pītiyā, yathā gatiṃ me*
> *abhisambhavetha.*

> As your attachment to sexual pleasure was abandoned instantaneously, I am obliged to provide you an opportunity to renounce. Pervade your entire body with immense rapture, and let that energy extend out so that you can experience my state. (*The Past Lives of the Buddha* 2.17.88, *The Story of Sarabhaṅga*)[263]

Through the practice of vipaśyanā meditation, energetic vibrations arise throughout the body, as if a stream of tiny wavelets is flowing. As soon as meditators experience such a state for themselves, they can partake of the same state as their teacher, since the teacher is also in a state in which he is experiencing such energetic vibrations. This is how a meditation practitioner has a vision, constituted by Dharma, of his teacher. Making this the goal, the Blessed One states:

> *yo kho, Vakkali, dhammaṃ passati so maṃ passati; yo maṃ passati so dhammaṃ passati.*

> Vakkali, whoever sees the Dharma sees me. Whoever sees me sees the Dharma. (*The Connected Discourses* 2.3.87, *Discourse to Vakkali*)[264]

This is the vision of the Buddha's Dharma-body, which is entirely distinct from a vision of his physical body. At a high level of meditation, this vision of the Dharma-body brings benefit to a meditation practitioner. A vision of the physical body, that is the material body, is merely an externally attractive symbol.

The Difference between the Dharma-body and the Material Body [of the Buddha]

One incident:

At one time the Blessed One was wandering between Ukkaṭṭhā and Setavya. He always walked with bare feet. The earth on which he was walking was flat and soft. Both the soles of the Blessed One's feet were also flat. In them were stamped wheels, each with a hub and one thousand spokes. These marks on his feet were clearly imprinted on the soft earth. A brahmin by the name of Droṇa saw the marks in the footprints and was greatly amazed: "How wonderful, how remarkable! Certainly this cannot be the foot of a human being. Let me see who the person is that has these footprints."

Eager to know about this, he came to the source of the footprints, and there was the Blessed One at the base of a tree, deep in meditation. Droṇa looked unblinkingly at the Blessed One. He had never before seen a person with such marks on his body: "This is truly no ordinary person." Then, out of curiosity, he questioned the Blessed One:

devo no bhavaṃ bhavissati?—Might you be a deity?
na kho ahaṃ, brāhmaṇa, devo bhavissāmi—Brahmin, I am not a deity.
gandhabbo no bhavaṃ bhavissati?— Might you be a *gandharva* (a celestial musician)?
na kho ahaṃ, brāhmaṇa, gandhabbo bhavissāmi—Brahmin, I am not a gandharva.
yakkho no bhavaṃ bhavissati?— Might you be a spirit?
na kho ahaṃ, brāhmaṇa, yakkho bhavissāmi—Brahmin, I am not a spirit.
manusso no bhavaṃ bhavissati?— Might you be a human?
na kho ahaṃ, brāhmaṇa, manusso bhavissāmi—Brahmin, I am not a human.

"If you are not a deity, a gandharva, a spirit or a human, then what are you?"
buddho ti maṃ, brāhmaṇa, dhārehi—Brahmin, know me as the Buddha.[265]

The Blessed One responded precisely. Because it is the highest point in the entire universe, it is known as the pinnacle of existence. All mortal beings, from the highest brahmas of the immaterial brahma realms to the lower realms—including those of deities and humans—are being crushed in the wheel of existence. A fully awakened buddha, on the other hand, has become liberated from the wheel of existence. This is his final birth.

> *natth' idāni punabbhavo ti.*
>
> After this, there is no additional birth. (*The Connected Discourses* 3.5.498, *Discourse on the Enlightened One*)[266]

It is not proper for such a liberated person to call himself a deity, a gandharva, a spirit, a brahma, or a human, as such beings are mortal. A buddha is liberated and therefore unique; he is distinct from others. He is not involved in the flow of existence, as others are.

> *puṇḍarīkaṃ yathā vaggu, toyena n' upalippati,*
> *n' upalippāmi lokena, tasmā buddho 'smi brāhmaṇā.*
>
> Just as a beautiful lotus is not besmeared in water, so also I am not besmeared in the world. Therefore, Brahmin, I am a buddha. (*The Numerical Discourses* 1.4.36, *Discourse to Doṇa*)[267]

The Difference between [a Buddha] and a Wheel-Turning Monarch

A wheel-turning monarch also has the mark of a wheel with one thousand spokes on the flat soles of his feet. A person seeing such a footprint in the earth might similarly ask, "Who are you?" Yet how could he say, "I am not a human being," when he is still subject to mortality? He is still, indeed, ensconced in the wheel of existence.

This is the particularity of a buddha. When the body of enlightenment—that is, the Dharma-body—is awakened in the material body of the bodhisattva at the base of the tree of enlightenment, the bodhisattva becomes a fully enlightened buddha. This is what makes him a manifestation of Dharma. This is why he is in a state above ordinary living beings, supreme among them, distinct from them. This is because of all of the qualities of a buddha. The qualities of the Buddha are the Buddha's Dharma-body. A vision of the qualities of the Buddha is a vision of the Buddha himself. A vision of the Buddha is a vision of the Dharma.

What Are the Qualities of a Buddha?

The qualities of the Buddha are manifold, but nine among them[268] are the primary causes for his becoming world-famous. They are the reasons why the Buddha will be remembered in human history and why he became so well known during his own lifetime. The reputation of the Blessed Buddha spread so much, even in his lifetime, that merely upon hearing of his renown, and without seeing him, people were drawn to him. Even many of those who were drawn to him so as to counter [his teachings] became his followers.

The reputation of other teachers of those days also spread, but the Buddha's reputation is different from the panegyrical reputations of those teachers. All of them were celebrated panegyrically in the following way:

> *ayaṃ, deva, Makkhali Gosālo saṅghī ceva gaṇī ca gaṇācariyo ca, ñāto, yasassī, titthakaro, sādhusammato bahujanassa, rattaññū, cirapabbajito, addhagato, vayo-anuppatto.*
>
> Great king, this Makkhali Ghoṣāl is the leader of a community, the leader of a group, the teacher of a group; he is well known, famous, a guide, respected greatly by many people, with many years of experience, having renounced social life a long time ago. He is a senior who has traveled far on the path of life. (*The Long Discourses* 1.152, *The Discourse on the Fruits of Asceticism*)[269]

Whoever has not properly and fully understood the actual qualities of the Blessed One, because of their wrong and incomplete understanding, might think—like a certain ascetic wanderer, Sabhiya—that:

> *ayam pi kho samaṇo Gotamo saṅghī ceva gaṇī ca gaṇācariyo ca, ñāto, yasassī, titthakaro, sādhusammato bahujanassa...*
> This ascetic Gautama is the leader of a community, the leader of a group, the teacher of a group; he is well known, famous, a guide, respected greatly by many people...

Those who understood did not assess the Blessed One on the basis of these qualities. But Sabhiya was ignorant, and so he grouped the qualities of the Blessed One with the panegyrics of other teachers, even though he could see that the ascetic Gautama was much younger than they were. Other teachers were old and developed, patriarchs of a ripe old age:

> *jiṇṇā vuḍḍhā mahallakā addhagatā vayoanuppattā.*

On the other hand,

> *samaṇo Gotamo daharo ceva jātiyā, navo ca pabbajāya.*

> Ascetic Gautama (in comparison) is young and new to renunciation.

Will he be able to answer my questions when these other senior, experienced teachers cannot? But then the following came into his mind:

> *daharo pi cesa samaṇo Gotamo mahiddhiko hoti,*
> *mahānubhavo.*

> However young the ascetic Gautama might be, he is very powerful and a great glorious meditator. (*The Suttanipāta* 3.6, *Discourse to Sabhiya*)[270]

"In that case, [thought Sabhiya], why don't I see if I can question him?" In the eyes of the ascetic wanderer Sabhiya, it was important that the Blessed Buddha was the leader of a community, famous, and so forth. Since he was of lesser age and experience, he was deficient. Stuck in this state of confusion, Sabhiya had heard nothing about the actual qualities of the Buddha. Knowledge of these qualities would be for him an encounter with the Blessed One. Since he had not come in contact with the Blessed One, he remained under the delusion that he was like other teachers, [since he was] a leader of a community, famous, and so forth. He did not understand how much greater than these ordinary qualities the actual qualities of the Buddha are.

The king of Koshala, Prasenjit, was also uneasy about the deficiency of the Blessed One's young age. Then, upon crossing paths with the Blessed One and witnessing the clarity with which he spoke, Prasenjit proclaimed:

> These ascetics and brahmins are each leaders of a community, leaders of a group, teachers of a group; they are well known, famous, guides who are worshipped by many people and have lived long lives. But one does not attain full perfect enlightenment merely by having these characteristics.

So, with them

> *te pi mayā anuttaraṃ sammāsambodhiṃ abhisambuddho ti paṭijānāthā ti puṭṭhā samānā.*

Upon being asked whether they have attained the knowledge of unsurpassed full perfect enlightenment,

They give this answer:

anuttaraṃ sammāsambodhiṃ abhisambuddho ti na paṭijānanti.

The knowledge of unsurpassed full perfect enlightenment has not been attained.

And then:

kiṃ pana bhavaṃ Gotamo daharo ceva jātiyā navo ca pabbajāya.

You, Gautama, are young, new to renunciation. So how can you make this claim? (*The Connected Discourses* 1.1.112, *Discourse on the Young*)[271]

After close contact for many years, Prasenjit's doubts disappeared because he had understood and tested the actual qualities of the Blessed One in various encounters. When he had matured in age and established a Dharma relationship with the Blessed One, he would speak of him with praise:

sammāsambuddho bhagavā—He is a Blessed One, a full and perfectly enlightened person.
svakkhāto bhagavatā dhammo—The Dharma of the Blessed One is well stated.
suppaṭipanno bhagavato sāvakasaṅgho—The community of disciples of the Blessed One is well practiced.

There are three yardsticks to assess any guide—that is, a teacher:

1. How is the guide himself? Has he experienced for himself what he teaches?
2. How is his Dharma taught? Is it clear so that anyone can understand it and get benefit from applying it? Alternatively, is it entangled with the speculative beliefs of sectarian dogma that are based on blind faith?
3. How are his disciples? Are they actually following his teachings? Or are they exploiting people with a sectarian con?[272]

We will find extensive answers to these three questions in the Tipiṭaka. Now, we will catch merely a few glimpses of them.

First let us take a bird's-eye view of the Blessed One's nine qualities, on the basis of which he became *dhammakāyo* [one whose body is Dharma], *dhammabhūto* [Dharma manifest], *brahmakāyo* [one whose body is Brahman], *brahmabhūto* [Brahman manifest]; *cakkhubhūto* [vision manifest], and *ñāṇabhūto* [knowledge manifest].

These nine primary qualities of the Buddha were certainly well known to people during his own lifetime, and they are the reason that the Blessed Buddha became world renowned. The nine qualities were:

iti pi so bhagavā arahaṃ sammāsambuddho vijjācaraṇasampanno sugato lokavidū anuttaro purisadammasārathi satthā devamanussānaṃ buddho bhagavā ti.

Let us use the evidence of his beneficial teachings to make an exploration of this panegyric of the qualities of the Buddha and take a look at some of their delightful portrayals.

CHAPTER 14

The Land of My Birth

from *Blessed Baba!*

Blessed Baba! *is one of S.N. Goenka's autobiographical works. Published in 2002, it contains reminiscences of his early life in Burma and reflections on how his family ended up emigrating there from India. The work is structured around a series of poetic couplets in Goenka's Rajasthani mother tongue. They are dedicated to his grandfather, Basesarlal Goenka, whom he called Baba. The opening pages of the book, in which Goenka imagines his grandfather's journey over land and sea to seek a livelihood in Burma and then describes in florid detail the beauty of the land in which he himself was born, are presented here.*[273]

You Happily Made a Home of Burma

I look out through the window of the past, and a lovely imaginary vision rises to the surface of my mind. It is a vision of a historical event that took place 125 years ago.

An eager young man, around the age of eighteen, set out from the city of Churu in the state of Bikaner on a difficult journey to an unknown country far away. The journey was truly difficult. But the young man's untamed eagerness drove him on, step by step. In those days, there was no train to Churu. So, at times on foot and at times riding a camel, by way of sandy desert roads, he left the state of Bikaner and came to a railway station of the British colonial government. From this remote station, he caught a train departing for Calcutta [now Kolkata]. This was the young man's first journey. He left home for the first time in his life—going out to seek a livelihood—and came to Calcutta. Many people from Churu and its environs were living and working there. He also could have stayed there had he wanted to. But he felt some invisible force urging him to go farther. Next came a long and perilous ocean journey. The young man had never before traveled by rail or boat. Nevertheless, because of his extraordinary eagerness and firm resolve, he completed what was in those days a long, perilous journey on a small vessel and came to Rangoon [now Yangon].

As soon as this vision forms in the imagination, a couplet comes to mind:

> *dar kūṃcā dar maṃjalāṃ, dar cālyo parādes* |
> *kit Barmā kit murdharā, jaṃgalā maṃgalā des* ||

> From one lane to the next, from one destination to the next, constantly braving difficulty, he proceeded [to a foreign land]. Crossing that inhospitable barren land of Marwar, he took a contented breath upon arriving in an auspicious, hospitable land, that verdant jungle of Burma.

Then another couplet breaks through the surface of the mind:

> *kālī kosāṃ āviyo, pāyo kasṭ anek* |
> *potā to sukh pāviyā, milī Dharam rī ṭek* ||

> In making such a long difficult journey, you risked great peril. But the result of this is that your descendants got

the auspicious ground of beneficent pure Dharma. They became happy.

In this connection, another couplet breaks through:

aur des jā biṇājatā, dhan to pātā bhot |
paṇ Bābā! Birmā binā, kaṭhai Dharam rī jot ||

If you had settled in some other country, you would still have earned abundant wealth because of your hereditary skill in trade and your hard work. But without Burma, how would your descendants have attained the light of pure Dharma in the form of vipaśyanā?

The wisdom of vipaśyanā, which brings welfare to all and gives immediate results, had not only completely disappeared from India, the land of your birth, but also from the other places where it had gone in times past. Only the saints of this one Dharma country, Burma, preserved it in its pure form for centuries. Because Baba settled in Burma, I was born in this Dharma land. Otherwise, I might have continued to take birth after birth somewhere away from contact with True Dharma.

In the mythological books of India, it was said that taking an ocean voyage was a faulty thing to do.[274] However, you violated this prohibition and crossed the ocean. Only because of that were we able to attain this beneficent vipaśyanā, the True Dharma. Inspired by these feelings, another couplet emerges:

sāṃc Dharam sai dūr hī, hotā jaḷm anek |
jai Bābo nā toḍto, kāḷai pānī rekh ||

Another couplet arises in connection with this one:

Bābā! raito bhaṭkato, lakh corāsī jūn |
hoto pramukh pradhān nit, āṭo pāṇī lūṇ ||

If one does not attain the True Dharma, certainly that person continues to wander in 840,000 wombs, with the sole aim of seeking out sustenance—flour, water, and salt—to fill the belly. Because of this, that person remains unaware that there is a high spiritual wisdom that supplies us with the nectar of the deathless.

In expression of gratitude for Baba's boundless beneficence, another couplet reverberates:

Bābā terai kāraṇai, pāyo subaraṇ des |
an dhan rā toḍā nahīṃ, milgyo Dharam ases ||

Baba! Because of you we came to reside in this Golden Land (Suvarṇabhūmi). We enjoyed enough food and resources, and here we also got the great opportunity to attain Dharma in its completeness.

The completeness of Dharma does not come simply from obeying morality. It does not come from getting absorbed in deep concentration. Rather, the completeness of Dharma comes only from engaging in vipaśyanā, which is awakening to wisdom constituted through direct knowledge and through which one completely uproots rebirth-producing karmic forces—in the form of dormant defilements—collected and stored up in the subconscious mind in many births. This is the complete Dharma that we were able to attain here.

With reference to this, another couplet emerges:

Buddhă Dharam ar Saṃgh par, sraddhā jagī aṭūṭ |
Bābā! milī vipassanā, pīyūṃ imarat ghūṃṭ ||

> What an ignorance-filled life it was, with respect to the Buddha and his teaching! Upon the discovery of vipaśyanā, indestructible faith for the Buddha, the Dharma, and the Sangha was awakened.

Faith in the Buddha was not awakened because, through repeated prostrations to a statue of him, or through repeatedly reciting his name, or through singing songs of praise to him with an attitude of devotional surrender, he will become pleased and liberate me from the suffering of existence. Rather, it was awakened because he discovered a form of wisdom such as vipaśyanā, which brings swift results. Becoming liberated himself through this wisdom, by teaching it, he paved the path of liberation—which is scientific and brings welfare to all—for others.

Faith in the Dharma was awakened, not because there is a ritual order [to follow] in the name of Dharma, not because of some wrongly held philosophical belief based on blind trust, not because of some deceitful program to confine people within a sectarian enclosure, and not because of the outcome of mere acceptance at the level of faith or intellect of a theoretical tenet of Dharma. Rather, it was awakened because all importance was given to the practical aspect, so that Dharma might be taken up, so that it might enter one's daily life and become part of one's life.

Faith in the community [of the Buddha's disciples] was not awakened because these people are associated with our sect. Rather, it happened because these people have taken up Dharma and are living ideal lives. Such dharmic persons, whether they are renunciants or householders, are indeed the community (*saṃgha*). They are saints. As such they are worthy of worship.

Morality and concentration can also be attained by other means. But one remains far from vipaśyanā, which is constituted by wisdom. One remains far from the nectar of the deathless, [the nectar] of liberation from existence.

When one plunges into the confluence of [the three streams of] morality, concentration, and wisdom, one attains the invaluable gem of liberation, the true fruit and true form of complete Dharma.

sīl samādhi gyān rā, ratan milyā anmol |
Bābā! dāḷad miṭ gayā, suphaḷ huī yā khoḷ ||

Through the attainment of worldly wealth, one escapes worldly poverty. But, Baba, even the [more elemental] poverty of suffering while wandering through existence after existence is removed by attaining the invaluable gem of the complete Dharma!

This human birth truly becomes fruitful only when one obtains these three gems and is able to access liberation from existence.

In acknowledgment of gratitude for Baba's beneficence, another couplet peels off:

the Birmā bhal bāsiyo, sārā miṭgyā sok |
Bābā! donūṃ sudhargyā, lok aur paralok ||

Baba! If you had settled somewhere else, you would have earned much wealth and happily accepted the erroneous aim of this-worldly advancement. But you chose this country of Dharma, where [you] in fact advanced in both this-worldly and otherworldly spheres, and where all the suffering of existence after existence is eradicated.

As I become animated with this feeling, another couplet flits into the mind:

cāṃdī sā cāvaḷ aṭhai, īṃ sonai rai des |
tīn ratan jagmag jagai, gūṃjai budh saṃdes ||

This Golden Land, which yields abundant wealth, is replete with enough resources to remove worldly suffering. But three invaluable jewels—in the form of the Buddha, the Dharma, and the Community [of Disciples]—also continue to sparkle in this country. The words of the Buddha continue to reverberate here on the earth and in the sky, and those who obey these words find deliverance from the suffering of repeated existence. The gem of the Buddha is itself included in the words of the Buddha.

And further:

Bābā! Birmā bās kar, karyo dhaṇo kalyāṇ |
Buddh Dharam Saṃgh rī, saraṇ milī sukh khān ||

Truly, Baba, how beneficent you were to us! You settled in this Dharma country so that, by taking refuge in the Buddha, the Dharma, and the Community [of Disciples], we got the treasure of supreme happiness. Truly life has become enriched.

Remembering Baba's abundant beneficence, a cloud of boundless gratitude thickens in the sky of the mind:

tero pun puratāp hai, vā rai Bābā vāh |
sut potā paḍpotarā, paḍyā Dharam rī rāh ||

Truly, Baba, because of your glorious merit, your children, grandchildren, and great-grandchildren have become travelers on the auspicious path of pure Dharma.

As I become inspired by these feelings [of gratitude], another couplet forms:

pāṃc pīḍhiyāṃ tar gayīṃ, sāṃc Dharam rai pāṇ |
āgai nai tirasī kitī? Bābā! putr mahān ||

Thanks to you, we have been walking on the path of pure Dharma, and it has crossed five generations [of our family]. Is there any doubt as to how much further it might reach in the future? This is indeed the glorious result of your great merit.

Mother, Land of My Birth

How much love does one feel for one's birth mother? In the same way, one feels such love for the land in which one is born, one's native soil. The magnificence of both is like heaven. The land of my birth is indeed magnificent like heaven. It seems to me that it is as beautiful as the Grove of Delight in heaven. Overcome by this feeling, a couplet forms:

yadi dhartī par surag hai, Naṃdanvan surdhām |
to Bābā! Birmā jiso, aur na des lalām ||

Baba! If someone were to say that there is indeed a deity realm—including a Grove of Delight—on earth, what country other than Burma could they be praising?

Truly, if there is a heaven on earth and a Grove of Delight in heaven, Burma is indeed it. There is no other country like it.

Another couplet flickers into being in connection with the glory of the land of my birth:

Mahāmuni rī saraṇ maṃh, ratanpuṃj so dhām |
jaḷmabhūm Bābā milī, kisī' k sukhad lalām ||

Baba, my destiny awoke when I attained as the place of my birth a city such as Mandalay, the capital city—the jewel in the crown—of the Burmese king. It is truly an abode of Dharma, a holy place of pilgrimage. This is so because of the holy vibrations of going for refuge that pervade the pure, peaceful atmosphere of the ancient temple of Mahamuni Buddha. They fill mind and body with thrilling shivers. They flow in a tide of holy waves of rapture and delight-filled happiness. It is very beautiful, very delightful!

With a feeling of gratitude toward the land of my birth, another inspired verse surfaces:

Sveḍagon maṃdir bhalo, Birmā bhalo sudes |
Bābā! bhalī vipassanā, bhalo Buddh saṃdes ||

Among countries, Burma is the most wonderful. It is truly excellent, unparalleled. This is because it has the excellent, unparalleled Shwedagon Pagoda, where the remains of the Blessed Gautama Buddha and the holy relics of the three other buddhas of this aeon are enshrined. In every village and every city, in the homes of householders and in the monasteries of monks, the auspicious words of the Buddha's true instructions continue to reverberate throughout the country. And beyond all of this, the beneficial wisdom of vipaśyanā—sought out and disseminated by the Blessed

Buddha—was saved and preserved in this country in its pure form for millenia.

With reference to this, therefore, another couplet materializes:

īṃ dhartī rai garbh maṃh, bharyā ratan āgār |
paṇ Bābā! anămol to, Dharam ratan bhaṃḍār ||

How abundant is this land of my birth, this beautiful treasure mine filled with a hidden treasure—the most valuable diamonds, emeralds, and jewels. But the most special resource of all here is the invaluable gem of the Dharma.

How could one assign a value to it? Because of this gem, my motherland is the wealthiest place in the universe.

Baba! I have traveled the earth many times in the service of trade and commerce. I have seen many countries. It is difficult to account for the beauty of the many countries of the world, but nowhere have I found beauty like that of my motherland. Moved by this supreme beauty, this couplet surfaces:

dekhyā des-disāvarāṃ, phiryo ghaṇā pardes |
paṇ Bābā! Birmā jiso, milyo na manahar des ||

Fortunately, since childhood, I have had many opportunities to explore my motherland. At the age of twelve, we went to Kalaw in the beautiful hills of Shan State to refresh ourselves from [the heat of] Mandalay, and between the ages of twelve and eighteen, I traveled from Mandalay to Maymyo (Pyin Oo Lwin) many times. Once I also took a journey from Nawnghkio to Goke Hteik. The views of the beautiful mountains and plateaus made a deep impression on my mind. As a student, between the ages of twelve and sixteen,

I would travel to Myitkyina and celebrate the holiday of the hot season with my eldest brother. I would go to bathe on the banks of the murmuring Irrawaddy (Ayeyarwady) River, flowing down from the high peaks of the Himalayas. The river's course was not very wide before the beginning of the rainy season. The bank of the river was filled with large rocks—worn smooth by the river—from the paths on the hills along the river. These rocks would show clearly through the pure, translucent water. My mind would fill with delight when I would dip into the fast-flowing river there. When I returned to Mandalay, the Irrawaddy River would become enormous. In the rainy season, its path became very wide, its current became very fast, and it became very dangerous. Nonetheless, I never tired of dipping into it again and again. I also took delightful journeys along this beautiful river, traveling to Minbu, Magway, Alamyo, Bagan, and Prome (Pyay) by boat. These trips left lovely impressions on the surface of the mind that remain to this day. How alluring!

A train journey from Mandalay to Monywa; by boat from Monywa to Kalewa on the Chindwin River; the long journey from Kalewa to Tamu, sometimes sitting on a bullock cart and sometimes walking alongside it. How inclement it was, and yet this journey in the unseen parts of my country touched my heart. The impression from this journey of the past in the northwestern region of the country will remain seared on the surface of the mind.

Similarly, there are alluring memories of visiting Hinthada, Pathein, Bago, and Mawlamyine in the South. They have also become like adamant on the surface of the mind. Praise is sung of the delightful visions of the openhanded abundance provided by the magnanimous natural environment of my motherland, with its flowing wheat fields lined with various types of fruit-laden trees spreading out across it far and wide, its "brilliant waters," "abundant orchards," and "rich dark fields."[275] Such fertility and natural wealth may be seen in beautiful abundance in other countries as well, but none is a match for my motherland. This earthly body of mine has been formed from the dust of its earth, its food and water, its fruits and flowers. The holy vibrations of this sacred land gave me life. How could the land of any other country match it?

It is natural for my heart to feel boundless attraction and a strong sense of attachment toward that piece of earth where I took birth, where my umbilical cord was cut and the train left the station. But when one also gets to take a second birth on that land and become twice-born, boundless gratitude arises.[276] My second birth occurred in this Brahma-land. In the first birth, I came out of my mother's womb. In the second, I got to break the shell of ignorance at Sayagyi U Ba Khin's vipaśyanā meditation center on Inya Myaing Road. What can I say about that second birth? I got this second birth in my motherland, Burma. This was my actual birth. It is just like when a bird takes birth from its mother's belly in the form of an egg. Its real birth is when it breaks the shell of the egg and emerges from it. For this reason, we refer to it as twice-born. We refer to it as a being that has been born two times. In the same way, when I broke the shell of ignorance and emerged from it through the practice of vipaśyanā—thanks to the benevolence of my teacher—at that time my second birth occurred. It was a real birth. With my good fortune, I became a twice-born. Where else in the world besides this beneficial land might I have attained such a second birth? I am very grateful, therefore, to this holy land of my birth. I am very grateful to my Dharma-father, Sayagyi U Ba Khin.

CHAPTER 15

The Floodgates of Dhamma Open

from the *Vipassana Newsletter* (May 1997)

When he first arrived in India to teach vipaśyanā, S.N. Goenka taught entirely in Hindi. In no time, however, he was providing guidance in English to a range of foreign students, most of whom were hippies from America and Europe. In this article from the Vipassana Newsletter, *Goenka recounts the first course in which he gave a formal Dharma talk in English, and some of the forces he had to deal with in that moment.*[277]

SAYAGYI U BA KHIN, my revered teacher, strongly believed that 2,500 years after the Buddha's *mahāparinibbāṇa* (final passing away of the Enlightened Ones), the second *Buddha-sāsana* (cycle of teaching) will start again in the land of its origin, and from there spread throughout the world for the boundless benefit of humankind.

Dhamma will again arise with the practice of vipassana. For millennia, Vipassana was lost to India. But it was preserved in its pristine purity in Myanmar (Burma).

Close to the end of this 2,500-year period, the historical Sixth Council was held from 1954 to 1956 in Yangon (Rangoon). It was during this time—from September 1 to 11, 1955—that I got my Dhamma birth. I sat my first Vipassana course.

After benefitting me immeasurably for fourteen years, vipassana returned to India on June 22, 1969, with the blessings of my teacher. An interval of about two thousand years had passed. In spite of all the self-doubts about my ability, Dhamma started to take root in India.

I am merely a medium. Dhamma is doing its own work. "The clock of Vipassana has struck," Sayagyi often said. "At this time, many people endowed with abundant pāramitā have been born in India and in the other countries of the world. The ticking of this vipassana clock will attract these people towards Dhamma."

So it happened. Innumerable people from different countries, religions, beliefs started participating in courses. So too did leaders of various religions. All of them accepted this technique as their own; none of them felt that it was alien.

These initial Vipassana courses were taught only in Hindi, since the majority of courses were held in North India. After a few months, a few Westerners also started participating in these courses.

After giving the Dhamma talk in Hindi, I used to give them a five- or ten-minute discourse summary and instructions. These students were very hard working, and this brief guidance was enough for them to achieve surprisingly good results.

Gradually, words of praise of vipassana spread amongst Western travelers. A year later, a group of tourists staying at Dalhousie requested me to come there and conduct a course exclusively for them.

It was difficult for me. The entire course would have to be conducted in English. To talk a few English sentences of guidance and to clear their doubts would have been simple. But to give an hour-long discourse fluently in English, or to give long, inspirational instructions throughout the day, as I did in Hindi, was impossible for me.

In Rangoon, I used to read out a written speech whenever I had to give a talk in English as president of the Chamber of Commerce and Industry, or at any important public function. I neither had the experience nor the ability to give a talk in English without reading from a text.

And a talk on meditation, in which I have to give English equivalents of technical terms of Indian spiritual traditions, was even more difficult for me.

So I expressed my inability to conduct a course in English and advised them to keep joining courses conducted in Hindi in small numbers. They argued that whereas Hindi-speaking students benefited greatly from the inspiring discourses and instructions, the foreign students were deprived of this benefit. Besides, they were convinced I knew enough English to conduct the course.

When I still refused, they contacted Sayagyi U Ba Khin and complained to him about me. "Sir, outside Burma, only one of your representatives is teaching this technique, and he is not accepting our request," they told him. "Where can we go to learn this technique?"

Besides, in those days, one could not get a visa to Burma for more than three days. So they pleaded with Sayagyi that he should order me to conduct courses in English.

I was in Bombay then. My revered teacher telephoned me and ordered that I should go to Dalhousie to conduct that course. He told me with loving firmness, "You must go. Whatever English you know will be enough. You will be successful. Dhamma will help. All my mettā is with you." After getting such a powerful reassurance, I went to Dalhousie.

I had nothing against going to Dalhousie. In fact, I had reasons to look forward to the trip. This would be my first course in the lap of the Himalayas. Sayagyi used to say, "Who knows how long in how many lives we have meditated in the serene caves of the Himalayas?"

That is why on reaching there, my mind was filled with rapture. My self-doubts began to melt.

The course started. For the first two days, while sitting on the Dhamma seat, I experienced an inexplicable feeling of suffocation. As a result, I was unable to speak for more than fifteen minutes the first evening.

On the second evening, I had to struggle to speak for about twenty-five minutes. I felt suffocated again. Although I found no cause for it in the surface layers of my mind, I felt that maybe the inferiority complex of having trouble speaking English was creating obstacles at the deepest level.

But the actual cause turned out to be something else. This was a small course with eleven students. It was conducted in a little bungalow called Shanti Kutir. The group sittings and discourses were held in a small room. The student who had invited me for the course lived in the adjacent room.

On the third day, I felt strong, impure, anti-Dhamma flowing from that room and polluting the adjacent meditation room.

With the pure vibrations of the Himalayas on the one hand and the powerful mettā of my revered teacher on the other hand, I could not understand what could cause these anti-Dhamma vibrations.

That afternoon, when I went to that room to check the student, I was startled to see a human skull on his table. Nearby was a blood-stained *khūkhrī* [curved knife used by Gurkhas].

The student explained he was the disciple of some local tantric [member of a mystical cult]. Only three nights ago he had gone to the cremation ground and had made an animal sacrifice with this khūkhrī as part of a tantric ritual. His guru had told him that his meditation would be very successful if he kept the skull and khūkhrī close to him.

Now I understood the cause of the suffocating, negative vibrations pervading the meditation room. Only after much persuasion by me did he throw that khūkhrī and skull in some cavern far away. And only then was the anti-Dhamma force eliminated from Shanti Kutir.

That afternoon, I meditated on the Dhamma seat for a long time. The time for the evening discourse approached. I saw that the entire atmosphere, washed by the purifying waves of the breeze from the Himalayas, had become even purer with the mettā-filled Dhamma vibrations from my revered teacher.

Just a few moments before the start of the discourse, Dhamma vibrations flooded my being through the top of the head. I began the discourse, and I found I spoke English as fluently as I speak Hindi. I spoke for an entire hour.[278]

After the five-minute break, I gave long instructions with the same fluency. I could see that all meditators—male and female—were absorbed in deep meditation. At 9:00 P.M., when the day ended, their faces were radiant. I was wonderstruck.

It was Sayagyi's mettā that gave me the Dhamma strength to turn what seemed impossible to possible. The first-ever vipassana course in English became successful. What Dhamma desired happened.

After this, all courses were bilingual. Daily, I gave Hindi discourses in the morning and English discourses in the evening. Instructions too were bilingual.

More courses and courses with more students were conducted. The number of foreign students progressively increased. Courses in places like Bodh Gaya, Kushinagar, Varanasi, and Rajagir had almost only foreign students. Word spread to many Western countries. Groups of foreigners came to learn Vipassana. With courses often running full, many had to wait for the next course.

In a few years, thousands from about eighty countries came for Vipassana courses. Students came from neighboring Sri Lanka and Thailand. The time had come for the prophecy and Dhamma wish of Sayagyi to come true.

Vipassana will spread throughout the world. Perhaps that is why it became possible to conduct courses in English. Without this, Vipassana would not have spread among the people of foreign countries.

I felt contented. The Vipassana floodgates had opened, and the infinitely beneficial Ganges of Dhamma also flowed to students outside India, to the world.

CHAPTER 16

On Concentration (*Samādhi*)

from a Dharma Talk on Day Ten of a Thirty-Day Meditation Course at Dhamma Giri, Igatpuri (1989)

The question of the role of jhāna, states of deep concentrated absorption, in S.N. Goenka's teachings is somewhat controversial. Goenka often dissuaded his students from getting involved in practice traditions that make jhāna a requisite for the practice of vipaśyanā. Goenka's teachers, Sayagyi U Ba Khin and Mother Sayama, trained many of their students in jhāna, but they also made a clear distinction between such states and states of liberatory wisdom. The logic of the relationship between the practice of deep states of concentrated absorption and the practice of insight into the nature of reality in Goenka's teaching model is laid out here in a somewhat technical Dharma talk from one of Goenka's advanced courses.

...[279] One gets progressively liberated from misery as one proceeds on the path, and ultimately one reaches the stage where there is no more misery. The path of paññā [wisdom] is for that purpose. Even when one starts practicing sīla [morality], practicing samādhi [concentration] in the proper way, one starts coming out of misery little by little. When one starts practicing paññā, one starts eradicating the misery at the deeper levels of the mind, and as the cause of the misery gets eradicated for the root level, it becomes easy for someone to reach the final goal where there is no more misery, because the cause of misery is totally eradicated.

This is what an enlightened person does. He rediscovers the path, the path of liberation. He purifies the path so that people walk on the pure path without getting deviated here or there. It becomes easy for the people who work seriously to come out of misery because the path has now been made very clear.

Between one *sammāsambuddha* [perfectly self-enlightened buddha] and another sammāsambuddha, there is such a big interval, such a big gap of period, that people lose the real path. Only the words remain. And also the echo of the words remains. Most of the time it is misinterpreted and creates confusion, because the period between one sammāsambuddha and another is so much, so great. And there are *kalpas* [eons; Pali: *kappa*] where there is no sammāsambuddha at all. There are kalpas where there is only one sammāsambuddha.

Fortunately, this is the *bhaddakappa* [auspicious eon], where you have five sammāsambuddhas; the fourth one passed away twenty-five hundred years ago. Another will be coming later on. But when we say, "later on," such a big interval. So also the interval between the third and the fourth, such a big interval, such a big gap. The echo of the teaching remains. People accept the fact that we must live the life of sīla; this is accepted. People accept the fact that we must develop mastery over our mind. This acceptance is there. People accept the fact that we must get our mind purified, eradicate the impurities, the craving, the aversion.

So although the actual teaching in detail, the practice in detail, gets lost, still a general outline is there that sometimes gets polluted, distorted. Words do not carry the meaning they originally carried.

And because the practice is lost, people cannot get any benefit even if the words remain. . . .[280]

Every part of Dhamma should grow simultaneously to reach the final goal. This gets lost during this period, this interval, the long interval. Samādhi is essential. All right, one starts practicing samādhi. The first jhāna, the second jhāna, the third jhāna, the fourth jhāna—very meticulously, very seriously, one is practicing. And then the fifth, the sixth, the seventh, the eighth. But a slight deviation is made. If the goal is one hundred thousand miles away and there is a straight road to that, [if] you deviate just one inch at the starting point, you will not only miss the goal, you will be miles away from the goal. And this is what happens.

The first jhāna to the eighth jhāna, the purpose of jhāna is lost. The purpose of sīla is that you should abstain from all physical and vocal unwholesome actions because such unwholesome actions are performed by generating impurity in the mind. You don't kill a visible being, and, on the other hand, when you see a visible being, you develop so much mettā, so much compassion, love: "A miserable being, how can I kill?" You feel like saving this being. So *cāritta* [acting], *vāritta* [abstaining]: In both ways the sīla develops. And that helps you to develop your samādhi, [the] proper way of concentrating the mind. And if it is properly done, then that helps you to develop your paññā.

But if all that is lost, then the aim of samādhi is just to get the mind concentrated, from [the] first jhāna to [the] eighth jhāna—deep absorption samādhi. Paññā is missing. A buddha finds that out. He practices all the different things that are common to the society at that time, tortures his body to any extent, to a great extent, and finds nothing. [He] practices jhāna, all eight jhānas, and finds that he is still not liberated; something [is] wrong.

Then [he] finds out the reason. He changes the whole technique of eight jhānas. Even from the first jhāna, *sampajañña* [awareness of impermanence] starts. By the time one reaches the third or fourth jhāna, one becomes perfect in sampajañña. Paññā is there. Otherwise, mere concentration, mere concentration, will give good results. One will get birth in a *rūpabrahma-loka*, the brahmic plains where the matter is there but [is] very fine matter, or *arūpabrahma-loka*, the higher brahmic plane where there is no rūpa, no matter, only mind. And aeons upon aeons, kalpas upon kalpas, one lives a very peaceful life.

But that is not the final goal. Still the impurity is there. At the depth of the mind, *anusaya kilesa* [latent defilements]—the sleeping volcanoes of the past *saṅkhāras* [karmic forces]—are there. One did nothing to eradicate them. So at the end of the life of arūpabrahma-loka—the highest plane of the brahmic plane—again one has to fall down, and the circle continues, the circle continues, the cycle of life and death, life and death. Because one deviated from the real path.

The first jhāna: *vitakka, vicāra, pīti, sukha, citta-ekaggatā*. One takes an object of meditation—vitakka. The object is the object of any sense door, bodily sense door—eyes, ears, nose, tongue, touch of the body. Vitakka. One keeps on repeating, repeating, repeating, keeps on rolling, rolling in this object. Does not take attention here or there. Only this object, only this object—vicāra. And as the mind gets concentrated—citta-ekaggatā—there is pīti—mental happiness, sukha—at the body level, very pleasant sensations. And like that one continues, the vitakka goes away, only vicāra remains; the vicāra goes away, only pīti, and sukha and ekaggatā remains.

An example: Someone takes the object of a word, that is vitakka, that is the object. And one keeps on repeating it, repeating it, repeating it, reciting it, reciting it, reciting it—*vicaraṇ*, vicāra. And as one continues, continues, the word gets lost, there is just an echo. The echo gets lost, there is only vibration. Vitakka, vicāra—both have gone, and there is a pleasant vibration in the body, a pleasant feeling in the mind, and the mind is concentrated. There is no understanding of anicca [impermanence] at all. Very pleasant, very pleasant.

As one proceeds, proceeds, [the] mind becomes calm, tranquil. The pleasant feeling with very high waves goes away, and there is a subtle, pleasant feeling in the body that also goes away. Mind is just concentrated—citta-ekaggatā—one reaches the fourth jhāna. What to do now? So after [the] fourth jhāna, the concentration is so deep, the samādhi is of such great absorption, [the] body stops working. All the five sense doors stop—eyes, ears, nose, tongue, body—the mind is there.

And the object for the fifth jhāna to [the] eighth jhāna cannot be [the] object of these five sense doors, which are no longer working now. So the mind starts imagining. There cannot be a material object, so the sky. Sky is just [a] vacuum, there is no matter: *ākāsa, ākāsa. Ananta ākāsa, ākāśa anantyāyatana.* Infinite sky, infinite sky, one keeps on expanding one's mind—infinite, infinite, infinite.

That is over. Now what to do? Oh, how this mind spreads. The mind spreads. So mind is important. *Viññāṇa* is important. The viññāṇa spreads. And some philosophical teaching is given, and that conditioning is there—that throughout the universe it is only viññāṇa, which is permanent. And like my viññāṇa, there is viññāṇa all around. Like this consciousness, there is a consciousness, cosmic consciousness, throughout the universe there is consciousness, and one starts imagining that, and expanding—consciousness, consciousness, consciousness; viññāṇa, viññāṇa, viññāṇa; ananta viññāṇa, infinite viññāṇa. The sixth jhāna.

Now what to do? Again, the echo of Buddha's words remains, but the meaning gets lost. The path takes you to the stage where there is no *ālambana*, no *ārammaṇa—nirālamba*, nothing to hold. When someone experiences nibbāna, there is nothing to hold. And because the actual experience of nibbāna is lost, so nothing to hold, *natthi kiñci*—there is nothing. Now I must practice that there is nothing. And one starts imagining there is nothing, there is nothing, there is nothing. *Akiñcana*, akiñcana; natthi kiñci, natthi kiñci. And expands this idea—natthi kiñci, natthi kiñci, natthi kiñci. Ananta—infinite. The seventh jhāna.

Now what to do? Let me see, that on this viññāṇa, is there anything that is arising in the viññāṇa? Is there *saññā* [perception]? He doesn't examine anything in the body because connection from the body is totally cut. From fifth to eighth jhāna, all connection from the body is cut. All body faculties stop working. So what is in the mind? Saññā. Oh, the saññā is so weak, so weak, but still it is there, sometimes it looks as if it is not there, but it is still there, so weak, so weak. *Nevāsaññā-nāsaññāyatana*—one cannot say there is saññā, at the same time one cannot say there is no saññā, it is so feeble, so feeble. Eighth jhāna. Very high stage of concentration no doubt, one has come out of all the bondages of rūpa. The material bondage—one is out of that. And one is experiencing in this very life what one will experience in arūpabrahma-loka, the higher brahmic plane where [there] is no matter at all. A very high stage. But a blind alley. [One] cannot go further.

A buddha before he becomes Buddha is a *bodhisatta*; he practices everything that is common and then finds out, "No, this is not the actual path." And then because of the pāramitās [karmic perfections] of the past, which are now developed to such an extent that they start helping him, he starts investigating the real path, real path. He sits under a tree, and it is the past pāramitās that help him. And the first thing he remembers [is] that, "as a child sitting under a tree, I had practiced ānāpāna [awareness of resperation]." Yes, as a child, hardly about five years old, an occasion arose where he was sitting under a tree, nobody was around, and he started practicing ānāpāna. He remembers that. Because of the past pāramīs, because of the past practices, and [he] starts working with ānāpāna, ānāpāna.

And as one starts working with ānāpāna, paññā starts developing simultaneously. As you practice ānāpāna, you start feeling sensations on the body. And because of his past pāramī, the sensation was not taken as a sensation [with which] to play games. The sensation was taken to understand wisdom, develop wisdom; this is anicca, this is anicca. With the help of ānāpāna, and with the help of this paññā of anicca, *anicca-vijjā-ñāṇa* [knowledge of the wisdom of impermanence], anicca-vijjā-ñāṇa, progressing [with] the anicca-vijjā-ñāṇa, anicca-vijjā-ñāṇa, all the *avijjā* [ignorance] was broken, eradicated. The *nibbāna-dhātu* [nirvana-element], he came in contact with nibbāna-dhātu, experienced nibbāna, became fully enlightened. The correct path was found.

Therefore, afterward when he started teaching, even from the first jhāna, sampajañña was added. By the time one reached the third jhāna, sampajañña became very strong. By the time one reaches the fourth jhāna, one not only attains the jhāna *samāpatti* [attainment of absorption] of the fourth jhāna, one attains the *nirodha* samāpatti [attainment of cessation] also—the phalasamāpatti [attainment of the fruit] of *sotāpanna* [stream-entry], the phalasamāpatti of the sakadāgāmī [once-returner], the nirodha samāpatti of *anāgāmī* [non-returner], the nirodha samāpatti of arahant. The path became so clear.

There were people around him who came to learn [the] technique. To some, vipassanā was given right away; of course with the base of sīla. Vipassanā was given right away. Samādhi develops along with vipassanā. No special practice is done for samādhi. And that is called *sukkha vipassanā*, the dry vipassanā. Someone is fit for that.

Samādhi is given to someone—wet vipassanā—first jhāna, second jhāna, third jhāna, fourth jhāna—as one develops in these jhānas, one practices paññā and gets liberated. Then not even the first jhāna but still samādhi, *khaṇika-samādhi* [momentary concentration], or *upacāra-samādhi* [access concentration], so that there is little bit of samādhi at least to start. And the samādhi develops as paññā develops, but it is not totally sukkha, not totally dry.

This tradition is working in this way. There must be upacāra-samādhi. One is not taken to four jhānas first and then given vipassanā. Partly because [for] a householder it is so difficult; it takes such a long time to develop these four jhānas or eight jhānas, and it is so difficult for the ordinary householder to find that much time. Even a monk, even a nun, will get bored, it becomes so difficult. And another danger, that if one practices these four jhānas, and if vipassanā is not added, sampajañña is not added at the earlier stage, the bliss, the ecstasy, even in the third and fourth jhāna is so high, what to talk of the fifth to [the] eighth. One feels like remaining submerged in that. One does not feel like coming and starting vipassanā. One misses vipassanā entirely. One does not work at all in vipassanā. There is a danger.

Another danger: by the time one reaches the third or the fourth jhāna, some of the mental faculties increase so much, one develops different kinds of psychic powers. This supernatural power, that supernatural power. There is every possibility—if paññā is not there, if vipassanā is not added—that this person will lose track. He will develop ego because of these supernatural powers and will be far away from full liberation.

So this technique very rightly wants you to start with khaṇika-samādhi, or better, with upacāra-samādhi. Even [if] it come[s] to *appanā-samādhi* [absorption concentration], the first stage of appanā-samādhi, the first jhāna of appanā-samādhi, is good enough. And then working with vipassanā, working with vipassanā, one reaches the first phalasamāpatti of sotāpanna, the second phala-samāpatti of sakadāgāmī. Then all importance is given to these four jhānas or eight jhānas. Partly because after becoming sakadāgāmī, it doesn't take much time. Mind has become much purer. A purer mind can get concentrated easily. So these four jhānas and eight jhānas have become easy for one who has become sakadāgāmī. And partly because one has practiced vipassanā, practiced nibbāna, there is no danger of this person going mad in any way. It becomes easy. So it is only after sakadāgāmī that the jhānas are being practiced—four or eight.

At this stage, for a meditator, upacāra-samādhi is good enough. You are aware of the object continuously, continuously. Although you didn't get the absorption samādhi of the first jhāna—some may get [it], some may not get [it]—still upacāra is there. Continuously, continuously. It is not just like a few seconds. Now you are aware of your object for a minute, for two minutes, five minutes, ten minutes, fifteen minutes, in some cases one hour. Good enough. This is good enough for you to start practicing vipassanā, and this will take you to the deeper level of vipassanā. And you will be moving toward the final goal of liberation, nibbāna, nibbāna.

The technique has worked; people have gotten benefit. The technique is tried by so many. Work with confidence. With the base of proper sīla, right sīla, pure sīla, and with the samādhi, samādhi of the reality that you experience on this area. No imagination involved, no speculation involved. No philosophical dogma involved. Everything that you accept, you accept because you experience it. The paññā is not merely sutapaññā [wisdom heard], it is *bhāvanāpaññā* [the wisdom of meditative cultivation]. *Anubhavana, anubhavita*: experience—then it becomes *bhāvanā-mayā paññā* [wisdom constituted through meditative cultivation]. . . .[281]

CHAPTER 17

On a Vipaśyanā Pagoda

from *The Global Pagoda Souvenir*

In the last two decades of his life, S.N. Goenka took on a major project—the construction of a large pagoda in the vicinity of Mumbai. This pagoda was and is dedicated to raising awareness about the Buddha's teachings, and Goenka hoped it would serve as a place for vipaśyanā meditators to congregate and practice together. Relics of the Buddha were enshrined in the pagoda in a public ceremony, and the site became an important gathering point for Goenka and his disciples at the end of his life. But the building of the pagoda was somewhat controversial for a variety of reasons, one being that many thought the building of such a structure would lead to the development of a vipaśyanā sect. In a series of articles from the late 1990s, eventually collected in a book titled The Global Pagoda Souvenir, *Goenka addressed his students' various concerns about the construction of the pagoda. Translations of the second article in that collection, along with a series of prescriptive quotations by Goenka about how to properly conceptualize the pagoda, is presented here.*[282]

Sayagyi U Ba Khin and the Vipaśyanā Pagoda

In the history of humanity, rarely does a good person take birth who carries out work so important for the benefit of people that its influence continues to affect people's lives for many centuries. Sayagyi U Ba Khin was just such a person of Dharma, a saintly person. Burma preserved the wisdom of vipaśyanā—passed down in a lineage of teachers and pupils—in its pure form for centuries, and he was a shining star of that lineage. While it is true that unparalleled compassion for the entire world flowed forth from his heart, still his love for India was without comparison. It was unique. He used to say that he must have been born many times in India and meditated many times in the hills and caves of the Himalayas. In the sixth decade of this century, when there was famine for two years continuously in Bihar, an ocean of compassion for the people of that region afflicted by hunger overflowed in his mind. Near the Dharma hall at the vipaśyanā center in Rangoon, there was a replica of the Himalayas that had been made by a skilled artisan. Every day, after waking up at four in the morning and meditating, Sayagyi U Ba Khin would stand by the sculpture and generate auspicious loving-kindness for a long time:[283] "May the people of India be liberated from suffering, may they obtain the Dharma, and may they be benefited. How afflicted, how impoverished, how distressed are the people of that country where Siddhārtha Gautama attained perfect enlightenment, not just for himself but for the supreme benefit of the whole world! What is happening there in the name of Dharma? How much violent conflict can continue to go on between those of different castes, different groups, rich and poor, different ideologies, and different sects? Indeed, how large can the terrible shadow of enmity and inhumane violence grow on that sacred land where the pure True Dharma in the form of vipaśyanā arose, in the country that for many centuries distributed this wisdom to the suffering people of the world? Today that country has been completely cheated of the benefits of this wisdom. How terribly unfortunate it is that the people of that place have forgotten even the word *vipaśyanā*, remaining far removed from being able to attain the benefits of this great wisdom! If this great country were to again obtain this ancient spiritual wisdom of its own, all such conflicts would cease of their own accord."

He again and again spoke of how, centuries before, Burma obtained this invaluable gem from India: "Now the time has come for me to repay the debt, to give to India that invaluable heritage that our masters strove so hard to preserve, to return it to India." With a mind of compassion, he again and again expressed this beneficent intention and wanted to come to India himself to repay the debt. But because of the political situation, he could not come to India. Nonetheless, again and again, these words of Dharma emerged from his mouth: "Now the drum of vipaśyanā has been struck. Very soon it will return to India." He had complete confidence that the prediction of some saint from the past made success certain: it had been stated that this wisdom would be preserved in Burma until twenty-five hundred years after the Tathāgata, and from there it would return to India, where many wise people with meritorious perfections would happily accept it. Then it would spread from India around the globe, and it would bring great benefit to people.

Though he was powerless to come to India himself, Sayagyi U Ba Khin nonetheless fulfilled his auspicious dream. He trained his Dharma-son of Indian origin as much as he could, brought him to maturity as much as he could, and sent him to India as a proxy. After an interval of approximately two thousand years, the blessed wisdom of vipaśyanā returned to this great country. During the last thirty years or so, not quite enough work has been done, but a start has indeed been made. And things have started well. I am thankful, very thankful, to that great saint, due to whose devotion and diligence this invaluable treasure that had been lost to India has been recovered. How can we forget the debt owed to this saint? How can we overlook it?

The plan is simply this: first, to become mature in this wisdom ourselves; and second, to help in the work to bring more and more people in contact with this wisdom so they might be able to benefit from it. This was the beneficent wish of my teacher (Gurudev). This was his life's auspicious objective. It was important and dear to him. Next year is the birth centenary year of that great saint, Sayagyi U Ba Khin. An auspicious resolution was made to build a massive stupa in the great city of Mumbai. As a result of this, the family of a powerful meritorious vipaśyanā meditator donated a very valuable piece of land out of deep faith. This Dharma stupa will be built there, and it will become a particularly influential medium for the propogation of vipaśyanā. In accordance with the last order of the Blessed Buddha, his bone relics will be enshrined in a massive Dharma hall of the stupa. Approximately ten thousand vipaśyanā meditators will be able to participate in group meditations there, taking the benefit of the Dharma vibrations of the relics. We will also regularly hold one-day courses there.

Some intelligent people may ask, "Why should this massive building be built as a replica of a pagoda? Why shouldn't it be built in the form of some Indian temple?" They should understand why things are being done in such a way.

If the inner structure of the stupa is round, the vibrations of meditation are more permanent and more powerful. And since this Dharma stupa is being built for vipaśyanā meditation, it can't be built in the form of just any temple. No image will be enshrined in it. There will be no ceremonies of worship for the treatment of disease, no devotional chanting and singing, no oblation ceremonies, no lighting of incense and lamps, no offerings of flowers and things of that sort, no banging of bells and gongs in a ceremony of prayer to anyone, and no other form of sectarian ritual whatsoever. Only meditation practitioners, in great numbers, will meditate inside the stupa, and they will certainly not meditate on any statue or image. They will not do any chanting of names or mantras. Otherwise, all of this will become sectarian. This stupa will be used only for vipaśyanā meditation, where meditators practice to remain vigilantly aware of the cause of their internal defilements and the method of counteracting such causes. This practice of vipaśyanā is not sectarian. It has not been associated with any one sect. Its universality is axiomatic. In this respect, it is absolutely unnecessary to be initiated into any sect. Just as yogic postures and breath control are exercise for the body, so vipaśyanā is exercise for the mind. Anyone of any sect may practice it and get the same results, reap the same fruits. The art of living a pure life gets taken in hand. Life becomes filled with happiness and peace. Such evidence is before us. People of various sects, in large numbers, have joined in vipaśyanā courses and are benefiting from them. The construction of a vipaśyanā stupa is never for the establishment of a sect. On the contrary, it is for the establishment of a life of good conduct, which results from leaving behind various sectarian bonds and following a morality that is acceptable to all. And it is for purifying wisdom that comes about by making the mind one-pointed. The purpose of this Dharma stupa is for vipaśyanā meditators to come here to develop themselves further in vipaśyanā and for those who are not meditators to attain inspiration to get involved in vipaśyanā.

My teacher, Sayagyi U Ba Khin, was not eager to send some sect from Burma to India. He was eager to send vipaśyanā, which is for the welfare of all people. [He said,] "Listen, there are many, many sects here. Those that are here, and the results that are coming from them, stand before us. The meaning of the word *sect* (*sampradāy*) is 'to bestow harmony' (*samatā pradān karnā*). But these sects—regardless of who they are—are bestowing discord in society instead of bestowing harmony. In such a situation, if one more sect were to be created there, what good would it do for that country?" My teacher understood this issue well. The Dharma that is universal is for the benefit of India and the world. This was his expectation, and that is why the construction of a vipaśyanā Dharma stupa in his sacred memory is to fulfill his beneficent wish.

Still one question arises: While it makes sense to construct a vast Dharma hall—with a round ceiling unobstructed by pillars—for ten thousand meditators, what is the point of constructing it so that its external structure is a replica of the Shwedagon Pagoda in Yangon? What is the reason for that?

This also should be understood. When one begins to comprehend the purity of Dharma, one will also begin to comprehend that gratitude is an important aspect of Dharma. The country of Myanmar preserved this invaluable treasure of our country in its pure form with great care for approximately two thousand years, and now, for our good, it has been returned. Acknowledging the service of that country, it is absolutely necessary that a feeling of gratitude should arise. This accords with Dharma.

In the past, when this wisdom went to neighboring countries, the people of those countries built stupas replicating the form of the stupas of those days here in India. The primary reason for this was so that when people of those various countries would see the stupas built in their own countries, a feeling of gratitude toward India would continue to arise in their minds for centuries. Even now it arises. In just the same way, since we have obtained this wisdom from Burma, when people from here see this stupa built in the form of the famous Burmese stupa, they will arouse a feeling of gratitude toward Burma. And this gratitude will continue to arise for centuries. This structure of the stupa should be accepted because this is the intention behind it. Surrounded by magnificent architectural structures, this grand, sky-high stupa will attract many people from India and around the world, raising its head [to represent] the ancient spiritual wisdom of India. It will invite them, and many among those who come onto this sacred land will become connected to vipaśyanā and reap its benefits for themselves. This is also one of the primary sacred purposes of the construction of the Dharma stupa. More and more people should benefit from vipaśyanā! The violent conflicts of the entire world will be removed—not just those of India! May the sacred Ganges of Dharma, of vipaśyanā, once again flow powerfully, so that its influence brings great benefit to the world. Catalyzed by this Dharma intention, this auspicious effort is an expression of my deep gratitude to that great householder saint, Sayagyi U Ba Khin.

Gratitude is certainly the most auspicious thing. People should also understand the pure intention, on my part, to make an offering after the ways of ancient India, as I pour the oblation in this historically monumental Dharma sacrifice. In the field of pure Dharma of ancient India, the tradition of giving was very holy, virtuous. We must establish that holiness so that the glory of the country will increase and people will also benefit.

According to ancient tradition, when a monk went out for alms in a city, he would wander with bowl in hand, eyes down, from one house to another in silence, stopping for a few minutes in front of each one. He would not say, "Give alms," nor would he cry out, "Mother, I am hungry. Father, give me some bread. Mother, give me some bread." In ancient India, a monk was not a beggar. There is a great difference between a monk and a beggar. A person who has destroyed the suffering of the flowing of existence through the practice of vipaśyanā is called a monk: *bhindati dukkhaṃ ti bhikkhu!* He does not wander to beg, but stops in front of every house to provide an opportunity to householders to produce merit in accordance with the tradition of pure Dharma. Waiting for about a minute, if no one were to come out, he would proceed onward, wishing them well with a contented mind. When someone would come out to offer food for his bowl, he would also proceed farther in the same way, wishing them well.

And it was often that householders would wait eagerly in front of their homes when monks were making their rounds, just as it happens in neighboring countries in the present day. Householders endowed with Dharma are thankful that monks provide them with the opportunity to offer food. Based on this sacred custom, the low intention of begging does not arise in the mind of a monk, and a sense of self-importance does not arise in the mind of the householder. Both giving and receiving donations remain faultless. They remain replete with Dharma. All donations associated with the True Dharma are offered with such purity. First the intention must arise in the mind that "I am not giving a donation simply to fulfill the present purpose. Rather, I am doing it so that millions of people of future generations, for centuries to come, will be attracted to vipaśyanā. A donation with foundations of this kind will become powerful and bear fruit for centuries to come. How fortunate it is that I am getting this unique opportunity to acquire merit that will give fruit for such a long time." It is necessary that this kind of intention be aroused in the mind of every donor. Another good intention must arise in the minds of vipaśyanā meditators who want to make a donation: "How would I have benefited were it not for our guru-grandfather giving this beneficial wisdom to India! So whatever amount of support—large or small—that I am offering to this undertaking, within my capacities, is simply a small effort to make known my gratitude to that great saint, Sayagyi U Ba Khin. May the meritorious work of benefiting people through beneficial vipaśyanā continue to be carried out for a long time in India and in the world, and may he fulfill his Dharma desire to benefit all people."

Whatever help is offered with this Dharma intention—whether it is large or small—will certainly bear much meritorious fruit. May India's ancient glory again arise with dignity. Placing this invaluable crown jewel of the wisdom of vipaśyanā on her head, may this practical training of nonviolence that is for the peace of all people be shared throughout the entire universe! May the entire world be safe due to its influence! May the entire world be well! May the wisdom of vipaśyanā spread throughout the world! May the suffering of people in pain be removed! May all attain peace and happiness! May all be well and safe! May all be fully liberated! May all be fully liberated!

My gratitude to all Dharma teachers, from Śākyamuni Gautama Buddha to Sayagyi U Ba Khin, is boundless. If they had not communicated the Dharma and preserved it in its absolutely pure form, how would I have obtained this invaluable jewel of the Dharma in this life?

I bow my head in their memory as an expression of deep devotion and boundless gratitude.

SAYAGYI S. N. GOENKA

The Vipaśyanā Meditator and the Vipaśyanā Pagoda

- Any meditator who has learned vipaśyanā from Sayagyi U Ba Khin by means of his proxy and Dharma-son (Respected Goenkaji) is a mobile monument to Sayagyi U Ba Khin.
- Someone is able to truly become a mobile monument to Sayagyi U Ba Khin when he is established in Dharma and lives an ideal life, such that more and more suffering people are attracted to the sacred path of liberation from suffering.
- Every meditation center in this tradition, wherever it might be in the world, is indeed a local monument to Sayagyi U Ba Khin.
- The Vipaśyanā Pagoda under construction in the village of Gorai in Mumbai will not be merely for attractive and beautiful appearance. It will be a functional Dharma stupa;

this practical aspect is primary. Thousands of people will sit to meditate together here and attain many fruits. Separate from the stupa, there will be an exhibition hall where true incidents from the life history of the Blessed Buddha will be displayed and where the actual truth of his beneficial teachings can be brought to light.

- The vipaśyanā stupa is a global undertaking. Information about it is being spread through the entire world for the benefit of meditators. Not even a small amount of pressure should be exerted to collect money for it.
- Everyone should get the same opportunity to take part in any such great meritorious work, as has been the ancient tradition of the True Dharma. This is also the purpose for continuing to provide information about the stupa's construction—so that every vipaśyanā meditator might have the opportunity to make his gratitude to Sayagyi U Ba Khin known. Whether the donation is small or large is of little importance. What is important is the sacred Dharma intention, by which we are establishing a strong basis, through this wholesome activity, to attract people to vipaśyanā for centuries to come—not just those living in India, but those living around the world. By this intention we are also contributing in some small part to the great Dharma wish of Sayagyi U Ba Khin.
- It is very important for the person who becomes a participant in this meritorious Dharma sacrifice—by making any type of offering as a manifestation of gratitude—to understand that he should never do so because of pressure to offer time or money. Rather, he should always do so happily, with a pure Dharma volition.

CHAPTER 18

Seeing the Dharma

from *Dharma: The Basis of an Ideal Life*

Dharma: The Basis of an Ideal Life *was one of S. N. Goenka's first books introducing the Hindi-speaking Indian public to his teachings. It was originally published under the title* Dharma: The Art of Living *(*Dharm: Jīvan Jīne kī Kalā*), not to be confused with the English-language book by Goenka's Canadian disciple William Hart. Published in 1976, it contains the principle ideas, doctrines, and experiential outlook that remained the hallmark of Goenka's meditation teachings to the end of his life. "Seeing the Dharma" is the eighteenth of twenty chapters that make up the book, and it does indeed present the reader with Goenka's vision of the Dharma. It encapsulates his understanding of the nature of reality, where that understanding fits in human history, how to practice to develop such an understanding, and how to live a life in accord with that reality.*[284]

Seeing the Dharma (*dharmadarśan*) means seeing the truth. Here *darśan* does not mean "philosophy"; it is not an interpretive model of reality, nor is it the seeing of some material form. Here *darśan* means "the direct experience of the truth." Seeing the Dharma is becoming aware, through direct experience, of the truths of the animate universe, of the all-pervasive order of nature. It is seeing the truth.

Dharma is for obtaining relief from suffering, and seeing (darśan) is the scientific practice of doing so. The purpose of seeing the Dharma is to become aware of, understand, accept, and mold ourselves in accordance with the law of nature, to which we are directly connected, acting on us at every moment. To the extent that we become mature in this process through the practice of seeing, we become established in Dharma and become true masters of happiness. Seeing the Dharma is our pathway to spiritual progress.

Dharma comprises the laws of nature that are directly connected to our suffering and liberation from suffering, our bondage and liberation from bondage, laws that we must become aware of and make use of for our own good. Dharma is the solution to the cause of suffering and the application of methods for liberation from suffering. It brings us into harmony with the all-pervasive order of things, for our own welfare and the welfare of others. The natural order of cause and effect is applicable to all. This order does not get angry with or favor anyone. The power of creation does not pay deference to anyone. Whoever breaks the law gets punished. Whoever obeys the law gets rewarded. The Dharma of fire is to burn. This is the order of nature. Because of our misunderstanding, we misuse fire and harm ourselves in various ways. When we use it correctly, we benefit immensely. Our suffering and its cessation depends on our ignorance or understanding. There is no sense in taking sides with anyone in the order of the universe, the Dharma of the universe. It is without qualities, without shape, free of identification, all-pervasive, and infinite. This order is uniformly applicable to one and all. Whoever comes into harmony with it becomes free from suffering. As much as we are in harmony with it, that is how much we become free from suffering. Until we fully understand this fact, we continue to get sidetracked and harm ourselves. Once we fully understand it, we get on track. We should make efforts to obey the order of things, the Dharma, so that we can remove the difficulties that arise from ignorantly carrying out actions that go against the order.

Generally, we remain healthy in body by understanding and following the regulations of creation that are related to the necessities of survival, such as food and drink. In quite the same way, we can achieve an internal happiness and peace when we understand the regulations and obey them at a subtler level.

When we don't know the cause of the disease, we can't combat it. We will get caught up with things that are not related to removing the disease. It is this ignorance that does not allow us to be free of the disease. When we become familiar with the actual cause of the disease and begin to combat it, what doubt is there that we will become free of the disease?

When human knowledge and expertise were in their infancy, enchanted humans saw only mystery in every aspect of nature. They were beguiled by its pleasing aspects and terrified of its fierce aspects. In that state of not knowing about true causes, terrified humans—by recourse to their imagination—understood the cause of the destructive play of nature to be the anger of an invisible god. They came to solicit his happiness so that he might protect them, singing songs in praise of him, and performing rites of worship to him. They did not simply offer food oblations to him, but they also bloodied the ground with offerings of meek, innocent animals and even humans. But how can there be a cure for a disease when the actual cause is not understood? The few humans who disregarded these blind beliefs and discovered the truth obtained the proper fruit of their striving. They discovered many mysteries about the truths of nature. They became familiar with the true causes of the great epidemics, such as the plague, cholera, and smallpox. Wise people exerted all of their power to eradicate these diseases. Instead of simply holding the hand of those who were helpless in the face of famine and floods, they used their intellects and roused people to ultimate human aims. They dammed the rivers. In this way, this truth-seeking human intelligence uprooted blind beliefs in various fields and began to advance the pleasure, resources, and wealth of humanity. This human research campaign into the truth—now advancing in giant leaps to measure space—is laudable.

But it is necessary to go beyond this external investigation. The investigation of inner space—the discovery of the truths of the cosmos relating to oneself—remains important. These are the truths that cause us to suffer and those that allow us to become free from suffering. When we are unaware of these truths, the causes of the difficulties in our daily lives are attributed to the discontent of gods and goddesses or a creator god, and the prevention of those difficulties is attributed to the contentment of those beings. Because of this, whenever suffering comes—be it major or minor—in a mental condition of naivety or fear, we plead for their mercy, we make offerings to them, we make pilgrimages to their abodes, we recite stanzas of exaggerated praise. We create and carry out countless rituals in order to please these imagined creators of the universe.

But an enlightened class of humans remains engaged in the search for inner truth. In many periods there were many such seers, sages, wise men, enlightened people, and victors[285] who explored inner space and proved that the root of our suffering, and the method of uprooting it, is inside us, not outside. They saw that when the stream of mind is impaired by the defilements of anger, envy, fear, clinging, covetousness, and so on, we are afflicted by suffering, and when these defilements are removed, we become free from suffering. Ultimately, they sought to answer the question, "Why do these defilements get produced?" They found that craving was the source of all the defilements—craving to attain what is desirable and craving to avoid what is undesirable. Craving is generated in the form of desire for a desirable, pleasant sensation that has awakened deep within or in the form of aversion for an undesirable, unpleasant sensation that has awakened deep within. Continuing the search, they wanted to know, "Why do these desirable and undesirable, pleasant and unpleasant, sensations ultimately arise?" Then they saw that whenever the six faculties of the eye, ear, nose, tongue, skin, and mind came into contact with their respective objects—a sight, sound, smell, taste, touch, or thought—deep within the complex of body and mind, innumerable subtle vibrations of various kinds are produced. Depending on our karmic inclinations and experiences from the past, we identify these vibrations as desirable or undesirable. The enlightened ones also saw that even when the eye, ear, nose, or tongue makes no contact with an object, and as a result no sensation is produced by such an interaction, as long as there is life, there continues to be sensations of contact at the level of body and consciousness at every moment. Taking these sensations to be desirable or undesirable, we continue to react to them with craving or aversion.

Further, the victors saw that the entirety of this activity is happening at the level of the subconscious mind, the level at which we remain unaware. That is, we remain unaware of when [sense] contact occurs. As a result of this, we also remain unaware of when a sensation has arisen and when we get immersed in the stream of craving or aversion in reaction to it, of when the knots of bodily tension begin to get tied, and of when the suffering begins to accumulate. The sages saw that even upon becoming aware at a superficial level of this process, we unintentionally continue, at every moment—in a state of unconsciousness, unknowing, ignorance, delusion deep within—to discharge defilements of craving or aversion into this stream of mind. It is like the discharge of pus constantly oozing from an abscess. For this reason, we carry on, immersed in suffering.

So the research continued. The wise men saw that whenever they remained aware at those depths of the subconscious mind—whenever they remained vigilant, free from unknowing, ignorance, and delusion, seeing this impermanent flow with a feeling of impartial detachment—at those moments new craving and aversion would not arise in the mind-stream. As a result, the old discharge is exhausted, and the previously accumulated defilements are cleared away. The enlightened ones saw that with the repeated practice of equanimous awareness, the mind-stream becomes free of defilement. As the mind-stream becomes more and more pure, it automatically becomes replete with good qualities. When it has become absolutely pure, it becomes replete with every possible good quality.

In this way, those researching the truth looked, with the power of their own experiences, and asked the question, "What is the root cause of the disease, and what is the method to prevent it?" The cosmos opened the entirety of its secret, its mystery, and placed it before them. They saw that in this process of researching the truth, their mind-streams had become free from discharge, free from defilements. They realized that any person who takes up this process of introspection, this process of self-realization, becomes pure of mind and is liberated from suffering. This direct benefit of researching the truth remains a great human accomplishment.

At times another question arises: "Scientists' discoveries about the external physical world have brought with them many benefits. Though we do not ourselves undertake this research in practice, it seems that we benefit directly from its accomplishments. Can we not get the benefits that come from discoveries of the internal, mental world in the very same way? If we accept the truth discovered by them and have faith in it, then enough, the work is complete. Why should every person among us participate in the process of research for himself? Why should one practice to see the Dharma for oneself?" The answer to this question is that this research process itself was their discovery. And it is the cure for the disease. We can't be liberated from suffering without carrying out an inspection of the self. Only when we have realized for ourselves the defilements of our minds can they be uprooted. This is the medicine that we must take. It is just like when a medical scientist discovered the cause of malaria and that quinine is the cure for that cause. Now, whatever the quality of the quinine, when sick people take it, they become free from malaria. In this way, trying out various kinds of methods, those meditators seeking the highest goal discovered the medicine of seeing the Dharma, which would still be necessary even if one had the remedy of one thousand of Rama's arrows.[286] The compassion of those pure, enlightened, liberated great men was so great that they found a path. We will have to walk it as well. No one can carry us on their shoulders to reach the destination. The point of believing that "your liberation is in your hands" is not to become egotistical. Rather, with a sense of humility, one must accept full responsibility for oneself.

Meditators! I am speaking on the basis of my own experience, and the experience of thousands of meditators I know, when I say that this course of practice involves no supernatural miracles. Whatever accomplishment there is comes from one's own hard work. I have with me an unclean mental cloth. Fortunately, I have obtained this method in the form of soap. As much as I make use of the soap, that much of the dirt is washed off, no more. To the extent that there is any dirt remaining, I suffer. It is not some miracle such that I don't do any work, or I do only a little bit of work, and the dirt gets entirely washed off. Actually, this is a lifelong project. One must remain self-aware and self-attentive for life. One must remain vigilant. In truth, the work is difficult. But there is also no other path.

Still, in our naiveté we seek some miraculous path. We seek a miracle of the sort that will allow us to avoid difficult effort and still attain success. In such a state, we again begin to concoct fantasies.

After the discovery of ultimate truth by such wise people, it must be accepted that the cause of our suffering is not some deity or creator god. The cause is simply our own stock of karmic reactions. But we are attached to the hope that, despite our committing thousands of impure actions, some all-powerful being, some ocean of compassion, may somehow take delight in removing all our suffering. With this hope, we run the gambit of practices such as flattery, visitation, making offerings, and so on. We have no idea what we are doing. Under the power of blind devotion, we dishonor that poor god that we have fashioned. What kind of a god becomes happy because of receiving our respect, who swells and gets puffed up from invocations of praise? The answer comes: "Sir, he keeps a protective eye out for those who are ostentatious in their flattery. He rains down dowry on those offering gifts. Pleased with those who praise him, he clears away their offenses. He treats the guilty cheater in the same way as he does the innocent." The effigy of the "I" is such that should someone forget his name, simply upon its invocation, he is immediately ready on the line. Such is the attachment he has to his name. And such is the attachment he has to his sect! He takes the side of the person of the sect whose god he is. We have set up different gods who are partial to different sects. I say, is there any limit to our foolishness? Is the state of this great world in fact in the hands of some ruler or rulers—arbitrary arbiters who, in their partiality, pride, and despotism, overturn the way of things, the order of Dharma? Bad qualities are indeed then a source of bad qualities. If one were to believe this, then some deity, full of good qualities, must make this place of bad qualities so that one might reflect on his qualities, be inspired, and develop all those qualities. Then benefit is brought about. But in our foolishness, we carry out inauspicious practices. Liberation from suffering comes about only through purity of mind. Only when one has accepted this order of things may the mind become pure. It will not become pure when it is caught up in the foolishness of trying to please some despotic creator who is beyond the order.

The practice of seeing the Dharma pulls these misunderstandings out of us. The cause of suffering is impurity of mind, and becoming liberated from these impurities is itself liberation from suffering. The clearer this unwavering law and order of the cosmos becomes, the farther we advance on the path of Dharma, because we recognize that the only aim is purity of mind. Then simply obeying the order of things becomes primary for us. The truth (*satya*) itself becomes God (*nārāyaṇ*).[287] Dharma itself becomes the creator. The idea of placating some god—who might subvert the order of things, the law, the truth, the Dharma, or who is distinct from these—does not even come to mind. When Dharma is forgotten, afflictions upon afflictions come to awareness. When Dharma is applied, blessings upon blessings come to awareness.

Once we recognize that truth itself is the creator and maintain a detached faith in it, then, when we practice to see the Dharma, we are liberated from suffering to the extent that we are able to see the Dharma—that is, see the truth. In that state, we come into harmony with the infinite subtle realities of nature. Because these realities of nature are bound by their own laws, they begin to protect us automatically. When we take it on, Dharma automatically protects us. This is the law of Dharma. When our minds are entangled in bad qualities, and they generate vibrations of impure mental activity, they come into harmony with the impure vibrations that pervade the entire universe and, as a result, proliferate suffering. In the same way, when our minds are pure because they are free of bad qualities, when they are full of good qualities and begin to give rise to vibrations of good mental activity, then the pure, Dharma-constituted, virtuous vibrations of virtuous deities and brahmas—among the seen and unseen living beings in this infinite universe—come to meet us. They provide us strength, amplify our happiness, and protect us. This is the law, the order of things. It can be experienced directly.

The governmental order of a country is the Dharma of that country. In the very same way, this global, universal, eternal order of the universe is the Dharma of the universe. When a citizen of a country lives a life in accordance with its legislative order and does not break the law, there is then no fear of the wrath of the lawgiver. Additionally, without being entreated, the government is entirely responsible for the protection of the country. If someone systematically disrupts the order of things, breaks the law of the state, and then placates the lawgiver or ruler with flattery or the scattering of flower petals, such a person is proven to be a danger, not only to himself, but also to the happiness and peace of the entire country and society. That person is a danger to the system. Happiness and peace will shine forth in the country, in the society, where people attentively obey the law of the state. In the same way, in this great kingdom of the universe, what else can be the means of achieving happiness and peace aside from obeying the Dharma in its manifestation as the law and order of the universe?

For this reason, we should take on Dharma, not only for our own happiness and peace, but for the happiness and peace of all. We should live a life in accordance with the order of the universe, and we should make our minds free from defilements by the practice of seeing the Dharma with unwavering devotion. Whatever obstacles come in the way of this practice—however delightful they may be, however much they may accord with our various accepted beliefs—we should remove them without identifying with them and continue to again and again make tireless efforts to purify the mind exclusively: "When one job is accomplished, all is accomplished."

This is the order of the bounteous ultimate truth contained in every single particle of the infinite.

Truth, Dharma, the Lord of the World

The law of creation is neither kind nor angry.
One suffers with a defiled mind, one is happy with a pure one.
Who should I worship? What deity or Lord God?
I should worship the truth. Truth is Dharma, the Lord of the world.
When the order of things is ignored, disorder reigns, and forms become primary.
Enmeshed in the forms of the order, the fool forgets the order itself.
What God should I worship, when Dharma is not with me?
What God should I worship if it is?
Obeying a moral code is difficult, while praying to the Lord is easy.
How foolish the person who might pray to the Lord, upon straying from the moral code.
In obeying the rule of Dharma, whatever obstacles there might be,
As delightful as they are, relinquish them. Be free of identification.

Acknowledgments

FIRST AND FOREMOST, I would like to thank S. N. Goenka for authorizing and encouraging the research from which this book emerged and which has been ongoing since 2008. When I met Goenka in 2008 to discuss why I think it is important to contextualize his mission historically and to understand his approach to meditation in light of the broader context of Asian history, culture, and traditions of practice, he expressed his approval in one of his characteristic turns of phrase: "I am certain that your research work will be successful." Illaichidevi Goenka also gave me her blessing at that time. In writing this short book on the life and works of my teacher, I hope that it will indeed be successful in helping people to understand S. N. Goenka, his teachings, and his mission to spread them.

I would like to express my sincerest gratitude to Michael Jordan and Leslie Gray for first encouraging me to practice vipaśyanā meditation, and to Ram Singh for facilitating my initial formal entry into this path of practice.

I am grateful to Barry Lapping, Bill Hart, Sharda Sanghvi, Ruth Senturia, O. P. Pathak, and numerous others in Igatpuri, Mumbai, Pune, and elsewhere in India, the United States, Europe, and Myanmar, who facilitated my research over the past decade or so. Bill Hart in particular made important research materials available and revealed to me a number of community attitudes that informed my research. Sharda Sanghvi was also particularly helpful by ensuring that I had access to and permission to use and reproduce transcripts of Goenka's oral discourses.

I am also very grateful to John Beary, Thomas Crisman, Karen Donovan, Kathy Henry, Paul Fleischman, Bill Hamilton, Bill Crecelius, Nirmala and Hamir Ganla, Dhananjay Chavan, Rohi Shetty, and Edward and Junko Giorgilli. These vipaśyanā administrators, and quite a few others not named here, helped show me why a book like this is of such crucial importance for today's community of practitioners.

I am grateful to Sriprakash Goenka for providing permission to translate and/or reproduce a number of S. N. Goenka's written works. Many of these works can be found at the following website: www.vridhamma.org. Specific details for the publications from which the individual writings are drawn can be found in the notes to the individual chapters.

Funding for the research that formed the foundation of this book was provided by the American Institute of Indian Studies (2009–2010), the University of South Carolina (2013–2016), the Robert H. N. Ho Family Foundation with the American Council of Learned Societies (2016–2017), and the Fulbright Program (2017). Without the generosity of these funding bodies, this book would never have been written. I am grateful to Mahesh Deokar as well, for hosting me at the Department of Pali and Buddhist Studies at the Savitribai Phule Pune University during my stint as a Fulbright scholar.

For her untiring support and brilliant editorial help, I remain ever indebted to my wife, Mari Jyväsjärvi Stuart. Without her, this book would never have been completed.

For informing me of and sharing with me important historical sources on the life of Sayagyi U Ba Khin, thanks go to Roberto Mannai and Joah McGee.

For help with translation, I am grateful to Swe Mon, Jenny Ko Gyi, Mukul Agarwal, Harpreet Singh, and Narendra Bokhare.

For her caring ear, I am grateful to Cristina Bonnet.

Finally, I would like to thank those who supported me at Shambhala. Nikko Odiseos put his faith in me when he commissioned this project, and Robert Pryor was very kind to suggest that he do so. Matt Zepelin and Emily Coughlin were unbelievably supportive, and their thoughtful editing helped me bring the manuscript to its final form in the gentlest of ways.

Surely many others whom I have not mentioned helped me get to where I am today so that I might bring out a book such as this. I express my gratitude to and request forgiveness from anyone I may have overlooked in this regard.

Notes

1. Gelles, "Overlooked No More."
2. Michaelson, "S.N. Goenka." It is perhaps of interest here to note that Michaelson teaches Buddhist meditation and is a student of Leigh Brasington, a meditation teacher whose lineage can be traced back to S. N. Goenka's teacher, Sayagyi U Ba Khin.
3. Braun, "S. N. Goenka, Pioneer." Perhaps even more telling than this analytically cryptic obituary is Braun's treatment—or lack thereof—of Goenka in his 2013 book, *The Birth of Insight*. Goenka's identity and that of his teacher Sayagyi U Ba Khin are too complex for the simple one-sided narrative that Braun attempts to tell in that monograph, a narrative that largely obliterates the complex agencies of its colonized Asian actors, even its main target, the Ledi Sayadaw. So he simply removes the most complicated actors from the equation for the most part, though they are integral pieces of the story of the development of modern global insight meditation.
4. According to the Hindu lunar calender, Goenka's date of birth was Māgh Śuklă 12, 1924. Goyankā, *Kalyāṇămitră Satyanārāyaṇ Goyankā*, 11.
5. The revered monk is reported to have passed away on the full moon day of Waso (June 27), 1923 (Htay Hlaing, *Rahantā-Nhaṅ'ʻ-Pugguil'-Thū"-Myā"*, 327; and Nyanissara, *A Short Biography*, 18). There seems to be some confusion about this date, however, arising from accounts of the funeral proceedings (see Candima, "A Study of the Life and Work," 14–15).
6. On the process of haveli construction as a mode of establishing identity and ancestral ties to place among Marwari diaspora communities, see Hardgrove, *Community and Public Culture*, particularly chapters 1 and 3; and Nakatani, "Hometowns of the Marwaris."
7. The historian Thant Myint-U (*The Making of Modern Burma*, 89–90) notes that Burmese of Indian origin were classed by ethnic Burmese as

kala, a category used to identify all non-Burmese foreigners, including Europeans.

8. Goyankā, *Ātma-Kathan*, *Bhāg 1*, 49.
9. Vipassana Research Institute, *Sayagyi U Ba Khin Journal*, 147.
10. Goyankā, *Dhanyă Bābā!*, 71.
11. Goyankā, *Dhanyă Bābā!*, 1.
12. Goyankā, *Dhanyă Bābā!*, 71–72.
13. On the historical development of the system of the four *āśramas* ("stages of life") in Hindu tradition, see Olivelle, *The* Āśrama *System*. On the historical nebulousness of the category of "forest hermit" (*vānaprastha*) in Vedic tradition, see particularly Olivelle, *The* Āśrama *System*, 109–111.
14. Goyankā, *Dhanyă Bābā!*, 72.
15. Goyankā, *Dhanyă Bābā!*, 73.
16. Goyankā, *Ātma-Kathan, Bhāg 2*, 51–2; see also "Contact with Arya Samaj," *Vipassana Newsletter (VRI Edition)*, 28, no. 13 (December 22, 2018): 1.
17. For a brief and incisive description of the Arya Samaj and its historical formation, see Hansen, *The Saffron Wave*, 71–74.
18. The notion of cultural nationalism was perhaps first formulated by Friedrich Meinecke in 1907 (based on the concept of a *Kulturnation*) in his book on German nationalism entitled *Weltbürgertum und Nationalstaat: Studien zur Genesis des deutschen Nationalstaates* (Virginia Beach, VA: Spencer, 2014). Meinecke distinguished between political nationalism and cultural nationalism, suggesting that the latter claims to be apolitical and is usually based on some common cultural form, such as language, while the former is usually based on civic structures. There is often, but not always, an overlap in these forms of nationalism in the formation of modern nation-states.
19. Hansen, *The Saffron Wave*, 74. On the role of Swami Dayananda Saraswati's disciple, Swami Shraddhananda, in this process, see Clémentin-Ojha, "Secularizing Renunciation?"
20. See Dayānand Sarasvatī, *Satyārth Prakāś*. The book was first translated into English in 1906 (see Bharadwaja, *Light of Truth*), though Goenka would have read it in its original Hindi.
21. Goyankā, *Ātma-Kathan, Bhāg 2*, 44.
22. Goyankā, *Ātma-Kathan, Bhāg 1*, 50–63; Goyankā, *Ātma-Kathan, Bhāg 2*, 44–48 and 80.

23. Goyankā, *Ātma-Kathan, Bhāg 1*, 51–55.
24. Goyankā, *Ātma-Kathan, Bhāg 2*, 44–45; Vipaśyanā Viśodhan Vinyās, *Mettavihāriṇī Mātājī*, 6; Goyankā, *Kalyāṇāmitrā Satyanārāyaṇ Goyankā*, 17–19.
25. Goyankā, *Ātma-Kathan, Bhāg 2*, 45.
26. Savarkar, *Hindutva*, 18–29. On this treatise and Savarkar's life, see Bakhle, "Country First?" and Sampath, *Savarkar*. The influential early twentieth-century leader of the Arya Samaj, Swami Shraddhananda, publicly lauded and embraced Savarkar's book not long after it was written (Savarkar, *Hindutva*, vi). On this historical moment and its role in the development of violent nationalism, see Pandey, *Routine Violence*, 106–14.
27. Goyankā, *Ātma-Kathan, Bhāg 1*, 1–49.
28. Goyankā, *Ātma-Kathan, Bhāg 1*, 1–49.
29. Goyankā, *Ātma-Kathan, Bhāg 2*, 9.
30. Goyankā, *Ātma-Kathan, Bhāg 2*, 7.
31. Goyankā, *Ātma-Kathan, Bhāg 2*, 39.
32. Vipaśyanā Viśodhan Vinyās, *Mettavihāriṇī Mātājī*, 6.
33. *Vipaśyanā* 36, no. 9 (March 2007): 1; see also *Vipassana Newsletter (VRI Edition)* 17, no. 3 (March 2007): 1.
34. See Leonard, "Family Firms in Hyderabad."
35. *Vipaśyanā* 36, no. 9 (March 2007): 1; see also *Vipassana Newsletter (VRI Edition)* 17, no. 3 (March 2007): 1.
36. Goyankā, *Ātma-Kathan, Bhāg 2*, 45; see also *Vipassana Newsletter (VRI Edition)* 28, nos. 10–12 (November 2018): 1–2.
37. Vipaśyanā Viśodhan Vinyās, *Mettavihāriṇī Mātājī*, 6–7, 121.
38. Tinker, "A Forgotten Long March," 1–2.
39. Tinker, "A Forgotten Long March," 2.
40. Goyankā, *Ātma-Kathan, Bhāg 2*, 42–43; see also "Some Memorable Episodes," *Vipassana Newsletter (VRI Edition)* 28, no. 9 (August 26, 2018): 3.
41. Goyankā, *Ātma-Kathan, Bhāg 1*, 3–12.
42. Goyankā, *Ātma-Kathan, Bhāg 2*, 42; Goyankā, *Ātma-Kathan, Bhāg 1*, 5.
43. *Katras* are quadrangular buildings that form part of the market area of Chandni Chowk.
44. Goyankā, *Ātma-Kathan, Bhāg 1*, 3–4.
45. Goyankā, *Rāj-dharm* (see also *Vipaśyanā* 29, no. 3 [September 1999]: 1–3); Goenka, *Defense against External Invasion*; Goenka, *How to Defend the Republic*; and Goenka, *Why Was the Sakyan Republic Destroyed?*

46. Flood and Martin, *The Bhagavad Gita*, xvii–xxii, xxvi–xxvii.
47. For some useful sources on Gandhi's relationship with the Bhagavad Gita, see Majmudar, "Mahatma Gandhi and the Bhagavad Gita."
48. Goyankā, *Ātma-Kathan, Bhāg 1*, 13. For the complete poem, entitled "When Might I Free Mother [India] from Her Shackles?" see Goyankā, *Barmā Meṃ Likhī*, 68–70. The poem as it appears there differs slightly from what is presented here.
49. On the history of this organization and its role in the development of Indian nationalism, see King, "Forging a New Linguistic Identity."
50. Goyankā, *Ātma-Kathan, Bhāg 1*, 4.
51. Goyankā, *Ātma-Kathan, Bhāg 1*, 13–14.
52. See "Alvidā Mere Bhaiyā!," *Vipaśyanā* 41, no. 5 (November 2011); "Farewell, My Brother," *Vipassana Newsletter* (*VRI Edition*) 21, no. 11 (November 10, 2011).
53. Goyankā, *Ātma-Kathan, Bhāg 1*, 17–18; Goyankā, *Kalyāṇāmitrā Satyanārāyaṇ Goyankā*, 14–16.
54. See Goyankā, *Ātma-Kathan, Bhāg 2*, 42–44; see also "Profound Faith in Lord Krishna," *Vipassana Newsletter (VRI Edition)* 28, no. 9 (August 26, 2018): 2–3, and *Vipassana Newsletter (VRI Edition)* 28, no. 10 (September 25, 2018): 1.
55. Goyankā, *Ātma-Kathan, Bhāg 2*, 42.
56. For a useful example of such ideas among Bengali religious literati already in the last quarter of the nineteenth century, see Wong, "Universalising Inclusivism."
57. Goyankā, *Ātma-Kathan, Bhāg 2*, 53–54; see also "Some Memorable Episodes," *Vipassana Newsletter (VRI Edition)* 28, no. 13 (December 22, 2018): 2.
58. See Savarkar, *Hindutva*, 18–29.
59. Goyankā, *Kyā Buddh Nāstik The?*, 10.
60. See Bhagavad Gita 2.54–72 (Flood and Martin, *The Bhagavad Gita*, 21–24).
61. Goyankā, *Kyā Buddh Nāstik The?*, 10–11.
62. Flood and Martin, *The Bhagavad Gita*, xii.
63. Goyankā, *Ātma-Kathan, Bhāg 2*, 55.
64. Goyankā, *Ātma-Kathan, Bhāg 2*, 56; see also "Contact with Arya Samaj," *Vipassana Newsletter (VRI Edition)* 28, no. 11 (October 24, 2018): 2.
65. Goyankā, *Kyā Buddh Nāstik The?*, 11.
66. Goyankā, *Ātma-Kathan, Bhāg 2*, 57.
67. Vipaśyanā Viśodhan Vinyās, *Mettavihāriṇī Mātājī*, 7–8.

68. "Infinite Devotion towards the Buddha," *Vipassana Newsletter (VRI Edition)* 29, no. 1 (January 21, 2019): 2.
69. Houtman, "Modern Burmese Buddhist Meditation Master," 313 (Ko Lay, *Myanmar's Excellent Person*, 67–68) and Vipassana Research Institute, *Sayagyi U Ba Khin Journal*, 8.
70. Houtman, "Modern Burmese Buddhist Meditation Master," 313–17 (Ko Lay, *Myanmar's Excellent Person*, 85) and Vipassana Research Institute, *Sayagyi U Ba Khin Journal*, 8–9.
71. On Ledi Sayadaw's charge to Saya Thetgyi to teach six thousand laymen, see Vipassana Research Institute, *Sayagyi U Ba Khin Journal*, 82 (Htay Hlaing 1987). On some aspects of the background of this historical moment, see Braun, *The Birth of Insight*; and Turner, *Saving Buddhism*.
72. Bischoff, *Selected Discourses*, 3–6.
73. *The Path of Purification* (*Visuddhimagga*), authored in Sri Lanka by the famous Indian exegete Buddhaghosa, is an important authoritative textual source on meditation practice within the Theravada Buddhist tradition. For an English translation of this important text, see Ñāṇamoli, *The Path of Purification*.
74. Ko Lay, *Myanmar's Excellent Person*, 86–88. I am grateful to Swe Mon for helping me translate this passage.
75. A description by a European student, Jan Van Amersfoort, indicates that he was able to attain the first stage of Buddhist awakening after merely a few hours of meditation over a night and a day (International Meditation Centre, "Practical Buddhist Meditation"). Another account by S. N. Goenka's close friend and family doctor, Om Prakash, relates that he attained the first stage of enlightenment after only two days of practice (Goenka, "Farewell Dhamma Brother").
76. On Burmese *weizzā* traditions, see Patton, *The Buddha's Wizards*. On the complexity of the category of weizzā, see particularly pages 1–17 of that monograph. On the notion of *dhāt-sī*—"riding the medium" or "channeling the saint" or "possession"—in weizzā tradition, see pages 73–78. U Ba Khin's teaching practices, particularly the many healings he performed, must be understood in connection with the broader spectrum of such weizzā practices.
77. In oral teachings recorded during one of his ten-day meditation retreats in the early 1960s (Ba Khin, "Discourses from a Ten-Day Vipassanā Course"), U Ba Khin spoke repeatedly to his students about the different kinds

of healing with which he and Mother Sayama were involved in at their meditation center. He spoke of what one might call exorcisms, the healing of allergic reactions, and the ability to bring mentally deranged people to sanity, among other things.

78. Ba Khin, "Towards Peace of Mankind," 1952. This document, as it has been made available by the Vipassana Research Institute, does not contain the entirety of U Ba Khin's communication.
79. On U Chan Htoon's role in the government of early independent Burma, see Taylor, *Dr. Maung Maung*, 110–17. U Chan Htoon was also an early postcolonial voice in the Buddhism, meditation, and science conversation (see Chan Htoon, *Buddhism and the Age of Science*).
80. Goyankā, *Ātma-Kathan, Bhāg 2*, 63–64; see also "Infinite Devotion towards the Buddha," *Vipassana Newsletter* 29, no. 1 (January 21, 2019): 2.
81. Goyankā, *Ātma-Kathan, Bhāg 2*, 65; see also "Infinite Devotion towards the Buddha," *Vipassana Newsletter (VRI Edition)* 29, no. 1 (January 21, 2019): 3.
82. "Infinite Devotion towards the Buddha," *Vipassana Newsletter* 29, no.1 (January 21, 2019): 3.
83. Goyankā, *Ātma-Kathan, Bhāg 2*, 66–67; see also "The Technique," *Vipassana Newsletter (VRI Edition)* 29, no. 2 (February 19, 2019): 1–2.
84. Goyankā, *Ātma-Kathan, Bhāg 2*, 69; see also "The Technique," *Vipassana Newsletter (VRI Edition)* 29, no. 2 (February 19, 2019): 2.
85. Goyankā, *Ātma-Kathan, Bhāg 2*, 70.
86. On the buddha Maitreya (Pali: Metteyya) in Pali Buddhism, see Stuart, *The Stream of Deathless Nectar*. On a public assertion in print that U Ba Khin was a bodhisattva, see Khit Sann Maung, "The Last Rites of Guru Ji," 57. There is also a record of U Ba Khin himself hinting at this idea. In a discourse on the fourth day of one of his ten-day meditation courses, he told the story of a monk, Mahāsiva, who was able to teach and bring others to arhatship even though he was not yet an attainer himself: "Ven. Mahāsīva was a *puthujana* [a person yet to attain one of the four fruits of the Buddhist path] but he instructed over twenty thousand monks to become arahants. Here, take note that a *puthujana* person can also instruct you to become an arahant. People ask me whether I am a *sotāpanna* [stream-enterer] or a *sakadāgāmi* [once-returner] or an *anāgāmi* [non-returner]. U Nu asks very often. They should not ask about it. I don't answer back." (Ba Khin, "Discourses from a Ten-Day Vipassanā Course," disc 3, track 1, 30:25–31:10).

87. For Goenka's own take on the "denialists" of Indian tradition, see chapter 10.
88. Goyankā, *Ātma-Kathan, Bhāg* 2, 70–72.
89. The phrase here "offer themselves" is a rendering of the Burmese *ap'naṅ*, "to place one's body down to be tread on," which is U Ba Khin's translation of the Pali verb *pariccaj-*, "to completely relinquish." This is an aspect of the formal ritual initiation that takes place at the beginning of all of Goenka's meditation courses (see Goenka, *The Gem Set in Gold*, 4, where the formula of initiation can be found: *imāhaṃ bhante attabhāvaṃ jīvitaṃ ācariyassa pariccajāmi*—"Sir, I surrender my life completely to my present teacher [for proper guidance and protection].").
90. Ba Khin, "Discourses from a Ten-Day Vipassanā Course," disc 5, track 1, 11:51–15:23.
91. Slightly adapted from "A New Birth," *Vipassana Newsletter (VRI Edition)* 29, no. 3 (March 21, 2019): 2, with reference to Goyankā, *Ātma-Kathan, Bhāg* 2, 79.
92. The term *dvija*, or "twice-born," refers in Hindu tradition to those members of the top three social classes (*varṇa*) who have undergone the coming-of-age ritual of getting invested with the sacred thread. Goenka makes reference to this issue of his caste identity in mentioning his second birth in the pages of his autobiography: "According to our traditional beliefs, I was, up until that time, still a *śudra* (one in the lowest of the four social classes), since I had never been invested with the sacred thread in a coming-of-age ritual. I refused to perform the ritual until all people of the society might be allowed to participate in it. Because of this resolve, I was happy to remain a *śudra* up until that time. But now I felt that I had become one who is truly twice-born. How does someone rightly become twice-born by completing the ritual of investment with the sacred thread? Here I truly became a twice-born when I attained a new birth by breaking through the shell of the egg of ignorance. I became blessed, supremely blessed" (Goyankā, *Ātma-Kathan, Bhāg* 2, 80).
93. Goyankā, *Dhanyă Bābā!*, 10 (see chapter 13).
94. It is noteworthy that this belief in a "second sāsana" was in fact found to be without traditional warrant by the scholar-monks who took part in the Sixth Council (Pranke, "On Saints and Wizards," 466, n. 32).
95. Adapted from "A New Birth," *Vipassana Newsletter (VRI Edition)* 29, no. 3 (March 21, 2019): 1, with reference to Goyankā, *Ātma-Kathan, Bhāg* 2, 73–74.

96. On the details of this "world tour," see Maharishi Mahesh Yogi, *Thirty Years Around the World.*
97. Maharishi Mahesh Yogi, *Thirty Years*, 212–13. While the Maharishi said that he spent "about ten days" in Rangoon, Goenka's account suggested that the teacher was a guest in his home in Rangoon for seventeen days (Goyankā, *Ātma-Kathan, Bhāg* 2, 126).
98. Benson and Klipper, *The Relaxation Response*; Komjathy, "Therapeutic Meditation"; Harrington and Dunne, "When Mindfulness Is Therapy." The latter article problematically omits the role of U Ba Khin and his students in the development of mindfulness as a therapeutic practice.
99. See chapter 3.
100. On Hislop's visit, see Chit Tin, *A Western Student's Meditation Experience.* Hislop notes in his account that Goenka helped to make arrangements for his travel and took him shopping in Rangoon after his meditation course. On the Webu Sayadaw's visit to the International Meditation Centre in May of 1960, see Bischoff, *Selected Discourses*, 6–19 and Vipassana Research Institute, *Sayagyi U Ba Khin Journal*, 89–101.
101. See Hislop, *Conversations*; Hislop, *My Baba and I*; and Hislop, *Seeking Divinity.*
102. On Goenka and Krishnamurti, see chapter 5, 94–96.
103. Chit Tin, *A Western Student's Meditation Experience*, 13–15.
104. Goyankā, *Ātma-Kathan, Bhāg* 2, 126.
105. I have omitted a somewhat technical sentence here referring to two key leaps in the process of meditation, one from the insight meditation stage of *udayavyaya* (Pali: *udayabbaya*; "arising and passing away") to that of *bhaṅga* ("dissolution"), and the other the leap to *nirvāṇa.* On the sixteen stages of insight knowledge in classical Theravada Buddhist meditation, see Ñāṇamoli, *The Path of Purification*, 626–725; Mahāsi Sayadaw, *The Progress of Insight*; and Mahāsi Sayadaw, *Manual of Insight*, 303–418.
106. Goyankā, *Ātma-Kathan, Bhāg* 2, 126–27.
107. Another anecdote about the Maharishi that I have come across in my fieldwork at S. N. Goenka's meditation centers in India pertains to advice Goenka gave the Maharishi during his visit to Rangoon. According to a number of Goenka's close students, Goenka encouraged the Maharishi never to get involved in selling meditation—charging a fee for his initiations—as it would be his downfall. I have never seen this anecdote in writing, and it seems likely that its telling can't be separated from a set

of pejorative attitudes among Goenka's disciples toward the Maharishi's teachings.

108. Goyankā, *Ātma-Kathan, Bhāg* 2, 127.

109. Vipaśyanā Viśodhan Vinyās, *Mettavihāriṇī Mātājī*, 8–9.

110. *Prasād* usually refers to a food item distributed at Hindu temples, events, and festivals. It is understood to be a material instantiation of the blessings of a God or deity.

111. Vipaśyanā Viśodhan Vinyās, *Mettavihāriṇī Mātājī*, 40.

112. Several examples of U Ba Khin's unique training methods can be found in Goenka, *For the Benefit of Many*, 51–53; see also "Adbhut Praśikṣaṇ [Wondrous Training]," *Vipaśyanā* 21, no. 10 (April 1992): 1–3.

113. Among the notable figures from abroad who passed through the International Meditation Centre were Dr. Elizabeth Knottingham, Dr. Huston Smith, Dr. Winston King, Dr. Padmanabh S. Jaini, Eliashiv Ben-Horin, and Anthony Brooke. A number of these visitors were scholars who went on to write books about Buddhist meditation and world religions (Khit Sann Maung, "What They Say About Sayagyi U Ba Khin," 66–78). The International Meditation Centre was also featured in the BBC documentary series *Men Seeking God* by Christopher Mayhew. On the context for this BBC series, see Jordan, "Another Man's Faith?"

114. Ba Khin, "'My Life Ambition'," 1.

115. U Ba Khin sent students to John Hislop to learn beginning meditation in the 1960s, and Leon Wright was authorized to teach the basics of Buddhism to students in America sometime before 1964 (Odgers, *The Sixteenth Burma-Bucknell Weekend*, 3).

116. Ba Khin, "'My Recent Experiments'," 1.

117. *Vipaśyanā* 24, no. 1 (July 1994): 1 (*Vipassana Newsletter [VRI Edition]* 8, no. 6 [June 1998]: 1).

118. Ba Khin, "'This Is to Certify That'."

119. Ko Lay, "An Informal Chat with U Ko Lay," 1:12:25–1:17:40.

120. Ko Lay, "An Informal Chat," 1:18:55–1:21:00. For a poetic rendering of this protective chant by Goenka in Hindi, see chapter 8.

121. Ba Khin, "'My Recent Experiments'," 2.

122. For an example of one way in which this distant control worked in practice in the context of Goenka's teaching, see chapter 15, 239 and 299n276.

123. Goyankā, *Ātma-Kathan, Bhāg* 2, 144. After the military coup of 1962, the Burmese government nationalized all private industry in 1963 (Taylor,

"Pathways to the Present," 17). With this process, Goenka and his family members in Burma lost many of their financial resources.

124. Goyankā, *Ātma-Kathan, Bhāg 2*, 144–45.
125. Wright, "'I Make Haste to Write'," 1.
126. "First Vipassana Course in India," *Vipassana Newsletter (VRI Edition)* 8, no. 6 (June 1998): 1 ("Vipaśyanā kī Rajat Jayaṃtī [The Silver Jubilee of Vipaśyanā]," *Vipaśyanā* 24, no. 1 [July 1994]: 1).
127. On the somewhat troubling history of the Ananda Marga, see Crovetto, "Ananda Marga, PROUT."
128. "First Vipassana Course in India," *Vipassana Newsletter (VRI Edition)* 8, no. 6 (June 1998): 1 ("Vipaśyanā kī Rajat Jayaṃtī [The Silver Jubilee of Vipaśyanā]," *Vipaśyanā* 24, no. 1 [July 1994]: 1).
129. Goenka noted that the solution to his father's concern about maintaining his ritual practices was to find someone else to perform the rituals for him while he participated in the meditation course.
130. In his autobiography, Goenka noted that many of his family members in India eventually came to practice vipaśyanā meditation. He made it clear, however, that not all of them did, emphasizing how his youngest brother, Shyamsundar Goenka, remained against it (Goyankā, *Ātma-Kathan, Bhāg 2*, 146).
131. Goyankā, *Ātma-Kathan, Bhāg 2*, 146.
132. Goenka, "Discourses of a Ten-Day Vipassanā Course," Day 10; see also Ganesha, "S.N. Goenka—Dhamma Discourses," 59:00–1:02:43.
133. "First Vipassana Course in India," *Vipassana Newsletter (VRI Edition)* 8, no. 6 (June 1998): 1 ("Vipaśyanā kī Rajat Jayaṃtī [The Silver Jubilee of Vipaśyanā]," *Vipaśyanā* 24, no. 1 [July 1994], 1).
134. Goyankā, *Ātma-Kathan, Bhāg 2*, 129–30.
135. Goyankā, *Ātma-Kathan, Bhāg 2*, 130–31.
136. Goyankā, *Ātma-Kathan, Bhāg 2*, 131.
137. Goyankā, *Ātma-Kathan, Bhāg 2*, 88–89; see also "The Profound Influence of Swami Vivekananda on My Life," *Vipassana Newsletter (VRI Edition)* 29, no. 5 (May 18, 2019): 1–2.
138. Goyankā, *Ātma-Kathan, Bhāg 2*, 90; see also "The Profound Influence of Swami Vivekananda on My Life," *Vipassana Newsletter (VRI Edition)* 29, no. 5 (May 2019): 2.
139. Vipaśyanā Viśodhan Vinyās, *Mettavihāriṇī Mātājī*, 29.
140. Goyankā, *Ātma-Kathan, Bhāg 2*, 147.

141. See Ram Dass, "Ram Dass with Buddhist Friends." Goldstein's path-breaking book, *The Experience of Insight*, was published not long after he returned from seven years living and practicing meditation in India under the guidance of Anagarika Munindra and Goenka. Sharon Salzberg was one of three formal founders of the Insight Meditation Society, along with Joseph Goldstein and Jack Kornfield. Daniel Goleman was instrumental in the scientization of Buddhist meditation and continues to be active in the ongoing dialogue around this relationship. (see Goleman, "Meditation as Meta-Therapy"; Goleman, "The Buddha on Meditation and States of Consciousness"; Goleman, "Mental Health in Classical Buddhist Psychology"; Goleman, "Meditation and Consciousness"; Walshe et al., "Meditation"; Goleman, "Buddhist and Western Psychology"; Goleman, Smith, and Dass, "Truth and Transformation"; and Goleman, "How I Helped Bring Mindfulness.") Mirabai Bush was a close associate of Ram Dass and has recently worked to bring meditation into mainstream social contexts (see Kucinskas, *The Mindful Elite*, 47–63 and 129–36; and Bush, "Ram Dass"). Wes Nisker is currently an affiliate teacher at Spirit Rock Meditation Center in California.
142. On the life of Anagarika Munindra, see Pryor, "Anagārika Munindra"; and Knaster and Pryor, *Living This Life Fully*.
143. See Goyankā, "Munidra—Merā Mitră," 2–3, and Goenka, "My Friend, Munindraji," 2–3. It is noteworthy that while Goenka suggested U Ba Khin did not want to teach Munindra for such political reasons, we have numerous examples of cases in which U Ba Khin overlooked his own policy. The case of U Ba Khin's close friend U Ko Lay is one example of this, and the case of U Ba Khin attempting to recruit U Rewata Dhamma, a scholar-monk and student of the Mahasi Sayadaw, is another.
144. Ba Khin, *Pariyatti 'akhrekhaṃ Nhan' ´ Paṭipatti 'aphre Mhan'*.
145. Munindra, "Dear Respected Sayagyi," 91; see also *Vipassana Newsletter (VRI Edition)* 14, no. 9 (August 2004): 3.
146. Munindra was virtually erased from this history in later retellings by Goenka and his students. This is starkly apparent in claims by Goenka, such as "That course in July 1969 marked the return of Vipassana to India," and claims of his close disciples, such as "July 3: Goenkaji begins conducting the first Vipassana course in India in modern times, at the Panchayati Wadi guesthouse in central Mumbai" (*Vipassana Newsletter [International Edition]* 46, no. 1 [April 2019]: 4, 6). Both of these claims are

objectively false if we take into account Munindra's teaching of Burmese vipassanā in the tradition of Mahasi Sayadaw.

147. Ba Khin, "YOU are the first'."
148. Fischer, "The Universal Meditation Technique."
149. U Ba Khin took recourse to a classic Pali scriptural passage in his discussion of the natural luminosity of mind, and this is also how Goenka understood the experience of "light": "Well, the Buddha taught that *pabhassaram idaṃ bhikkhave idaṃ cittaṃ*—'O monks, this mind is glitteringly pure always.' Mind has the quality of purity. *Āgantu upakkilesehi kilamathe*—'Because of impurities, which are known as *upakkilesa* and are like guests [of the mind], the pure quality of the mind is not revealed.' When we meditate, we try to cultivate the clarity of mind by detaching slowly from greed, hatred and delusion, which adhere to the mind. Then we get clarity of mind" (Ba Khin, "Discourses from a Ten-Day Vipassanā Course," disc 1, track 2, 2:10–2:50). On the layered nature of such notions in the history of Buddhist thought, see Anālayo, "The Luminous Mind in Theravāda."
150. Fischer, "The Universal Meditation Technique."
151. Knowledge and Vision—Ñana-dasana, "Reflections on Goenka/U Ba Khin Style Vipassana," 05:45–07:01.
152. On Krishnamurti's life and teachings, see Stuart Holroyd, *The Quest of the Quiet Mind* (Wellingborough, Northamptonshire: The Aquarian Press, 1980); Mary Lutyens, *Krishnamurti: The Years of Awakening* (New York: Farrar, Straus, and Giroux, 1975); Mary Lutyens, *The Open Door* (London: John Murray, 1983); Mary Lutyens, *Krishnamurti: The Years of Fulfilment* (New York: Farrar, Straus, and Giroux, 1988); Mary Luytens, *Krishnamurti: His Life and Death* (New York: St. Martin's Press, 1990); Pupul Jayakar, *Krishnamurti: A Biography* (San Francisco: Harper & Row, 1986); and Aryel Sanat, *The Inner Life of Krishnamurti*, (Wheaton, IL: Quest Books, 1999).
153. On John Coleman's encounters with Krishnamurti in the 1950s and 1960s, see Coleman, *The Quiet Mind*, 49–72.
154. Sramana, "Question to Acharya S. N. Goenka," 0:08–2:21; see also Agarwal, "The Buddha - Vipassana - J. Krishnamurti," www.buddhanet.net/bvk_study/bvk22c.htm.
155. Krishnamurti, "Brockwood Park," 4432–41.
156. Stuart, "Insight Transformed," 167, n. 16.

157. Stuart, "Insight Transformed," 168–171.
158. For an outline of some of these key institutional moments, see *Vipassana Newsletter (International Edition)* 46, no. 1 (April 2019) and 46, no. 2 (July 2019).
159. Goyankā, *Dharm: Jīvan Jīne kī Kalā*; and Goyankā, *Dharm: Ādarś Jīvan kā Ādhār*. For a translation of the eighteenth chapter of this important introductory work, see chapter 18 of the Writings and Teachings section.
160. The accounts that follow and much of the material in chapter 6 are recastings of historiographical analyses presented in an unpublished article manuscript by the author (Stuart, "Insight in Perspective").
161. On these figures, see Lerner, *Journey of Insight Meditation*, 5–72, 165–172; Coleman, *The Quiet Mind*; Zagato, "La Storia Di John Earl Coleman"; and Boucher, *Dancing in the Dharma*, respectively.
162. *Vipassana Newsletter (International Edition)* 1, no. 2 (Summer 1974): 2.
163. On this period of Goldstein's formation as a meditation practitioner, see Sam Harris, "The Path and the Goal," October 28, 2014, in *Making Sense* (previously *Waking Up*), podcast, www.samharris.org/podcasts/the-path-and-the-goal/.
164. This characterization of Goldstein at this time is drawn from an interview with an anonymous informant who practiced with Anagarika Munindra and Goenka in India during this time.
165. Personal correspondence between Joseph Goldstein and Shambhala Publications, February 13, 2020. It is noteworthy that despite this "something of a split" with Goenka, Goldstein nonetheless dedicated his first book, *The Experience of Insight*, to Munindra, Goenka, and Dipa Ma (Nani Bala Barua) as his teachers. It is worth reflecting here on the ambiguity that emerges when looking at these different representations of such a student-teacher relationship.
166. See Ñāṇamoli and Bodhi, *The Middle Length Discourses*, 145–55; and Walshe, *The Long Discourses of the Buddha*, 335–350.
167. On this point, see chapter 11; Goenka, *Discourses on Satipaṭṭhāna Sutta*, 25–27, 37–38, 47–48; and Vipaśyanā Viśodhan Vinyās, *Mahāsatipaṭṭhāna-sutta*, 12–14.
168. The debate about the distinctions between these introductory approaches to the foundations of mindfulness is more complex than this brief discussion allows. It should be noted that the differences appear less and less important in more advanced instructions within both traditions.

Nonetheless, these differences were used to draw lines of identity that had powerful historical implications.

169. Goldstein, *The Experience of Insight*.
170. This passage is drawn from chapter 13.
171. On the meditative challenges Goldstein faced working with Goenka and how his body became "once again blocked up," see Harris, "The Waking Up Podcast #4," 43:10–45:45.
172. *Vipassana Newsletter (International Edition)* 2, no. 3 (Summer 1975): 4.
173. *Vipassana Newsletter (International Edition)* 2, no. 3 (Summer 1975): 4. On this article and Denison's narration of this moment, see Boucher, *Dancing in the Dharma*, 152–53.
174. *Vipassana Newsletter (International Edition)* 4, no. 2 (May 1977): 1.
175. Erik Braun (*The Birth of Insight*, 164) has insightfully drawn attention to this key moment of fissure as retrospectively narrated by Jack Kornfield in a 2007 article entitled "This Fantastic Unfolding Experiment" (*Buddhadharma: The Practitioner's Quarterly* [Summer]: 32–39). Kornfield wrote: "From the very beginning we offered the practices of both Mahasi Sayadaw and U Ba Khin, with Ruth Denison and John Coleman leading retreats. We also asked U Ba Khin's great disciple Goenka if he would come and teach, because Joseph, Sharon, and others were very devoted to him. He responded in a letter saying, 'If you open a center and have more than one lineage teaching there, it will be the work of Mara, and it will be the undoing of the dharma.' Goenka's teacher U Ba Khin believed this. However, his letter came the day *after* we signed the mortgage—fortunately, it was too late." In presenting this passage, Braun zeros in on a key narrative of one of the most consequential moments in the history of modern meditation. This is not the place for an extended discussion on issues of authority and the way humans retrospectively narrate events to serve their own interests, but were I to do a complete analysis of what is going on in this narrative moment, those aspects would be central to my interpretation. Here I simply want to emphasize how this narrative implicitly acknowledges Goenka's powerful authority in this moment, even while suggesting that it was "karma or grace" that allowed the putative founders of the IMS to feel compelled to carry forward in their transgressive innovation under the onus of financial commitment.
176. See Braun, *The Birth of Insight*, 164–65; and Boucher, *Dancing in the*

Dharma, 141–66. Boucher's account is perhaps the most informative in terms of accounting for Hover's role.

177. Coleman, *The Quiet Mind*, 173–75. It is noteworthy that in his book Coleman did not explicitly mention Mother Sayama's role in helping to catalyze his enlightenment experience.
178. *Vipaśyanā* 8, no. 4 (October 15, 1978): 3.
179. *Vipaśyanā* 8, no. 5 (November 14, 1978): 3.
180. *Vipassana Newsletter (International Edition)* 6, no. 3 (Autumn 1981): 1.
181. *Vipassana Newsletter (IMC-UK)* Supplementary Issue (Spring 1982): 1.
182. Goenka, "I Cannot Forget Their Help," 3; see also Goyankā, "Jinkā Upăkār Na Bhūl Sakūṃ," 3. For a brief account of this event in Goenka's Hindi-language autobiography, see Goyankā, *Ātma-Kathan, Bhāg 2*, 151.
183. Houtman, "Traditions of Buddhist Practice in Burma," 203 (Ko Lay, *Myanmar's Excellent Person*, 119–21).
184. All of the foregoing quotations are drawn from Confalonieri, *The Clock of Vipassana Has Struck*, 18–20.
185. This idea was discussed retrospectively—and in a historically and culturally decontextualized fashion—in a recent English-language *Vipassana Newsletter*: "Whatever the reason, people of all backgrounds came to Goenkaji and filled the courses he conducted. And soon he had another surprise: the people sitting before him did not progress in the same way as meditators at Sayagyi's center in Yangon. There it was said that not a single course of Sayagyi's went "dry"; that is, in every course someone experienced *nibbāṇa* for the first time. Goenkaji tried working with some of his more serious students, as Sayagyi had done. He stopped when Sayagyi explained that Goenkaji had a different role. If someone was going to reach the highest stage, they had all the tools and did not require his guidance. In his later years, Goenkaji was not even interested if people reported that they had experienced *nibbāṇa*. It was too easy to be misled, he felt. If someone really had reached that stage, the confirmation would come from a change in that person's life" (*Vipassana Newsletter [International Edition]* 46, no. 2 [July 2019]: 2). Note how this framing of Goenka's mission tacitly absolves him and his assistants of any responsibility for providing guidance to students who have the sincere aim of attaining the final goal of the Buddha's teachings. It also reveals how Goenka and his community attempted to sidestep the knotty problem of how to assess attainment in Buddhist practice contexts.

186. See chapter 5, p. 81–82.
187. Goenka, "Discourses of a Ten-Day Vipassanā Course," day 10; see also Ganesha, "S.N. Goenka—Dhamma Discourses," 59:00–1:02:43.
188. Two exceptions to this are U Chit Tin and U Tint Yee; see Chit Tin, *Anecdotes of Sayagyi U Ba Khin*, 42–43.
189. See www.dhamma.org/en-US/locations/directory.
190. *Vipaśyanā* 11, no. 5 (November 11, 1981): 3.
191. In the one formal treatise that U Ba Khin wrote on the relationship between meditation practices and theoretical knowledge of such practices in texts, he referred only once to the foundations of mindfulness, and this was in the context of a discussion of the establishment of awareness of bodily states (*kāyagatā sati*). His primary textual source was *A Comprehensive Manual of Abhidhamma* (Cf. Bodhi, *A Comprehensive Manual of Abhidhamma*).
192. On the historical challenges of interpreting this text, see, for example, Schmithausen, "Die vier Konzentrationen der Aufmerksamkeit" and Anālayo, *Satipaṭṭhāna*, 73–97.
193. See Ñāṇamoli and Bodhi, *The Middle Length Discourses*, 941–48, 1087–96.
194. Goenka, "Discourses of a Satipaṭṭhāna Meditation Course," day 1.
195. Goenka, "Discourses of a Satipaṭṭhāna Meditation Course," day 1.
196. *Vipaśyanā* 11, no. 7 (January 9, 1982): 3; see also *Vipassana Newsletter (International Edition)* Winter 1982: 1.
197. *Vipaśyanā* 11, no. 12 (June 6, 1982): 2–3; see also *Vipassana Newsletter (International Edition)* Spring 1982: 1–2.
198. In Indian-language contexts, Goenka's Hindi-language instructions and discourses were translated; while outside of India, his English-language instructions and discourses were translated.
199. Over the years, an organizational hierarchy of assistant teachers developed, primarily for the sake of dividing up administrative and organizational duties within Goenka's organization. There developed five tiers of responsibility: (1) assistant teachers (*sahāyak ācāryă*); (2) senior assistant teachers (*variṣṭ sahāyak ācāryă*); (3) full teachers (*ācāryă*); (4) center teachers (*kendrīya ācāryă*); and (5) coordinator area teachers (*samanvayak kṣetrīya ācāryă*). The term *ācārya* ("full teacher") became more of an administrative title—as opposed to a title referring to someone's capacities as a meditation teacher—once Goenka's organization fully developed its institutional structure by the mid-1990s. For a partial picture of the

institutional structure of Goenka's network of meditation centers, assistants, and regional responsibilities approaching the time of his death, see *Vipassana Newsletter (VRI Edition)* 22, no. 13 (December 28, 2012): 2–6.

200. See *Vipaśyanā* 11, no. 7 (January 9, 1982) through 12, no. 7 (December 30, 1982).

201. English-language parallels to these summaries appeared some years later; see *Vipassana Newsletter* 11, nos. 4 (October/November 1984) through 13, no. 3 (September 1986); and Goenka and Hart, *The Discourse Summaries*.

202. It is noteworthy that while English versions of the discourse summaries were published only a few years after the first Hindi versions were made, English translations of the Buddhist liturgical texts chanted by Goenka on his retreats were not published until many years later in 2006 (see Goenka, *The Gem Set in Gold*). The reasons for this delay are not clear, but it seems likely that it was a deliberate public relations choice to avoid the issue that the content of Goenka's liturgy is largely devotional, contains explicit supplications to his teacher, and invokes a range of supernormal forces in a religious fashion that is explicitly tied to traditional Buddhist protective rituals and domestic Buddhist ritual practice. The material in this liturgy does not appear to fit with the image—presented particularly to Goenka's English-speaking followers—of a tradition that is (as Goenka states in the standard discourses of his ten-day retreat) "logical, pragmatic, scientific . . . [without] any kind of guruism involved, [without] any kind of dogma or belief involved[,] . . . a pure science of mind and matter."

203. *Vipaśyanā* 13, no. 7 (January 19, 1984): 3.

204. On the connection between Robert Hover and Jon Kabat-Zinn, see Stuart, "Insight Transformed," 160–66 and 173, n. 26.

205. See, for example, Goleman, "Meditation as Meta-Therapy"; Goleman, "The Buddha on Meditation and States of Consciousness"; Goleman, "Mental Health in Classical Buddhist Psychology"; Goleman, "Meditation and Consciousness"; Goleman, "Buddhist and Western Psychology"; Goleman, Smith, and Dass, "Truth and Transformation"; Goleman, "How I Helped Bring Mindfulness"; Kornfield, "The Psychology of Mindfulness Meditation"; Walsh et al., "Meditation"; Kabat-Zinn, "An Out-Patient Program"; and Kabat-Zinn et al., "The Clinical Use of Mindfulness" and "Four Year Follow-Up."

206. *Vipaśyanā* 15, no. 2 (July 31, 1985): 3–4.

207. On the development of a Pali studies program, see *Vipassana Newsletter (International Edition)* 13, no. 1 (April 1986): 3–4; *Vipassana Newsletter (International Edition)* 13, no. 4 (December 1986): 8–9; *Vipassana Newsletter (International Edition)* 14, no. 4 (December 1987): 3. On the development of health-related research, see, for example, "Mind and Body: Healthy Living the Vipassana Way," *Vipassana Newsletter (International Edition)* 12, no. 3 (September 1985): 4; "Seminar on Vipassana Meditation," *Vipassana Newsletter (International Edition)* 14, no. 1 (April 1987): 2–3; "Papers from the Seminar on Vipassana Meditation," *Vipassana Newsletter (International Edition)* 14, no. 2 (June 1987): 1–4; "Vipassana Meditation in the Practice of Medicine," *Vipassana Newsletter (International Edition)* 15, no. 2 (June 1988): 3; and "A Report on Health Seminar," *Vipassana Newsletter (VRI Edition)* 1, no. 3 (January 1991): 10. Nearly all of the "papers" presented at these seminars and published in the newsletters and in various booklets of the Vipassana Research Institute involved no research and are best understood as missionary propaganda. For Goenka's take on textual learning in this particular historical context, see, for example, *Vipaśyanā* 14, no. 5 (1985) through 15, no. 7 (1986), and especially *Vipaśyanā* 15, nos. 8/9 (February 24, 1986): 1–2 (*Vipassana Newsletter* 13, no. 1 [April 1986]: 1–2).
208. In recent years, a few original peer-reviewed papers looking at the connection between vipaśyanā and sleep have been published by scholars at the National Institute of Mental Health and Neurosciences (NIMHANS) in Bangalore in collaboration with the Vipassana Research Institute. See, for example, Nagendra et al. 2012 ("Meditation and its regulatory role on sleep," *Frontiers of Neurology* 3, no. 54) and Maruthai et al., 2016 ("Senior Vipassana Meditation practitioners exhibhit distinct REM sleep organization from that of novice meditators and healthy controls," *International Review of Psychiatry* 28, no. 3: 279–287).
209. Vipassana Research Institute, *Sayagyi U Ba Khin Journal*, 246.
210. Hart, *The Art of Living*, 14.
211. The entirety of this chapter of Goenka's first book has been translated in chapter 18.
212. Ba Khin, *Pariyatti 'akhrekhaṃ Nhan' ´ Paṭipatti 'aphre Mhan'*, 21. This passage was translated by Jenny Ko Gyi with the editorial assistance of Daniel Stuart.
213. Ba Khin, *Pariyatti 'akhrekhaṃ Nhan' ´ Paṭipatti 'aphre Mhan'*, 37–38. This

passage was translated by Jenny Ko Gyi with the editorial assistance of Daniel M. Stuart.

214. Goenka, ""Discourses of a Thirty-Day Meditation Course," day 10.

215. The author was present at this talk, and this quote as well as the following one come from his field notes.

216. See also chapter 17.

217. Goyankā, *Ātma-Kathan, Bhāg* 2, 161.

218. Global Vipassana Foundation, "Construction and Development," www.globalpagoda.org/construction-and-development.

219. The email together with the document—neither of which have been published—circulated openly as a single PDF among Goenka's assistant teachers and serious students in North America, Europe, and India in the years after its composition. It was brought to my attention by several friends and informants not long after it was sent out, and it became the source of much uncertainty, confusion, and self-searching within the community.

220. The Fleischmans' communication indicates that several senior vipaśyanā administrators from North America cautioned against "widespread emails that foment agitation or division." It also indicates that these administrators and others were themselves participants in the breakdown of communication within the community.

221. The breakdown of communication has not affected the organization's ability to put on courses and serve students who come to practice meditation at centers established by Goenka and his students around the world.

222. While I don't want to downplay the problems entailed in Goenka's choice to intermingle his family business with his role as a meditation teacher, I can't say that I was surprised to hear about this issue in the course of my research. In fact, Goenka's mission and his family business were intermingled from the very beginning, since it was his family who supported him and financially underwrote most of his teaching activities in the first decade in India.

223. I do not think it is mere coincidence that the Hindu nationalist ideologue Narendra Modi recently used the same unfortunate phrase ("the new India") in a speech calling for unity after a controversial supreme court ruling in favor of Hindu Nationalist groups advocating for the construction of a temple on the site of the Babri Masjid (see Abi-Habib

and Yasir, "Court Backs Hindus on Ayodhya"). The mosque was unlawfully destroyed by mobs of zealous Hindu nationalists in 1992, and its demolition triggered riots all over India. While Fleischman is not an advocate of violence of the sort enacted by such nationalist agendas, the language he deploys participates in a civilationalist ideology that does epistemic violence to practices, traditions, and cultures of which he remains willfully ignorant.

224. For Goenka's own take on this issue, elucidated in his 1995 magnum opus written in Hindi, see chapter 13, 214–16.

225. These poems were selected and translated from Goyankā, *Barmā meṃ Likhī Gayīṃ Merī Kavitāeṃ*. The original Hindi titles of the poems and their respective page numbers in that volume are as follows: 1. *Śraddhā-Bal* (43–45), 2. *Ājādī kā Mahāparv* (74–79), 3. *Hindustānī* (82–87), 4. *Bhārat Bhūmā Ke Bhavyă Bhānu (Mahātmā Gāndhī)* (97), 5. *Māṃ Durgā* (133–36), and 6. *Uttam-Maṅgal* (46–47). I am grateful to Mukul Agarwal for discussing my translations with me and making many helpful corrections and suggestions.

226. The narrative context for this poem is a famous episode from the *Rāmāyaṇa* in which an army of bears and monkeys (*vānara*), supporters of Rama, constructs a bridge between India and Sri Lanka. See Goldman, Goldman, and van Nooten, *The Rāmāyaṇa of Vālmīki*, 154–56 (*Rāmāyaṇa* 6.15.1–33).

227. Maharana Pratap, or Pratap Singh I (1540–1597), was a king of the Mewar region of northwest India.

228. The Khalsa is the name for the congregation of Sikhs under Guru Gobind.

229. Dasahara, or Vijayadashami, is the name of a Hindu festival day. It marks the last day of Navaratri, the festival of "nine nights," celebrated annually in the autumn in honor of the goddess Durga.

230. "Deathless nectar," or just "the deathless" (*amṛt*), is one way of speaking about the state of nirvāṇa.

231. This poem was inspired by the *(Mahā)maṅgalasutta*, a protective chant (paritta) in Pali. On this text, see Nunamaker, "An Exploration of the *Mahā-Maṅgala Sutta*," and Goenka, *The Gem Set in Gold*, 55–57.

232. This chapter is a translation of the short opening chapter of Goyankā, *Ātma-Kathan, Bhāg 1*, 1–2.

233. Throughout the text Goenka uses the honorific *-jī* at the end of Gandhi's name when referring to him. I have not included this honorific element in the translation.

234. Subhas Chandra Bose was the leader of Azad Hind ("Free India"), an Indian provisional government established in occupied Singapore in 1943 and supported by the Axis powers. It was a uniquely militaristic faction of the independence movement during the Second World War.
235. S. N. Goenka, *Was the Buddha a Pessimist?* (Igapturi, India: Vipassana Research Institute, 2001).
236. The four sections of this chapter are drawn from Satyanārāyaṇ Goyankā, *Kyā Buddh Nāstik The?* (Igatpuri, India: Vipaśyanā Viśodhan Vinyās, 2008). The original Hindi titles of the excerpts and their respective page numbers in that volume are as follows: *Vipaśyanā kā Vyāvahārik aur Gītā kā Saiddhāntik Pakṣ* (12–15); *Bhagavān Buddh dvārā Āstikavādī Saddharm kī Sthāpanā* (45–46); *Nāstikavād kā Virodh* (47–50); and *Buddh kī Prayogātmak Vipaśyanā Vidyā* (55–60).
237. See chapter 2, 36–39; see also Goyankā, *Kya Buddh Nastik The?*, 10–11. This episode is also recounted in Goyankā, *Ātma-Kathan, Bhāg* 2, 54–57, translated into English in "Contact with Arya Samaj," *Vipassana Newsletter* 28, no. 11 (October 18, 2018): 1–3. In this short chapter, Goenka recounts two incidents from before he himself became interested in the Buddha's teachings. The first took place after a public talk that he gave on the Bhagavad Gita. At that time his Burmese friend, U Ta Mya, suggested that the key teaching of "establishment in wisdom" (*sthitaprajñatā*) in the Gita had been plagiarized from the Buddha's teachings. The second took place at a gathering devoted to Burmese literature, where the respected Buddhist monk and scholar Bhadant Anand Kausalyayan was in attendance. Goenka's Hindutva sensibilities were offended when this learned monk also suggested that, not only the Gita, but also many other Hindu works were strongly influenced by the Buddha's teachings.
238. On "establishment in wisdom" (sthitaprajñatā), see Gita 2.54–72 (Flood and Martin, *The Bhagavad Gita*, 21–24).
239. *Dohavalı* 78 (Poddār, *Dohāvalī*, 28).
240. *Dohāvalī* 78 (Poddār, *Dohāvalī*, 28).
241. *Vinayapatrikā* 79.1 (Dvivedī, *Vinaya-Patrikā*, 161–62).
242. Here the term "spiritual" is a translation of Hindi *adhyātm*, which is perhaps more literally translated as "internal" or "pertaining to the self."
243. "Noble Dharma" is a translation of the loaded Hindi term *āryădharm* (Sanskrit: *āryadharmaḥ*; Pali: *ariyo dhammo*), perhaps more literally translated as "Aryan Dharma." The phrase has strong ethnolinguistic associations,

and the Buddha appears to have played on such associations when invoking the term in his teachings.

244. See Goyankā, *Dhamma-Vaṃdanā*, 80.

245. Cf. Bodhi, *The Numerical Discourses of the Buddha*, 1231–32 and 1813, n. 1801.

246. Cf. Bodhi, *The Connected Discourses of the Buddha*, 227.

247. Goenka almost always used the word "vibration" to translate Hindi *taraṃg*, which might be more literally translated as "wavelet."

248. This chapter is a translation of *Vipaśyanā* 2, no. 12 (June 15, 1973): 1–5.

249. In several places the Pāli of this passage, as printed in the *Vipaśyanā* newsletter, reads *rūpa* where it should read *rūpaṃ*. Similarly, in two places the text reads *rūppati* when it should probably read *ruppati*.

250. *The Connected Discourses* (III) 22.2.3.7, *The Discourse on Being Devoured* (see Bodhi, *The Connected Discourses of the Buddha*, 915 and 1070, n. 110).

251. Cf. *The Long Discourses* 22, *The Great Discourse on the Foundations of Mindfulness* (see Walshe, *The Long Discourses of the Buddha*, 337).

252. This phrase is an explicit invocation of the language of the *(Great) Discourse on the Foundations of Mindfulness* (see Walshe, *The Long Discourses of the Buddha*, 335–50).

253. *Rūp* is the modern Hindi form of Pali and Sanskrit *rūpa*.

254. It seems likely that the phrase *ruppa atyena rūpaṃ* is some sort of corruption in the text. Something like the phrase *ruppatīti rūpam* (from *The Connected Discourses* (III) 22.2.3.7, *The Discourse on Being Devoured*), found in the quote at the beginning of the article, was probably intended.

255. Cf. *Abhidhammatthasaṅgaha-mahāṭīkā* (75): *ruppatīti rūpaṃ. sītuṇhādivirodhipaccayehi vikāram āpajjati*. Cf. also *Aṅguttaranikāya-ṭīkā* (150): *ruppatī ti sītādivirodhipaccayehi vikāraṃ āpādīyati, āpajjatīti vā attho.*

256. For English translations of *The Discourse on the Foundations of Mindfulness (Satipaṭṭhāna-sutta)* and *The Great Discourse on the Foundations of Mindfulness (Mahāsatipaṭṭhāna-sutta)*, see Ñāṇamoli and Bodhi, *The Middle Length Discourses*, 145–55, and Walshe, *The Long Discourses of the Buddha*, 335–50, respectively.

257. This chapter is the author's translation of Satyanārāyaṇ Goyankā,. *Tipiṭak meṃ Samyak Sambuddh, Bhāg 1*, 5 vols. (Igatpuri, India: Vipaśyanā Viośodhan Vinyās, 2008), 81–90. An English translation of this entire book was recently published in two volumes by the Vipassana Research Institute, under the title *The Buddha As Depicted in the Tipiṭaka.*

258. Cf. Bodhi, *The Connected Discourses of the Buddha*, 545. The English titles of

texts referenced in the parenthetical citations in this chapter are my own translations of the Pali titles of the canonical collections and discourses provided in Pali in the original. The text numbers in the parenthetical citations refer to the Sixth Council edition of the Pali canon in Devanāgarī script published by the Vipassana Research Institute between 1993 and 1998 (see Vipaśyanā Viśodhan Vinyās, *Dhammagiri-Pāli-Ganthamālā*).

259. Cf. Walshe, *The Long Discourses of the Buddha*, 245.
260. Cf. Walshe, *The Long Discourses of the Buddha*, 245.
261. Cf. Bodhi, *The Connected Discourses of the Buddha*, 939.
262. Cf. Cowell, *The Jātaka*, Volume V, 78.
263. Cf. Cowell, *The Jātaka*, Volume V, 78.
264. Cf. Bodhi, *The Connected Discourses of the Buddha*, 939.
265. Cf. Bodhi, *The Numerical Discourses of the Buddha*, 425–26.
266. Cf. Bodhi, *The Connected Discourses of the Buddha*, 1678.
267. Cf. Bodhi, *The Numerical Discourses of the Buddha*, 426.
268. An analysis of these nine qualities forms the main exegetical content of the book from which this excerpt is drawn, and it follows the classical liturgical statement delineating nine descriptive aspects of the Buddha: *iti pi so bhagavā arahaṃ*... See below, 221.
269. Cf. Walshe, *The Long Discourses of the Buddha*, 91.
270. Cf. Bodhi, *The Suttanipāta*, 242.
271. Cf. Bodhi, *The Connected Discourses of the Buddha*, 164.
272. "Sectarian con" here is a translation of the term *ṭhag-vidyā*, which might more literally be translated as "swindler's wisdom."
273. This chapter is a translation of Goyankā, *Dhanyă Bābā!*, 1–10.
274. In traditional Hinduism, it is considered a violation of caste norms to take an ocean voyage.
275. These phrases come from the first verse of the well-known national song of India "Vande Mātaram": . . . *sujalām suphalām, malayajaśītalām, śasyaśyāmalām*. . . .
276. The term *dvija*, or "twice-born," also refers in Hindu tradition to those members of the top three social classes (*varṇa*) who have undergone the coming-of-age ritual of being invested with the sacred thread.
277. "The Floodgates of Dhamma Open," *Vipassanā Newsletter (VRI Edition)* 7, no. 3 (May 1997). This article first appeared in Hindi under the title "Bāṃdh Khul Gayā" in *Vipaśyanā* 26, no. 9 (February 1997). Goenka always capitalized the term *Vipassana* in his English-language writing.

278. The original Hindi is here more technical and also more revealing of the experiential aspects of Goenka's metaphysical relationship to his teacher in the contexts of his teaching: "A few moments before the discourse was to begin, when my attention went to the heart-base [*hṛdayavastu*, an energy center in the region of the solar plexus, considered to be the seat of the unconscious mind], I saw that the bhavaṃga [stream of basic consciousness] was very lively and palpable. The gate at the crown of my head [*brahmaraṃdhră*, another energy center considered to be a receptive opening for external cosmic forces] opened, and the Dharma vibrations of *maṃgal-maitrī* [auspicious loving-kindness] of my respected guru were flowing down into it. My entire body and mind were pervaded with a thrilling rapture. When I began to speak, I did so fluently and without stopping, just as well as when I was speaking Hindi" (*Vipaśyanā* 26, no. 9 [February 1997]: 2).

279. A few preliminary sentences, relating to the context of the meditation retreat, have been omitted here.

280. A discussion of the term *uposatha* and its distortion in the religious practice history of India has been omitted here.

281. A final exhortation to practice diligently has been omitted here.

282. This chapter is a translation from Global Vipaśyanā Phāuṃḍeśan, *Vipaśyanā Pagoḍā Smārikā. Mumbai: Global Vipaśyanā Phāuṃḍeśan* (Mumbai: Global Vipassana Foundation, 2000), 8–12. For a related piece available in English, see S. N. Goenka, "Why the Grand Vipassana Pagoda?" *Vipassana Newsletter (VRI Edition)* 7, no. 8 (October 1997), www.vridhamma.org/node/2470, originally published in Hindi in *Vipaśyanā* Patrika 27, no. 3 (September 17, 1997): 1–4.

283. This probably refers to a practice of chanting Buddhist stanzas while at the same time generating within oneself and radiating out from oneself a positive energetic force.

284. This chapter is a translation from Goyankā, *Dharm: Ādarś Jīvan kā Ādhār*, 72–79.

285. A "victor" (*jina*) is an enlightened person, one who has been victorious in the spiritual quest.

286. In Hindu mythology, Rama's arrows are understood to be able to cure any physical disease.

287. Note that here we find reference to Goenka's own name, Satyanārāyaṇ.

Bibliography

Abi-Habib, Maria, and Sameer Yasir. "Court Backs Hindus on Ayodhya, Handing Modi Victory in His Bid to Remake India." *New York Times*, November 8, 2019. www.nytimes.com/2019/11/08/world/asia/ayodhya-supreme-court-india.html. supreme

Adcock, Cassie S. *The Limits of Tolerance: Indian Secularism and the Politics of Religious Freedom*. New York: Oxford University Press, 2014.

Agarwal, Munish. "The Buddha - Vipassana - J. Krishnamurti: Research Study." Buddhanet: Buddha Dharma Education Inc. www.buddhanet.net/bvk_study/bvk002.htm.

Anālayo, Bhikkhu. "The Luminous Mind in Theravāda and Dharmaguptaka Discourses." *Journal of the Oxford Centre for Buddhist Studies* 13 (2017): 10–51.

——. *Satipaṭṭhāna: The Direct Path to Realization*. Birmingham, UK: Windhorse Publications, 2003.

Ba Khin, U. "Discourses from a Ten-Day Vipassanā Course with Sayagyi U Ba Khin at the International Meditation Centre." Yangon, Myanmar: International Meditation Centre, n.d.

——. "'My Life Ambition . . . ,' a Letter to John Coleman Dated April 24th, 1969." Rangoon, Burma. 1969. www.momentum-vitae.it/biografiedarangoon/letterautografe.

——. "'My Recent Experiments . . . ,' Authorization Letter to John Coleman Dated April 23rd, 1969." Rangoon, Burma. 1969. www.momentum vitae.it/biografiedarangoon/lettereautografe.

——. *Pariyatti 'akhrekhaṃ Nhan' ́ Paṭipatti 'aphre Mhan'* [The Right Answers to Practice with a Basis of Theory]. Rangoon, Myanmar: Vipassanā Association of the Office of the Accountant General of the Union of Myanmar, 1962.

——. "'This Is to Certify That . . . ,' Certificate of Authorization for S. N. Goenka to Teach Buddhist Meditation Abroad Dated June 20th, 1969." Rangoon, Myanmar: International Meditation Centre, 1969.

——. "'Towards Peace of Mankind,' Notice Issued by Sayagyi U Ba Khin, Dated October 23rd, 1952, Advertising Courses of Meditation." Rangoon, Myanmar: International Meditation Centre, 1952. https://www.dhamma.org/en/os/subk231052.jpg.

——. "'. . . YOU are the first . . . ,' a Letter to S.N. Goenka Dated August 28th 1970." Rangoon, Burma: International Meditation Centre, 1970. https://www.dhamma.org/en/os/subk280870.jpg.

Bakhle, Janaki. "Country First? Vinayak Damodar Savarkar (1883–1966) and the Writing of Essentials of Hindutva." *Public Culture* 22, no. 1 (2010): 149–86.

Benson, Herbert, and Miriam Z. Klipper. *The Relaxation Response*. New York: Avon, 1975.

Bharadwaja, Chiranjiva. *Light of Truth, or an English Translation of the Satyarth Prakash, the Well-Known Work of Swami Dayanand Saraswati*. Rev. ed. United Provinces of Agra and Oudh, India: The Arya Pratinidhi Sabha, 1915. First published 1906 by Union Printing Works (Lahore).

Bischoff, Roger. *Selected Discourses of Webu Sayadaw*. Dhamma Text Series. Heddington, UK: The Sayagyi U Ba Khin Memorial Trust, 2003.

Bodhi, Bhikkhu. *A Comprehensive Manual of Abhidhamma: The Abhidhammattha Sangaha of Ācariya Anuruddha*. Kandy, Sri Lanka: Buddhist Publication Society, 1999.

——. *The Connected Discourses of the Buddha: A New Translation of the Saṃyutta Nikāya*. Somerville, MA: Wisdom Publications, 2000.

——. *The Numerical Discourses of the Buddha: A Translation of the Aṅguttara Nikāya*. Somerville, MA: Wisdom Publications, 2012.

——. *The Suttanipāta: An Ancient Collection of the Buddha's Discourses, Together with Its Commentaries*. Somerville, MA: Wisdom Publications, 2017.

Boucher, Sandy. *Dancing in the Dharma: The Life and Teachings of Ruth Denison*. Boston: Beacon Press, 2005.

Braun, Erik. *The Birth of Insight: Meditation, Modern Buddhism, and the Burmese Monk Ledi Sayadaw*. Chicago: University of Chicago Press, 2013.

——. "S. N. Goenka, Pioneer of Secular Meditation Movement, Dies at 90." *Tricycle: The Buddhist Review*, October 1, 2013. https://tricycle.org/trikedaily/s-n-goenka-pioneer-secular-meditation-movement-dies-90.

Bush, Mirabai. "Ram Dass: Being Here." *Lion's Roar*, November 13, 2013. www.lionsroar.com/being-here-january-2014-review.

Candima, Venerable U. "A Study of the Life and Work of the Most Venerable

Ledi Sayadaw." Master's thesis, Bangkok, Thailand: Mahachulalongkornrajavidyalaya University, 2005.

Chan Htoon, U. *Buddhism and the Age of Science*. Kandy, Sri Lanka: Buddhist Publication Society, 1961.

Chit Tin, U, ed. *Anecdotes of Sayagyi U Ba Khin: Real Accounts of the Teachers*. Dhammadana Series. Heddington, UK: The Sayagyi U Ba Khin Memorial Trust, 1982.

———. *A Western Student's Meditation Experience Under the Guidance of Sayagyi U Ba Khin*. Heddington, UK: The Sayagyi U Ba Khin Memorial Trust, 1985.

Clémentin-Ojha, Catherine. "Secularizing Renunciation? Swami Shraddhananda's Welcome Address at the Congress Session of Amritsar in 1919." In *Religious Interactions in Modern India*, edited by Martin Fuchs and Vasudha Dalmia, 209–35. New Delhi, India: Oxford University Press, 2019.

Coleman, John E. *The Quiet Mind*. Onalaska, WA: Pariyatti Publishing, 2000.

Confalonieri, Pierluigi. *The Clock of Vipassana Has Struck: The Teachings and Writings of Sayagyi U Ba Khin, with Commentary by S.N. Goenka*. Onalaska, WA: Pariyatti Publishing, 1999.

Cowell, E. B. *The Jātaka, or Stories of the Buddha's Former Births, Volume V.* Cambridge: Cambridge University Press, 1905.

Crovetto, Helen. "Ananda Marga, PROUT, and the Use of Force." In *Violence and New Religious Movements*, edited by James R. Lewis, 249–74. New York: Oxford University Press, 2011.

Dvivedī, Devanārāyaṇ. *Vinaya-Patrikā (Mahākavi Gosvāmī Tulsidās-Kṛt)*. Vārāṇasī (Banāras), India: Jñānmaṇḍal Limiṭeḍ, 1962.

Fischer, Norman. "The Universal Meditation Technique of S.N. Goenka." *Lion's Roar*, February 27, 2009. www.lionsroar.com/the-universal-meditation-technique-of-s-n-goenka.

Flood, Gavin and Charles Martin. *The Bhagavad Gita: A New Translation*. New York: W. W. Norton, 2012.

Gelles, David. "Overlooked No More: S. N. Goenka, Who Brought Mindfulness to the West." *New York Times*, April 3, 2019. www.nytimes.com/2019/04/03/obituaries/sn-goenka-overlooked.html.

Goenka, S. N. *The Buddha As Depicted in the Tipiṭaka*. Mumbai, India: The Vipassana Research Institute, 2017.

———. *Defense against External Invasion*. Igatpuri, India: Vipassana Research Institute, 2003.

———. "Discourses of a Satipaṭṭhāna Meditation Course of S. N. Goenka."

Blackheath, Australia: Dhamma Bhūmi, 1990. Transcripts made available by the Vipassana Research Institute.

——. *Discourses on Satipaṭṭhāna Sutta*. Igatpuri, India: Vipassana Research Institute, 1999.

——. "Discourses of a Ten-Day Vipassanā Course of S. N. Goenka," 6th ed. North Fork, CA: Dhamma Mahāvana, 1991. Transcripts made available by the Vipassana Research Institute.

——. "Discourses of a Thirty-Day Meditation Course of S. N. Goenka." Igatpuri, India: Vipassana Research Institute, 1989. Transcripts made available by the Vipassana Research Institute.

——. "Farewell Dhamma Brother." *Vipassana Newsletter (International Edition)* 25, no. 3 (1998): 1–3.

——. *For the Benefit of Many: Talks and Answers to Questions from Vipassana Students, 1983–2000*. Igatpuri, India: Vipassana Research Institute, 2007.

——. *The Gem Set in Gold*. Onalaska, WA: Vipassana Research Publications, 2006.

——. *How to Defend the Republic*. Igatpuri, India: Vipassana Research Institute, 2003.

——. "I Cannot Forget Their Help." *Vipassana Newsletter (VRI Edition)* 18, no. 6 (June 18, 2008): 1–3.

——. "My Friend, Munindraji." *Vipassana Newsletter (VRI Edition)* 14, no. 9 (August 30, 2004): 1–3.

——. "Question Asked to Acharya S.N. Goenka on OSHO." May 13, 2017. YouTube video, 3:07. www.youtube.com/watch?v=18ThQ_pMpag.

——. *Why Was the Sakyan Republic Destroyed?* Igatpuri, India: Vipassana Research Institute, 2003.

Goenka, S. N., and William Hart. *The Discourse Summaries*. Igatpuri, India: Vipassana Research Institute, 1997.

Goldman, Robert P., Sally J. Sutherland Goldman, and Barend A. van Nooten. *The Rāmāyaṇa of Vālmīki: An Epic of Ancient India, Volume VI: Yuddhakāṇḍa*. Princeton, NJ: Princeton University Press, 2009.

Goldstein, Joseph. *The Experience of Insight: A Simple and Direct Guide to Buddhist Meditation*. Boston: Shambhala Publications, 1976.

Goleman, Daniel. "The Buddha on Meditation and States of Consciousness, Part I: The Teachings." *Journal of Transpersonal Psychology* 4, no. 1 (1972): 1–44.

——. "The Buddha on Meditation and States of Consciousness, Part II: A

Typology of Meditation Techniques." *Journal of Transpersonal Psychology* 4, no. 2 (1972): 151–210.

——. "Buddhist and Western Psychology: Some Commonalities and Differences." *Journal of Transpersonal Psychology* 13, no. 2 (1981): 125–36.

——. "How I Helped Bring Mindfulness to the Western World." Linkedin. 2016. www.linkedin.com/pulse/how-i-helped-bring-mindfulness-western-world-daniel-goleman.

——. "Meditation and Consciousness: An Asian Approach to Mental Health." *American Journal of Psychotherapy* 30, no. 1 (1976): 41–54.

——. "Meditation as Meta-Therapy: Hypotheses toward a Proposed Fifth State of Consciousness." *Journal of Transpersonal Psychology* 3, no. 1 (1971): 1–25.

——. "Mental Health in Classical Buddhist Psychology." *Journal of Transpersonal Psychology* 7, no. 2 (1975): 176–81.

Goleman, Daniel, Huston Smith, and Ram Dass. "Truth and Transformation in Psychological and Spiritual Paths." *Journal of Transpersonal Psychology* 17, no. 2 (1985): 183–214.

Goyankā, Bālăkṛṣṇă. *Kalyāṇămitră Satyanārāyaṇ Goyankā, Vyaktitva Aur Kṛtitva.* Igatpuri, India: Vipassana Research Institute, 2002.

Goyankā, Satyanārāyaṇ. *Ātma-Kathan, Bhāg 1.* Igatpuri, India: Vipaśyanā Viśodhan Vinyās, 2003.

——. *Ātma-Kathan, Bhāg 2.* Igatpuri, India: Vipaśyanā Viśodhan Vinyās, 2016.

——. *Barmā Meṃ Likhī Gayīṃ Merī Kavitāeṃ.* Igatpuri, India: Vipaśyanā Viśodhan Vinyās, 2013.

——. *Dhamma-Vaṃdanā.* Igatpuri, India: Vipaśyanā Viśodhan Vinyās, 2006.

——. *Dhanyă Bābā!* Igatpuri, India: Vipassana Research Institute, 2002.

——. *Dharm: Ādarś Jīvan kā Ādhār.* Igatpuri, India: Vipaśyanā Viśodhan Vinyās, 2008.

——. *Dharm: Jīvan Jīne kī Kalā.* Bombay: Sayājī U Bā Khin Memoriyal Ṭrasṭ, 1983. First published 1976.

——. "Jinkā Upākār Na Bhūl Sakūṃ." *Vipaśyanā* 37, no. 11 (May 19, 2008): 1–3.

——. *Kyā Buddh Nāstik The?* Igatpuri, India: Vipaśyanā Viśodhan Vinyās, 2008.

——. Mahāsatipaṭṭhānasutta (Bhāṣānuvād evaṃ Samīkṣā sahit). Igatpuri, India: Vipaśyanā Viśodhan Vinyās, 2008. First published 1996.

——. "Munidra—Merā Mitră." *Vipaśyanā* 34, no. 2 (2004): 1–3.

——. *Rāj-dharm: Kuch Aitihāsik Prasaṃg (Buddhavāṇī ke Paripreksy meṃ).* Igatpuri, India: Vipaśyanā Viśodhan Vinyās, 2003.

Hansen, Thomas Blom. *The Saffron Wave: Democracy and Hindu Nationalism in Modern India*. Princeton, NJ: Princeton University Press, 1999.

Hardgrove, Anne. *Community and Public Culture: The Marwaris in Calcutta*. New Delhi: Oxford University Press, 2004.

Harrington, Anne, and John D. Dunne. "When Mindfulness Is Therapy: Ethical Qualms, Historical Perspectives." *American Psychologist* 70, no. 7 (2015): 621–31.

Harris, Sam. "The Waking Up Podcast #4—The Path and the Goal: A Conversation with Joseph Goldstein." 2014. www.samharris.org/podcast/item/the-path-and-the-goal.

Hart, William. *The Art of Living: Vipassana Meditation, As Taught by S. N. Goenka*. 2nd ed. Igatpuri, India: Vipassana Research Institute, 1988.

Hislop, John S. *Conversations with Sathya Sai Baba*. Tustin, CA: Sathya Sai Book Center of America, 1979.

———. *My Baba and I*. San Diego: Birth Day Publishing Co., 1985.

———. *Seeking Divinity*. Andhra Pradesh, India: Sri Sathya Sai Publications, 1998.

Houtman, Gustaaf. "The Biography of Modern Burmese Buddhist Meditation Master U Ba Khin: Life before the Cradle and Past the Grave." In *Sacred Biography in the Buddhist Traditions of South and Southeast Asia*, edited by Juliane Schober, 310–44. Honolulu: University of Hawaii Press, 1997.

———. "Traditions of Buddhist Practice in Burma." PhD diss., London: School of Oriental and African Studies, University of London, 1990.

Htay Hlaing, U. *Anāgām' charā sak' kyī", sū' bhava| sū' tarā" nhaṅ'' sū' kye" jū"* [Anāgāmī Saya Thetgyi: His Life, His Teachings, and His Good Acts]. Rangoon, Myanmar: Amyui"sadhī" Pariyatti Ranh'puṃṅve, 1987.

———. *(Mran'mā nuiṅ' ṅaṃ paṭipattisāsanāvaṅ') Rahantā nhaṅ'' pugguil' thū" myā"* [Arahats and Extraordinary Individuals (of the Practice Traditions of Myanmar)]. Rangoon, Myanmar: Amyui"sadhī" Pariyatti Ranh'puṃṅve, 1993.

Ganesha. "S.N. Goenka—Dhamma Discourses, Day 10." November 25, 2013. YouTube video, 1:06:54. www.youtube.com/watch?v=oo8-2iQB8wU.

International Meditation Centre. *Practical Buddhist Meditation: Personal Experiences of Candidates (Buddhists and Non-Buddhists)*. Edited by International Meditation Centre (IMC). Rangoon, Myanmar: Vipassana Research Association, 1954.

Jordan, James. "Another Man's Faith? The Image of Judaism in the BBC Television Series *Men Seeking God*." *Jewish Culture and History* 12, no. 3 (2010): 463–76.

Kabat-Zinn, Jon. "An Out-Patient Program in Behavioral Medicine for Chronic Pain Patients Based on the Practice of Mindfulness Meditation: Theoretical Considerations and Preliminary Results." *General Hospital Psychiatry* 4, no. 1 (1982): 33–47.

Kabat-Zinn, Jon, Leslie Lipworth, and Robert Burney. "The Clinical Use of Mindfulness Meditation for the Self-Regulation of Chronic Pain." *Journal of Behavioral Medicine* 8, no. 2 (1985): 163–190.

Kabat-Zinn, Jon, Leslie Lipworth, Robert Burney, and W. Sellers. "Four Year Follow-Up of a Meditation-Based Program for the Self-Regulation of Chronic Pain: Treatment Outcomes and Compliance." *The Clinical Journal of Pain* 2, no. 3 (1986): 159–173.

Khit Sann Maung. "The Last Rites of Guru Ji." *The Maha Bodhi* 80, no. 4 (1972): 55–57.

——. "What They Say About Sayagyi U Ba Khin & The International Meditation Centre." *The Maha Bodhi* 80, no. 4 (1972): 66–78.

King, Christopher R. "Forging a New Linguistic Identity: The Hindi Movement in Banaras, 1868–1914." In *Culture and Power in Banaras: Community, Performance, and Environment, 1800–1980*, edited by Sandria B. Freitag, 179–202. Berkeley and Los Angeles: University of California Press, 1992.

Knaster, Mirka, and Robert Pryor. *Living This Life Fully: Stories and Teachings of Munindra*. Boston: Shambhala Publications, 2010.

Knowledge and Vision – Ñana Dassana. "Reflection on Goenka/U Ba Khin Style Vipassana." October 23, 2011. YouTube video, 28:06. www.youtube.com/watch?v=LSnadJDVZmU.

Ko Lay, U. "An Informal Chat with U Ko Lay." Unpublished audio recording. 1995.

——. *Mranmā guṇ' choṅ' pugguil thū" charā kyī" ū" bā khaṅ (attuppatti nhaṅ'' sasanā prulup' ṅhaṅ'" myā")* Myanmar's Excellent Person, the Extraordinary Sayāgyi U Ba Khin (His Biography and Missionary Activities). Rangoon, Myanmar: The Vipassanā Association of the Office of the Accountant General of Myanmar, 1980.

Komjathy, Louis. "Therapeutic Meditation: Herbert Benson's *The Relaxation Response*." In *Contemplative Literature: A Comparative Sourcebook on Meditation and Contemplative Prayer*, 593–638. Albany, NY: SUNY Press, 2015.

Kornfield, Jack. *Modern Buddhist Masters*. Kandy, Sri Lanka: Buddhist Publication Society, 2007.

———. "The Psychology of Mindfulness Meditation." PhD diss., Pasadena: The Saybrook Institute, 1977.

Krishnamurti, Jiddu. "Brockwood Park 2nd Conversation with Buddhist Scholars 28th June 1979, 'Death.'" In *Later and Unpublished Texts-1970s*, n.d., 4432–41. https://ilcorsaronero.me/tor/55031/Jiddu_Krishnamurti_Complete_collection_77_E_Books_PDF_ENG.

Kucinskas, Jaime. *The Mindful Elite: Mobilizing from the Inside Out*. New York: Oxford University Press, 2019.

Leonard, Karen Isaksen. "Family Firms in Hyderabad: Gujarati, Goswami, and Marwari Patterns of Adoption, Marriage, and Inheritance." *Comparative Studies in Society and History* 53, no. 4 (2011): 827–54. doi:10.1017/s0010417511000429.

Lerner, Eric. *Journey of Insight Meditation: A Personal Experience of the Buddha's Way*. New York: Schocken Books Inc., 1977.

Maharishi Mahesh Yogi. *Thirty Years Around the World: The Dawn of the Age of Enlightenment*. Fairfield, IA: MVU Press, 1986.

Mahāsi, Sayadaw, Venerable. *Manual of Insight*. Somerville, MA: Wisdom Publications, 2016.

Majmudar, Uma. "Mahatma Gandhi and the Bhagavad Gita." *American Vedantist*. 2014. https://americanvedantist.org/2014/articles/mahatma-gandhi-and-the-bhagavad-gita.

Mayhew, Christopher. *Men Seeking God: 2—Buddhism*. London: British Broadcasting Corporation, 1954.

Michaelson, Jay. "S.N. Goenka: The Man Who Taught the World to Meditate." *HuffPost*, September 30, 2013. www.huffpost.com/entry/sn-goenka-dead_b_4016374?guccounter=1.

Munindra, Anagārika. "Dear Respected Sayagyi." *The Maha Bodhi* 80, no. 4 (1972): 91–92.

Nakatani, Sumie. "Hometowns of the Marwaris, Diasporic Traders in India." In *Regional Routes, Regional Roots? Cross-Border Patterns of Human Mobility in Eurasia*, edited by So Yamane and Norihiro Naganawa, 63–76. Sapporo, Japan: Slavic Research Center, Hokkaido University, 2014.

Ñāṇamoli, Bhikkhu. *The Path of Purification (Visuddhimagga)*. Kandy, Sri Lanka: Buddhist Publication Society, 1991.

Ñāṇamoli, Bhikkhu, and Bhikkhu Bodhi. *The Middle Length Discourses of the*

Buddha: A New Translation of the Majjhima Nikaya. Somerville, MA: Wisdom Publications, 1995.

Nunamaker, Caralynn Rose. "An Exploration of the *Mahā-Maṅgala Sutta*: Content and Context." Master's thesis, University of South Wales, 2019.

Nyanissara, Ashin. *A Short Biography of the Venerable Ledi Sayadaw*. Sitagu International Buddhist Academy: Sagaing, Myanmar, 1996.

Odgers, Merle M. *The Sixteenth Burma-Bucknell Weekend*. Lewisburg, PA: The Bucknell University Christian Association and The Asia Foundation of San Francisco, 1964.

Olivelle, Patrick. *The* Āśrama *System: The History and Hermeneutics of a Religious Institution*. New York: Oxford University Press, 1993.

Pandey, Gyanendra. *The Construction of Communalism in Colonial India*. Delhi: Oxford University Press, 1997.

———. *Routine Violence: Nations, Fragments, Histories*. Stanford, CA: Stanford University Press, 2006.

Patton, Thomas Nathan. *The Buddha's Wizards: Magic, Protection, and Healing in Burmese Buddhism*. New York: Columbia University Press, 2018.

Poddār, Hanumān Prasād. *(Goswāmī Tulsīdāsjī Racit) Dohāvalī*. 45th ed. Gorakhpur, India: Gita Press, 2004. First published 1940 by the Gita Press.

Pranke, Patrick. "On Saints and Wizards: Ideals of Human Perfection and Power in Contemporary Burmese Buddhism." *Journal of the International Association of Buddhist Studies* 33, nos. 1–2 (2010): 453–488.

Pryor, C. Robert. "Anagārika Munindra and the Historical Context of the Vipassanā Movement." *Buddhist Studies Review* 23, no. 2 (2006): 241–48.

Ram Dass, Baba. *Be Here Now*. San Cristobal, NM: The Lama Foundation, 1971.

———. "Ram Dass with Buddhist Friends." May 19, 2014. YouTube video, 11:48. www.youtube.com/watch?v=ljFeu5-5RS8.

Sampath, Vikram. *Savarkar: Echoes from a Forgotten Past*. New Delhi: Penguin Random House India, 2019.

Sarasvatī, Svāmī Dayānanda. *Satyārth Prakāś*. Benares, India: Star Press, 1875.

Savarkar, Vinayak Damodar. *Hindutva: Who Is a Hindu?* 5th ed. Bombay: Veer Savarkar Prakashan, 1969. First published 1923 by V. V. Kelkar (Nagpur) under the title *Hindutva*.

———. *The Progress of Insight (Visuddhiñāna-Kathā)*. Translated by Nyanaponika Thera. Kandy, Sri Lanka: Buddhist Publication Society, 1973. First published in 1965 by the Buddhist Publication Society (Kandy).

Schmithausen, Lambert. "Die vier Konzentrationen der Aufmerksamkeit: Zur geschichtlichen Entwicklung einer spirituellen Praxis des Buddhismus." *Zeitschrift für Missionswissenschaft und Religionswissenschaft* 4, no. 76 (1976): 241–66.

Sramana. "Question to Acharya S. N. Goenka About Venerable J. Krishnamurti." November 3, 2017. YouTube video, 2:37. www.youtube.com/watch?v=MpsAMWIxdvo.

Stuart, Daniel M. "Insight in Perspective: A Stillbirth Revived by Karma in the Study of Modern Buddhism." Unpublished manuscript, n.d.

———. "Insight Transformed: Coming to Terms with Mindfulness in South Asian and Global Frames." *Religions of South Asia* 11, nos. 2–3 (2018): 158–81. doi:10.1558/rosa.37022.

———. *The Stream of Deathless Nectar*. Bangkok and Lumbini: Fragile Palm Leaves Foundation and Lumbini International Research Institute, 2017.

Taylor, Robert H. *Dr. Maung Maung: Gentleman, Scholar, Patriot*. Singapore: Institute of Southeast Asian Studies, 2008.

———. "Pathways to the Present." In *Myanmar: Beyond Politics to Societal Imperatives*, edited by Kyaw Yin Hlaing, Robert H. Taylor, and Tin Maung Maung Than, 1–29. Singapore: Institute of Southeast Asian Studies, 2005.

Thant Myint-U. *The Making of Modern Burma*. Cambridge, UK: Cambridge University Press, 2001.

Tinker, Hugh. "A Forgotten Long March: The Indian Exodus from Burma, 1942." *Journal of Southeast Asian Studies* 6, no. 1 (1975): 1–15.

Turner, Alicia Marie. *Saving Buddhism: The Impermanence of Religion in Colonial Burma*. Honolulu: University of Hawaii Press, 2014.

Vipassana Research Institute. "Dhamma Messenger of Compassion and Peace—Mataji Illaichidevi Goenka." *Vipassana Newsletter (VRI Edition)* 26, no. 1 (January 2016). www.vridhamma.org/node/2075.

———. *Sayagyi U Ba Khin Journal: A Collection Commemorating the Teaching of Sayagyi U Ba Khin, Published to Mark the Twentieth Anniversary of His Demise*. Igatpuri, India: Vipassana Research Institute, 1994.

———. "S. N. Goenka." n.d. www.vridhamma.org/S.N.-Goenka.

Vipaśyanā Viśodhan Vinyās. *Dhammagiri-Pāli-ganthamālā*. 140 vols. Igatpuri, India: Vipaśyanā Viśodhan Vinyās, 1993–98.

———. *Mahāsatipaṭṭhānasutta (Bhāṣānuvād Evaṃ Samīkṣā Sahit)*. Igatpuri, India: Vipaśyanā Viśodhan Vinyās, 2008.

——. *Mettavihāriṇī Mātājī: Śrīmatī Ilāyăcīdevī Goyankā*. Igatpuri, India: Vipaśyanā Viśodhan Vinyās, 2016.

Walsh, Roger N., Daniel Goleman, Jack Kornfield, Corrado P. Pensa, and Deane Shapiro. "Meditation: Aspects of Research and Practice." *Journal of Transpersonal Psychology* 10, no. 2 (1978): 113–33.

Walshe, Maurice. *The Long Discourses of the Buddha: A Translation of the Dīgha Nikāya*. Somerville, MA: Wisdom Publications, 1995.

Wong, Lucian. "Universalising Inclusivism—and Its Limits: Bhaktivinod and the Experiential Turn." *Journal of South Asian Intellectual History* 1 (2018): 1–43. doi:10.1163/25425552-12340002.

Wright, Leon. "'I Make Haste to Write . . . ,' a Letter to Sayagyi U Ba Khin Dated July 19th 1958." 1958. https://pariyatti.org/Free-Resources/Treasures.

Zagato, Fabio. "La storia di John Earl Coleman." *Visione Profonda: VipassanaItalia*. n.d. www.vipassanaitalia.it/la-tradizione/john-earl-coleman/la-storia-di-john-earl-coleman.

Index

LIVES OF THE MASTERS

"Since the time of Buddha Shakyamuni himself, Buddhists have been accustomed to recollect the lives of great teachers and practitioners as a source of inspiration from which we may still learn. The Lives of the Masters series continues this noble tradition, recounting the stories, wisdom, and experience of many accomplished Buddhists over the last 2,500 years. I am sure readers will find the accounts in this series inspirational and encouraging."

His Holiness the Dalai Lama

"The lives of the most important Buddhist masters in history written by the very best of scholars in elegant and accessible prose—who could ask for more?"

José Cabezón, *Professor of Tibetan Buddhist Studies*
University of California Santa Barbara

BOOKS IN THE SERIES

Atiśa Dīpaṃkara: Illuminator of the Awakened Mind
Gendun Chopel: Tibet's Modern Visionary
S. N. Goenka: Emissary of Insight
The Third Karmapa Rangjung Dorje: Master of Mahāmudrā
Tsongkhapa: A Buddha in the Land of Snows

Please visit www.shambhala.com
for more information on forthcoming titles.